In his new book, Ph[...] lored the
evidence surrounding [...] h insight
and skill. I found this [...] me in its
objectivity, and shock[...]

Whitley Streiber.

Nagaitis and Mantle's *Without Consent* is unique among British publications for its forthright documentation of mysterious experiences of profound importance that are affecting people in many parts of the world. Books like this are much needed to help break through the denial that surrounds the visitation phenomenon.

Dr. John Mack

Without Consent is an important book in the on-going attempt to understand the nature of the alien abduction mystery and presents case after case full of valuable and insightful testimony on this emotive controversy. For a subject that many see as being primarily an American one, the fact that the book concentrates on British-based accounts of alien abduction is a major and welcome plus.

Nick Redfern,
Author of "A Covert Agenda", "The FBI Files" and "Cosmic Crashes"

Since 1961, when an American couple, Betty and Barney Hill, reported being stopped in their car by a UFO during which encounter they believed they met with, and were intrusively examined by, aliens from another world, the phenomenon of *alien abduction* has been a prominent one. A virtual industry has blossomed in the years since typified by the success of television series such as *The X Files* and films such as *Communion* and *Fire in the Sky*, both based on the claims of American abductees.

But UFOs and *alien abductions* are not exclusively American phenomena; indeed there are world-wide reports. Mantle and Nagaitis in this book do a significant service to readers by reminding them that there have been many such accounts from Britain, equally fascinating, equally bizarre sometimes, and equally important. The book includes the detailed accounts of many British abductees and sets their claims into the global perspective showing both the similarities between British and American reports, and the differences.

It is an important and valuable contribution to the subject, which should be read by anyone interested in this modern enigma.

John Spencer
Director of Research for the British UFO Research Association

WITHOUT CONSENT

By Carl Nagaitis &
Philip Mantle

Published by
Beyond Publications

An imprint of Fortune Books Ltd 2002

Published in the UK by
Beyond Publications 2002

Beyond Publications is an imprint of Fortune Books Ltd
Sycamore House, Park Road, Colton, Leeds LS15 9AJ

Edited by Heather Pedley

Cover Artwork by Rob Townshend © Rob Townshend

Cover Design by Philip Shipley and Heather Pedley

Final Editing Assistance by Michael Landa

Printed and bound in Great Britain by Bell and Bain Ltd

ISBN: 1-903782-02-3

For reasons of privacy, some of the names in this
book may have been changed.

We dedicate this book to two much loved brothers who were taken suddenly during the writing of this project. Barry Nagaitis - a born seeker of truth, went in search of his own Holy Grail when he died after a tragic road accident aged 49, and Percy Mantle who at the age of 61, finally succumbed to a long battle with heart disease.

Both will be greatly missed and never forgotten,

Carl Nagaitis / Philip Mantle
2002.

ABOUT THE AUTHORS

Carl Nagaitis

During more than 25 years in journalism, Carl Nagaitis has covered just about every story it is possible to imagine. He has exposed scandals, worked under cover with a Fleet Street investigations team and has blown the lid on the secret antics of some dubious personalities.

The Manchester born *Cudlipp Award* winning writer has been an industrial correspondent, a diarist, a show-business writer, a literary editor and news editor. He was on the launch team of Europe's first trans-continental newspaper, *The European* and also news edited Britain's first national newspaper supplement for the Asian community.

Today he runs a PR & Publicity Consultancy in Cheshire but still prefers to describe himself as a *jobbing writer*.

Without Consent gave him the opportunity to combine a former hack's healthy cynicism with an open mind to take a fresh look at a modern mystery.

Carl lives in Winsford, Cheshire with his partner Helen, his daughter Heidi, and her teddy bear Buttons.

Philip Mantle

Born in West Yorkshire, England, Philip Mantle was Director of the *British UFO Research Association (BUFORA)* and the English representative for the *American Mutual UFO Network (MUFON)* for 10 years. Philip's interest in UFO research began in 1979 and since that time he has lectured around the world appearing on television and radio programmes, and writing features for newspapers and magazines including Daily Star, The Independent and The Guardian.

Over the last few years Philip has become known as one of the worlds leading UFO researchers and investigators.

CONTENTS

FOREWORD
By Nick Pope

Throughout human history, people have seen strange objects and phenomena in the skies. In 1947, a sighting attracted the attention of the American media, who coined the phrase *flying saucer.* In 1951 the United States Air Force adopted their own term, *unidentified flying object,* or *UFO* for short. Although precise numbers are disputed, even the most conservative estimates suggest that several hundred thousand UFO reports have been made in the last fifty years or so. Many of these reports involve a sighting that is either very brief, or involves an object at high altitude. There is, in a sense, a certain distance between the phenomenon and the observer.

But there is an exception to this. All around the world, thousands of ordinary people have claimed that they have had a much closer and more personal encounter, involving not just a UFO sighting, but interaction with the occupants of these craft. Most frequently, these people claim that they have been taken onto a UFO against their will. Some people claim to have undergone strange procedures, possibly medical in nature, while others report actual communication with extraterrestrial entities. The phrase *alien abduction* has been adopted to cover this phenomenon, and *Without Consent* tells the story of this most extraordinary of modern mysteries.

I first came across claims of alien abduction while I was working for the Ministry of Defence. From 1991 to 1994 I worked in a division called *Secretariat (Air Staff),* where my duties included investigating UFO sightings. Because of this, I found myself drawn into the debate over other mysteries such as crop circles, cattle mutilations and alien abductions. Initially, I was wary of getting too involved with the alien abduction phenomenon.

I had made progress with some of the more sceptical elements at the MOD. With a steady number of UFO cases involving military witnesses or radar evidence, I was convincing increasing numbers of colleagues to take a closer look at the issue. Then I began to be contacted by people claiming to have been taken onto UFOs, where they were subjected to some sort of medical procedure. I felt that such claims would result in ufology as a whole being perceived as a joke. I was worried that this would undermine my aim of getting the subject taken more seriously by people within the MOD, the military and the scientific community.

Ironically, it is surprising just how prevalent such a view is among ufologists, many of whom enjoy talking about UFO sightings by pilots, but shy away from anything more exotic. I overcame my initial prejudices and realised that I could not be selective. I had to go where the data took me. This is a philosophy that the authors of *Without Consent* have clearly followed. It is to their credit that their book does not attempt to weed out accounts that do not fit commonly held beliefs about the nature of alien abductions. Philip Mantle and Carl Nagaitis place their material before readers, inviting them to make up their own minds. This is not the only reason why *Without Consent* is such an important book.

It is perhaps unfortunate that most of the best-known researchers of the alien abduction phenomenon live in America. While investigators like *Budd Hopkins, John Mack* and *David Jacobs* are doing sterling work in this field, it does create the impression that we are dealing with a peculiarly American phenomenon. By concentrating on British cases, *Without Consent* will help show that these experiences are not confined to any particular country. The book places into the public domain details of cases every bit as extraordinary as some of the *classic* US abduction cases.

Refreshingly, *Without Consent* is a book about the abductees themselves, and not the researchers who have investigated their claims. Rather than telling their stories for them, Philip Mantle and Carl Nagaitis place the abductees at centre stage, drawing heavily on direct quotations from interviews and hypnotic regression sessions. The authors do of course offer analysis and opinion, but this is not intrusive. In this sense, this is a real researchers' book, with pride of place going to the evidence itself. Do not think, however, that this that the book is a dry, academic account.

It is highly readable and of equal value to seasoned investigators and those with no previous knowledge of this phenomenon.

So who are the abductees? To borrow a phrase from the film *Close Encounters of the Third Kind*, they are *ordinary people in extraordinary situations*. Certainly the few scientific studies into the mental health of abductees have found no evidence of psychopathology. Could we be dealing with hoaxers, *Walter Mitty* types, or people who want their fifteen minutes of fame? I suspect not.

I have worked with around one hundred abductees, either officially for the MOD or in a private capacity. Consequently, I am regularly contacted by production companies and TV shows wanting to put together items on alien abductions. I am asked how many people I know who would be willing to speak out concerning their experiences. Often, an appearance fee is offered. Yet, out of a hundred or so people, no more than half a dozen are willing to go public.

Could we be dealing with mass hysteria? Such a concept is not fully understood. There is, however, no evidence that would explain how thousands of people all around the world could come up with these highly complex narratives, often when they have no knowledge of similar reports.

On a personal note, I have met many of the people whose stories feature in this book. I can confirm that these are sincere individuals who genuinely believe that they have encountered something bizarre and - perhaps *otherworldly*. They do not strike me as mad, delusional or publicity-seeking. On the contrary, they have a certain quiet dignity about them. Sometimes they are critical of the authorities, either believing that they are involved in a cover-up of the truth about UFOs and abductions, or blaming them for not doing enough to protect them. Sometimes they are scathing about the sceptics who rubbish their claims without bothering to meet them or investigate their cases. All the abductees really want are answers.

So where does this leave us? The fact that this book is titled *Without Consent* reminds us that we are dealing with non-consensual experiences. These experiences are often intrusive and painful, so as well as dealing with a mystery, we are perhaps dealing with what should be regarded as a crime. *Without Consent* can therefore be regarded as a sort of detective story, where the authors examine what might in a literal sense be regarded as a crime against humanity.

Nick Pope
London
April 2002

PROLOGUE

Dateline: December 2001

Airline executive John Fraser (an assumed name) knew security nerves would still be jangling just 12 weeks or so after the Twin Towers attack that rocked the world. But when he inadvertently triggered a metal detector alarm at the Italian airport where he was due to board a flight back home, he was more shocked than anyone.

After a globe-trotting career with civilian and military airline companies, there was nobody more aware of the security requirements of international airlines. He knew the procedures to the letter and had carefully placed every metallic item in his possession through the metal detector separately before stepping through himself.

So how was he managing to set off the alarm system?

Slightly embarrassed by the unwanted attention he was now attracting, the 41 year old checked his pockets, removed his jacket and walked through the metal detection doorway once again.

The alarms immediately screamed into life, sparking a fresh frenzy of activity among the small group of Italian security personnel.

Again he was frisked and asked to check pockets for coins or any other pieces of metal that might set off the alert before going through once more.

"There I was standing just in my clothes with nothing metallic on me having set off the alarm on the metal detector arch at least four times when a security guard approached with one of the hand-held detectors," recalled John.

"He ran the detector up my right leg, along my torso and back down the left hand side. Then when it got to my left knee the buzzer went crazy!"

John paled visibly at the realisation. *For him, it was confirmation that alien beings had taken him, experimented on his unconscious body and planted un-earthly devices into the tissue around his left knee.*

The airport security men, convinced the Englishman did not pose any terrorist threat, assumed that the alarm had been triggered by a metal pin from some surgical procedure, and allowed John on his way.

1

John was sure that the security scare that he had sparked at a modern airport in the aftermath of the worst terrorist outrage in the history of the modern world was the work of alien life forms that, he believes, abducted him and implanted devices into his body a few years earlier.

When the report of John's experience landed on my desk it was the cue for me to call my co-author Philip Mantle to discuss the publication of an up-dated version of *Without Consent,* the first comprehensive survey of abduction phenomena in the UK that was originally published in 1994.

When we started the interviews for that book, nearly ten years ago, alien abduction was an unfamiliar term to most people. Then *The X-Files* hit our TV screens, along with many other US television and movie dramatisations which caused many to look at the subject with a new interest.

That new wave of interest resulted in more publications on the subject. New names entered the debate, including former Ministry of Defence man Nick Pope, and the subjects of Ufology and abductions were more widely discussed than ever before.

In 21st century Britain there can be few people who have never heard the term abduction. In fact abduction reports regularly flood in from all the country, like the West Midlands case that has just crossed my desk. It features an account from a 35 years old housewife who reports an alien visitation in her home. She produced a pen knife, presumably for self-defence, that she believes was zapped by a weird *rod of light.*

Extraordinary events are regularly reported by ordinary people. Without Consent aims to catalogue as many significant cases as possible, combine them with a wealth of information from various sources, and leave the reader to decide. I am led to believe readers find this a useful approach.

John Fraser's experience in an Italian airport brought home to me the fact that abduction is as much a 21st century phenomenon as it was a 20th century one. So an up-dated edition of Without Consent seemed appropriate.

Carl Nagaitis, March 2002

CHAPTER 1
Abduction - The Enigma

ABDUCTION: To carry off secretly. To draw away. To remove without consent. The dictionary definitions are chilling enough. The simple word often brings back memories of the sort of unpleasant events that, sadly, we have become used to reading in our newspapers: child abductions, abductions by terrorists, the abductions perpetrated by kidnappers, whether for political or financial gain. The very word is quite enough to strike fear into the hearts of most ordinary folk.

Yet today that very same word has a somewhat different meaning. Most now know that it has come to describe another frightening phenomenon that a growing number of people are experiencing . . . alleged Alien Abduction.

Alien abduction is the temporary taking of a person, or persons, by beings from beyond this world. Abductees, and there are many, often tell of being mysteriously transported to strange and unfamiliar places, perhaps spacecraft, where they undergo some form of examination, presumed to be medical in nature. Some victims, or to use the more correct term, *Abductees* are able to describe these events in great detail while others seem to bury their experiences in the depths of their minds, and that detail may only be accessible through hypnosis.

The majority of abductees are often only aware of experiencing *missing time.* They might find themselves arriving home much later than they anticipated; their last recollection being leaving work and with absolutely no idea of where they were or what they were doing in the intervening time. Some might seem to vanish off the face of the earth for short periods during their waking hours without a hint of a memory about those missing minutes or hours.

Others report possible nocturnal abductions - too real to be nightmares - in the form of visitations by alien beings or encounters with fantastic spacecraft. When amnesia locks away these experiences, hypnotic regression can provide the key which will admit the determined investigator to a treasure trove of abduction memories.

But what is the truth behind this bizarre affliction of the late 20th and early 21st century? Fact or fiction, a final frontier or a flight of fantasy?

Bizarre it is. But the 20th century cannot claim exclusive rights to the abduction mystery. It has been around for thousands of years. Gods and goblins, phantoms and fairies, they've all been blamed for the abductions that can be found scattered through ancient mythology and less ancient fairy tales.

So when did they become *alien* abductions? Well that all began on June 24, 1947 when American pilot Kenneth Arnold first coined the term *Flying Saucers* to described a group of nine UFOs he saw flying over Mount Rainier, Washington. He said they had *skimmed* over the horizon like saucers over water.

The birth of *flying saucers* spawned Ufology - the study and research of Unidentified Flying Objects.

By the early sixties there was widespread interest in the phenomenon and the number of Ufologists - the men and women who study the subject - had grown rapidly especially in America.

The possible link between abduction and UFOs came when Betty and Barney Hill, a young American couple reported a UFO sighting and a period of missing time during a long car journey from Canada to their home in New Hampshire.

The Hill's incident took place in 1961 after which both Barney and Betty suffered dreadful nightmares. They sought medical help and were introduced to a psychiatrist who decided to use hypnotic regression to discover what was disturbing them.

Under hypnosis Betty and Barney told an incredible story of being abducted by aliens which astonished both them and their doctor. They described their encounter in graphic detail: a meeting with aliens, a tour of a spaceship and a medical examination to boot.

Although reluctant, the psychiatrist allowed the couple to release their story in 1964. He wasn't convinced that their perception of events was accurate yet Betty and Barney were determined to go public.

When they did, they found their experience was not unique. At about the same time an Italian and a South American were also claiming to be alien abduction victims. And if their reports were to be believed, their abductions were even earlier than the Hill case.

The mystery abductions of the past were now Alien Abductions . . . suddenly they became a 20th century phenomenon.

And they are being reported in ever increasing numbers to this day.

The Establishment view? Alien Abduction Phenomena have been consigned to the trash can of twilight world twaddle along with ghosts, ghouls and fairies at the bottom of the garden. The fact that the flying saucer fraternity is involved only serves to further undermine its credibility as far as the cynics are concerned.

However Ufologists are well used to that sort of reaction. In response they have amassed an impressive array of statistics to support their case for research into abductions, which they regard as one small, but significant aspect of Ufology.

Since 1947 when flying saucer entered the English language, staggering *40 MILLION UFO sightings* have been logged. More than *30 UFO crash landings* have been reported and abduction reports run into an astonishing *TENS OF THOUSANDS*.

What on earth is going on out there? Well some people, Ufologists and others are trying to find out.

The vast majority of abduction reports come from America, where Ufology is something of a growth industry. In fact one observer recently calculated that some statistics suggest that as many as *ONE IN TEN* Americans have had some sort of encounter with a UFO and a significant minority of those claim abduction experiences.

The phenomenon is known throughout the rest of the world from Rio to Rotterdam, from Moscow to Memphis.

6

Individuals report alleged abductions from the frozen wastes of Northern Scandinavia to the humid hot spots of the Amazon Basin.

So what exactly do we mean by Alien Abduction? What series of events does an individual have to experience before we can call him the victim of an alleged alien abduction?

The variety of scenarios is virtually endless, but from exhaustive study of many hundreds of abduction reports from around the world Ufologists now accept that each abductee goes through a distinct series of stages.

The *classic* abduction, and there are some, goes something like this:

The witness or witnesses - *the Ufology term for anybody experiencing an encounter with an Unidentified Flying Object or its occupants* - finds himself in either an isolated or lonely place or in a normally busy but now deserted location and sights a UFO. The sighting may be preceded by a noise, often a humming, or strange lights or both.

If the witness is in a vehicle he may experience malfunctioning of the engine and electrical systems. Around this point he will either see signs of alien activity or encounter an alien who may then *escort* him into the craft. The escort may use encouragement, telepathic prompting or even a degree of force to get the witness into the object. Some witnesses recall being transported into the craft by various means which are beyond their understanding before encountering aliens inside the UFO.

The next stage involves examination of the witness, often some form of medical examination during which strange or apparently advanced implements or pieces of equipment are used. The examination is followed by some form of communication with the aliens. Interestingly, a large proportion of abductees claim that communication is not verbal but telepathic in nature. A tour around the craft then often follows with some abductees claiming visits to control rooms or engine rooms. More rarely a trip around *another world* or a strange environment may be undertaken.

Further communication between the witness and his abductors may involve questioning or warnings about the future, and promises of a return visit. The witness then leaves the craft, or loses consciousness and finds himself back where his adventure began or may even watch the craft take off into the beyond.

By no means do all abductees experience all of the above events, but all abductees experience at least one or more of them.

After returning to their own environment abductees may experience complete or partial amnesia which manifests itself as missing time.

Abduction amnesia varies dramatically. Approximately 50 percent of all witnesses recall all of their experience with some form of assistance, say hypnosis. Some may have forgotten everything and be aware only of a time loss. If they are curious enough, they can seek the help of a hypnotist who can regress their mind to the point at which their recall ends and allow them to *re-live* events once more. The value of this approach and the inherent dangers will be debated later. Other witnesses, with absolutely no recollection of the abduction, may suffer from disturbing dreams containing aspects of their experience. As in the Hill case, the recurrent nightmares may lead them to take medical advice to get them to the bottom of the problem. If their doctors suggest hypnosis, they could all be in for a shock.

A number of those whose memories of abduction are wiped out by total amnesia can develop flashbacks, or mental images of strange occurrences. These, combined with further images from the graphic dreams which can follow an encounter can fall into place like a jigsaw puzzle, with or without hypnosis.

So you don't have to have seen a UFO or an alien to be a possible abductee. In fact the most chilling aspect of this enigma is that if you had been snatched, for whatever reason, by beings, from wherever, the chances are you would not know about it.

Theoretically there is no limit to how many of us have been taken without consent.

A US magazine recently caused a mild panic when one of their *experts* took the above argument to extremes. Readers were told that if they could find any marks or scars on their body which they could not account for, then they were potential abductees. The publication was inundated with calls from anxious possible abductees.

Here in Britain the relevance of that theory was quickly demolished by the knobbly knee test. Delegates to a British UFO conference were asked to roll up their left trouser leg and hold up their hands if they could find a mark or scar for which they could not account. The response: 100 per cent.

The point of that exercise was that there was no room for wild claims and that sort of sweeping generalisation if modern Ufology was ever going to be taken seriously.

So, what are we to make of Abduction Phenomenon? Is it merely a part of UFO culture, or is it a phenomenon in its own right? In view of the fact that many of the abductees you will read about in this book had no involvement with Ufology until they began looking for reasons for their experiences and, as it is Ufologists who have gathered the majority of available data on the subject, have had no option, but to regard UFO culture and Alien Abduction as one and the same.

Furthermore, serious Ufologists contend, and we agree, that the phenomenon is a fact. There are just too many cases involving sane, sober, decent, honest and, above all, very ordinary people, for it to be discounted out of hand.

Whether the cause, or causes, of their experiences come from *Outer Space* or *Inner Space* is a matter for research and further debate. But the plain fact is that a growing number of people believe they have been taken away from their familiar surroundings, albeit temporarily, and introduced to something so strange, so odd that it often changes their outlook on life completely.

Those who don't write off their experiences as a *bad dream* or a *bout of temporary insanity* sometimes grasp the alien abduction theory with both hands because, at the very least, it offers them an explanation for the apparently inexplicable.

As we mentioned earlier, abductions didn't suddenly begin to coincide with the arrival of the term *flying saucer* back in 1947. People have been reporting mysterious abductions for centuries.

Back then the abductors were described as fairies or witches, even gods, some of whom liked to have their wicked way with the odd lesser mortal. The UFOs were variously described as magic carpets, flying castles and even *Chariots of the Gods,* as pointed out by author Erich von Daniken.

Stories of heroes being transported to the heavens, where they see myriad things magical and wondrous, abound in ancient literature. Folklore and fairy tales are full of references to children being taken off by the fairies.

Celebrated American astronomer Carl Sagan dug up the following folk tale from 1645, which illustrates the point: "A Cornish teenager, Anne Jeffries, was found groggy and crumpled on the floor. Much later she recalled being attacked by little men, carried paralyzed to a castle in the air, seduced and returned home. She called the little men *fairies.* The next year she was arrested for witchcraft . . ."

It is fair to speculate that a Middle Ages man confronted by a UFO would be stumped to find the words to describe it. A flying machine would have been a ludicrous concept in those far gone days so why not call it a flying castle? Some of the descriptions of aliens, allegedly encountered by some of the abductees we study in our book, make them sound not unlike the story book perceptions of goblins, or even elves. And by the time his story had been passed around the community, by word of mouth of course, it would certainly have been decorated with the usual embellishments these stories accumulate in the telling.

But let's face it, alleged abductions of long ago, are beyond investigation. No matter how easy it is to draw comparisons between modern day abductions and those in mythology and folklore, the latter remain no more than mythology and folklore.

Modern day abductions are fair game for thorough investigation. And thanks to 21st century communications technology today's abductees can, and sometimes do, find their reports flashed around the globe almost instantly.

Modern man can no longer blame fairies and goblins for those events and occurrences which his science is unable to explain. So UFOs can come in handy.

Ufologists have come up with a whole host of theories to try to explain both visitations and abductions. They range from the physical to the psychological and even the downright hysterical. Many Ufologists are less interested in UFOs and abductions than the reasons people report these things. Some privately admit that they believe there is little chance that the phenomenon is due to extraterrestrials visiting our planet. However they are prepared to keep an open mind.

Others find the alien evidence so compelling that they are convinced extra terrestrial activity is, indeed, the only possible explanation for the phenomena. Within this group alone, different theories abound.

One school of thought maintains that we Earth dwellers have been visited by intelligent life forms from the depths of space since time began. They believe they have monitored us through our development and have even nudged us in the right direction at the right time. This view of a philanthropic group of aliens who have taken on the role of guardians of our planet is appealing to some and indeed clues to support this theory can be found among the British cases which we have put under the microscope in this book.

However, although modern science accepts the likelihood that there is other life among the billions of stars in our universe, why would those life forms, assuming they have the ability, travel huge distances to oversee the inhabitants of an insignificant little planet like ours?

What's in it for them? Those questions remain unanswered.

Another school of though postulates the notion that our alien visitors come here for very selfish reasons. They have put forward the theory that the extraterrestrials behind UFO sightings and abductions are here to harvest a rich source of genetic material to enable them to continue their own race.

New York artist and world renowned Ufologist Budd Hopkins has put forward this view most forcibly in recent years. Whether the alleged aliens have found themselves down a genetic *cul-de-sac* forcing them to look elsewhere for the means to continue reproduction is, quite frankly, anybody's guess. But Hopkins, and others, point to various aspects of abduction phenomena which seem to support this genetic motive.

Many abductees report a high degree of alien interest in their sexual and reproductive organs during *on board* medical examinations. Some even claim to have had sexual relations with the visitors.

Add to that claims that human ova have been removed from some abductees and reports from others of mysteriously abandoned pregnancies coinciding with abductions - inferring the removal of tiny foetuses in the most mysterious circumstances - and it all adds up to the one of the most sinister scenarios imaginable.

Some of the British abductees you will read about later in this book add further fuel to the raging debate on the sexual/ human reproduction aspect of abduction.

This most disturbing of theories ties in with a spate of alleged mutilations of farm animals in the USA and England in recent years. Horses and cattle had whole sections of their reproductive systems removed with surgical precision, according to some reports from America.

The *operations,* it was claimed, had been conducted using some sort of laser instrument because of the cauterising effect on the animal tissue, researchers stated.

The British cases involved horses which had all been mutilated to some degree. In a number of cases genitalia were damaged, adding to speculation in Ufology circles, that the attacks could have some link with the alien genetic harvesting theory.

Intriguing, you'll agree. But because UFO research is undertaken largely by amateurs, some good, some not so good, gathering evidence to examine cases like these is extremely difficult. These are the sort of theories that we all know Ufologists will never prove, not unless they can first prove the existence of alien visitors piloting UFOs.

Thankfully in Britain and America we are lucky enough to have some well respected and experienced UFO investigators who are concerned with fact and not fiction.

And whether they are dealing with UFO sightings or alleged Alien Abduction Phenomena they are more likely to reject a case than put it up for serious consideration if it does not stand up to the test of a rigorous investigations.

Many alleged Alien Abduction cases are discounted because of *contamination*. No, they are not infected with some dreadful alien disease. The term simply means that their abduction experience could have been contaminated by the mass of readily available information, in the form of literature, films and TV programmes about other people's abduction cases.

Any abductee would be hard put to describe the myriad of new sights, sounds and sensations he experiences during an encounter. So if that abductee is familiar with, say Whitley Strieber's *Communion*, for example, or with any of the many books and the growing number of movies on the subject of abduction, he is likely to lapse into the relevant terminology.

If he describes the classic Streiber alien, slight, almond eyed, pinched nose, grey complexion, how can we know whether this is a description of what he has seen or what he thinks he has seen?

Is the sleek metallic craft he describes an account of a real experience or an imagined one based on a UFO picture or description picked up from a book or the TV screen? No matter how bona fide the abductee, no matter how graphic his description of events, the serious investigator must decide whether the evidence, the physical signs and any other factors sufficiently compensate for the level of contamination.

As with UFO sightings, the numbers of people reporting abduction phenomena is far greater in the United States than in the UK. This is not just because the population of America is far greater. It has more to do with the character of the nation.

A relatively new country, America is still more prepared to take on the unusual, to welcome the new and to be more open minded about strange concepts and ideas. After all, as we have already pointed out, it was an American who first used the term *flying saucer*.

Flying saucer witnesses in America are more likely to speak openly about their experiences than in stiff upper lipped Britain. They have a ready made audience, eager to hear the tiniest details in the form of the scores of UFO magazines published all over the country.

To the population of the nation which, for many years, led the space race, space ships are a reality. Maybe flying saucers are just the next step.

In fact some of the heroic astronauts from the National Aeronautics and Space Administration (NASA) have given a personal boost to the cause of Ufology.

One of the most interesting reports came from Gemini 4 astronaut James McDivitt, in June 1965. Orbiting 90 miles above the earth he saw a cylinder shaped object, with arms protruding from it, in apparent free flight over the Pacific Ocean . . .

Travelling at a higher altitude, the object moved along a parallel path to the Gemini, but seemed to be closing fast. McDivitt and fellow astronaut Edward White were preparing to take evasive action when the object disappeared.

McDivitt had taken a photo and some cine film of the object. The official version was that he had spotted the unmanned satellite *Pegasus*. But on checking, McDivitt discovered that would have been 1,200 miles away from his position when he sighted it.

Captain Ed Mitchell, the sixth man to walk on the moon, said in 1974: "I am completely convinced that some UFO sightings are real. The question is not where the UFOs are from. The question is, what they are?"

These are just two of an estimated 30 UFO sightings by astronauts. They became so common NASA came up with a codeword for them *Bogeys*.

These well publicised incidents and comments have given American Ufologists a credibility that can only be envied on the other side of the Atlantic.

Like UFO spotters, American abductees have come forward in their thousands to tell their stories or write their books.

This has much to do with the power of the mighty dollar. We remarked earlier on the way Ufology in the States has become something of a growth industry, and a good abduction case can mean that some abductees can cash in on the wider public interest. Lucrative book and film deals and radio and TV appearances offer celebrity status, albeit temporary, to many abductees and UFO witnesses in the States.

And if there is one thing American's love dearly it is a celebrity.

One of Hollywood's abduction success stories, in movie terms, was *Fire in the Sky*, which was a box office hit when it was released.

It followed the story of American logger Travis Walton who became an abduction victim in 1975. While his mystery vanishing act sparked a major police hunt, Walton was going through the classic stages of alien abduction. Police interviewed his workmates worried that Walton's disappearance could have been the result of foul play. But the bemused logger turned up just in time to prevent any miscarriage of justice and with a story that was literally out of this world.

Walton went on to write a bestseller about his abduction and when senior members of the Hollywood industry met with the humble logger to discuss the film project they said they had been impressed by his sincerity. After that meeting they had no hesitation in turning his account into a big screen production.

When he came to Britain to publicise his film, Walton

Without Consent

said he had found people anxious to hear his story and he was grateful for the assistance he had received from UFO investigators. He never once complained of the scorn and ridicule that many British abductees say they receive in this country.

Ironically the openness of the American approach to both UFOs and Abduction Phenomenon makes the reaction of British scoffers even more pronounced.

"Only the Yanks would fall for that nonsense," is the usual response when discussing the subject here. "Flying saucers and bug eyed monsters from Mars. They're only seen by loonies and crackpots." The dinner party crowd might not openly mock, but any attempt at a serious discussion on Ufology or Alien Abduction Phenomenon is received with the usual raised eyebrows and wry smiles.

"UFOs, flying saucers and abductions . . . just not British, are they old boy?"

With attitudes like that it is hard to blame British abductees for keeping their heads below the parapet. It probably explains why we have far fewer catalogued cases in this country than in the more open minded USA. Here, UFO investigators are convinced there are many, many more victims of alien abduction among us. However, they are often unwilling to admit their experiences, let alone talk about them. As one victim said recently: "For me, becoming an abductee was like contracting a socially embarrassing disease."

Why? Because he let it be known that he believed his abductors were not of this world. An intelligent and articulate man he has carefully considered who or what were responsible for a bizarre series of events he experienced some years ago and he has come to the sober conclusion that he was abducted by aliens who travelled to this Earth in a spacecraft.

He has no idea why they took him or why they examined him or where they came from.

He has eliminated all other rational explanations for his experience and settled for the only theory that seems to add up.

To the handful of people he confided in over the years, his story represents the rantings of a wacky weirdo, a member of the lunatic fringe with flying saucers on the brain. Scorned and derided by so-called friends, he quickly learned that silence was his best protection in a mocking world.

Today he is Mr Normal, Mr Middle Class, married, pursuing a safe and sensible career, he will deny any knowledge of Abduction Phenomenon except on the very rare occasions when he meets a fellow abductee. Even then he is reluctant to open up on the subject until he is assured that he has got a sympathetic ear.

However, the British reserve is not totally negative as far as our Ufologists are concerned. The fact that alleged abductees risk having ridicule heaped upon them when they talk publicly about their experiences must deter the cranks and the attention seekers.

The fact that some are willing to come out and talk about their abductions indicates a determination to get to the bottom of a phenomenon which has had an impact on their lives. They are prepared to risk the ridicule in the interests of research.

British abductees have much to lose and little to gain by going public. Unlike their American brothers and sisters they will not become temporary celebrities and they don't stand to get a fat cheque from a Hollywood producer.

For the purposes of this book we have persuaded abductees from across the country to tell their stories in the first ever complete catalogue of British abduction cases. Some have allowed us to use their real names; others have chosen to use pseudonyms for obvious reasons.

Some are coming forward for the first times and others have been prepared to reveal aspects of their cases they have never spoken about before. Each and every one of the following cases has been investigated and researched by Philip Mantle, Director of Investigations for the British UFO Research Association or by accredited investigators from BUFORA and other associated research groups.

We have reconstructed events as related to us in detail by the abductees or from the hundreds of pages of data from the files of BUFORA and other UFO organisations and researchers. Transcripts of scores of taped interviews and hypnosis sessions have been checked and cross checked to give the most accurate account possible.

Each of our abductees has their own theory about Abduction Phenomena, aliens and UFOs and those terms are used freely in their accounts. They have also been invited to give their own explanation of what they feel they went through.

We know how frustrating it can be to read of strange phenomena where the only cases available to illustrate events came from thousands of miles away. The stories of abduction from the United States and elsewhere in the world are legion but their remoteness means we sometimes have difficulty getting a grip on the subject.

In this book we present British cases involving ordinary people who find themselves caught up in extraordinary circumstances. They are all the sorts of people we can relate to, people like us living in typical British neighbourhoods, with typical jobs and typical interests. These are real people and to them their stories are equally real.

We take a neutral stance. Abduction Phenomenon is fact. Alien Abduction? Fact or fiction? We leave you to decide.

CHAPTER 2
CEIVs

Alien Abductions cases are known as Close Encounters of the Fourth Kind (CEIVs). Encounters of the First Kind (CE1s) are basically UFO sightings, but at relatively close range. Encounters of the Second Kind (CEIIs) are events where the UFO leaves some kind of mark on the environment, burn marks on the ground or any area of flattened vegetation to indicate the landing area of a vehicle.

Close Encounters of the Third Kind (CEIIIs) are understood by most people thanks to the Hollywood blockbuster of the same name. These events are sightings of UFOs where an occupant or alien being is involved.

Fourth kind encounters are the least common of UFO events, often the most dramatic and invariably the most difficult to investigate. They centre on the abduction of the witness or witnesses and therefore the credibility of those witnesses is crucial to establishing exactly what happened to them.

The UFO investigator, faced with an alleged abduction, will first scrutinise the abductee. Is he or she sane, free from drink or drug problems, of a stable background? He has to make sure that the trip experienced was not drink or drug induced and was not the result of a sick mind.

He will also need to check out the abductee's general state of health because if he or she were taking any medication, for whatever complaint, he will need to ascertain whether the drugs prescribed could have any side effects, like hallucination.

The general physical and mental check is a means of clearing the ground for the next stage of the investigation. Is the witness free from personal emotional crises?

Sadly there are some people who concoct stories to draw attention to them. Often they are the victims of personal problems and the creation of a fantasy scenario is their cry for help. They may just crave attention, want somebody to pay attention to them and spend some time with them. If that means fabricating a story so be it. Is the witness a publicity seeker, turned on by seeing his or her name in print? Is he or she out to make a fast buck? Some people, for whatever reason, will create an encounter not for personal attention, but public attention. The *celebrity status* they enjoy from local publicity is minimal, yet for some it is motive enough. Others mistakenly believe they can sell their UFO or abduction accounts to newspapers not matter how bizarre.

All these possibilities will go through the investigator's mind before he can begin the investigation proper.

The real work starts with the interview. Investigators spend a great deal of time in personal interviews with witnesses. He will take them through their experiences step by step, often probing for the sort of detail that the interviewee might regard as insignificant. Throughout this process, the interviewer will be paying great attention to the witness's body language, tone of voice and manner.

These can reveal much about the character of the witness. Sitting chatting in the home environment of the witness can provide useful background on the type of person making the claims.

So when the physical clues are sadly lacking, when the evidence, as is often the case, is very thin on the ground, the investigator can weigh-up the facts and make a balanced judgement on the case.

As one experienced investigator said recently: "After spending a great deal of time with a witness you can get a gut reaction. You may just know he is, or sometimes isn't, telling the truth."

When the investigator has completed his interviews, nearly always witnessed and tape recorded, he will then go through the witness statement with a fine toothed comb.

Did the UFO leave any physical mark on the environment in any way? Did the alleged occupants leave any kind of physical mark upon the witness? Did the witness have the opportunity to make any recordings or take any pictures of what or who he had seen? Although we don't know of any cases of witnesses being armed with tape recorders and cameras, one of those abductees who recounts his story in the following pages did indeed manage to take a snap of an alleged alien visitor.

Proving any abduction case is well nigh impossible at the present time. As former Director of Investigations for BU-FORA, Philip Mantle knows only too well that providing conclusive evidence of a Close Encounter of the Fourth Kind would also involve finding conclusive proof of the existence of UFOs and aliens . . . and nobody has managed to do that quite yet.

However an investigator can put forward a case for serious consideration if the witness or abductee is of sufficient quality. If they are decent, sound of mind individuals and if it can be demonstrated that they have nothing to gain, and in some cases much to lose, by talking about their experiences then they become candidates for our catalogue of study. The three cases we will now highlight are not untypical of many abduction reports. They all rely heavily on the testimony of the witnesses.

All three alleged abductees were alone when they experienced their encounters and there was no physical evidence to support their claims. In two of the cases there were no corroborating reports of sightings or events to support their perceptions.

However investigators were impressed by the sincerity of all three, none of whom sought publicity.

Each of these abductees stood to gain nothing by telling their stories and at least one of them suffered disturbing after effects in the form of nightmares in the months following his encounter. For ease of reference, each account begins with the name of the abductee, the date of their experience and the location of their encounter.

Elsie Oakensen
November 22, 1978
Church Stowe, Northamptonshire

Elsie Oakensen pulled her coat around her as she left her office at the Daventry Teacher's Training Centre at about 5.15 that chill winter's evening. The 50 year old working wife and mother felt the icy fingers of the North East wind sting her face as she stopped to buy a newspaper before making her way to her car.

She noticed that a sidelight on her vehicle was not working, so she decided to make the seven mile journey home driving with dipped headlights. A sensible woman, Mrs Oakensen was not one to take chances in the fast fading light. She had made the trip between her office and her home in the village of Church Stowe near Weedon so many times that she could have done it blindfolded. But the wife of a police officer knew better than to take chances when it came to road safety.

It was an uneventful journey until she joined the normally busy A5 just two miles or so from her home village. As she manoeuvred her car onto the highway she became aware of a sight she would never forget.

Ahead of her, about 100 feet above the smooth tarmac surface of the road was an object so strange, so unnatural that she had to struggle to find words to describe it.

A dumbbell shaped object, grey and plastic looking, with a brilliant red light in the left hand sphere and a green light in the right hand sphere just . . . well it just hovered there. It didn't move. It simply floated. From the way it spanned the entire width of the road, Elsie guessed this strange something to be at least 50 feet in length.

"I was absolutely fascinated by it," Elsie told us some time later. "But I just drove on as normal."

Gripped by a combination of both curiosity and awe, Elsie resolutely gripped the steering wheel and drove on, directly towards and then under the bizarre object. "I had to drive on so I could take my usual right turn off the A5 at Stowe Hill," she said.

"I remember at first thinking that it must be some kind of aeroplane and that it would zoom over my head and crash behind me. But it just hung in the air," recalled Elsie.

"Once I had turned off the A5, I looked back and thought it must have gone by now, but it hadn't. It was still there, those brilliant lights still shining."

The encounter had been so absorbing that Elsie could not recall seeing any other traffic on that section of the A5. But it would have been highly unusual for that busy section of road to be deserted at that time, when many people were returning home from work.

The darkness continued to close around Elsie's car as she proceeded with the final leg of her journey home. "How strange," she said to herself. "What could that have been all about?"

She made her way along the narrow, winding country road, taking a right turn at a T junction on the outskirts of Church Stowe. Completing the turn she changed up to third gear. Oddly the car seemed to slow down instead of speeding up.

Momentarily forgetting the mysterious object over the A5 she double checked she had the accelerator fully depressed and then in desperation changed down to first in a desperate bid to get the car moving.

At last the engine seemed to respond, but when she came to the end of a line of trees by the entrance to a farm at the perimeter of the village, the motor just cut-out.

Elsie found herself sitting in complete darkness, and complete silence. The engine had stopped and every light on the vehicle had been extinguished. Turning the ignition key was useless, the car was dead.

Elsie looked out of the car windows on total blackness. Putting her face close to the glass, so she could peer out, she thought she would catch a glimpse of the lights that normally shone in the houses and farm buildings she knew were so near. But she saw nothing. She could not even make out the shapes of any of the familiar buildings she drove by every day.

"I don't know why, but I wasn't frightened," she said later. But that was before the strange events of that dark and lonely night took an even more dramatic turn.

Suddenly a brilliant circle of pure white light appeared and illuminated the road by the passenger side of the car.

"Then as suddenly as it came on, it went off and I was in darkness once again," recalled Elsie.

Seconds later further circles of light, about a metre across, appeared first at the front of the car, then at the rear and then at each side. Punctuating the pitch darkness they flicked on, then off, then on again.

At one moment Elsie thought the glow from one of the circles illuminated the farm entrance, at another all she could see beyond the strange light was blackness.

Punching holes in the night, the circles of light danced around her car in an almost choreographed routine as if searching for something . . . or someone.

"Yes, they were searching," said Elsie. "They seemed to be searching the darkness. I would have called them search-lights, but I remember realising they couldn't have been caused by a searchlight because there was no beam."

Bizarrely, Elsie found herself 30 yards further down the road, the motor was running, the car was in third gear and she was behind the wheel and driving quite normally.

Her head was whirling. Moments ago Elsie was stranded in a broken down car, surrounded by darkness. Now she was back in control and driving home. But she had no idea of what had occurred in the intervening seconds.

As if to reassure herself she looked around and could see the shapes of the local church and other building silhouet-ted against the evening skyline. "Yes, I'm nearly home now," she said to herself. "Not far now."

As she parked up outside her home Elsie noticed her bro-ken side light was now working again. She glanced at her house and could see her kitchen lights were on. Good, that meant husband John was home and would be preparing the evening meal.

He had been working split shifts so it was quite normal for him to prepare the tea while waiting for his wife to re-turn home from work.

Elsie put the car in the garage and let herself into the house. It was then that she glanced down at her watch. She was stunned. Somehow her fifteen minute journey home had taken half an hour, twice as long as normal, although her car had seemed stationary for mere moments.

"I told John *I will just go upstairs to look out of the window and then I will tell you something you won't believe.*" From the bedroom window Elsie saw a flashing yellow light in the same position she had seen the dumbbell shaped object.

"I went down and told John exactly what had happened," said Elsie later. "He didn't say a word. He just dished out the meal. When I told him my story I didn't mention the word UFO. I don't think I had ever heard that word."

At exactly 7pm that evening Elsie felt a tightening sensation around her head. The band of pressure stretched across her forehead and around to the back of her cranium.

The strange restrictive sensation, like having a powerful elastic band placed around one's head, lasted about a minute and then disappeared completely. She suddenly recalled experiencing the same sensation at lunchtime that day.

That would have been the end of Elsie Oakensen's intriguing experience if it hadn't been for a young man at her office. Back at the Daventry Teacher's Training Centre next day the youngster overheard Elsie relating her experience to colleagues during a break for coffee. "Sounds like a UFO to me", he said suddenly, causing Elsie to sit up, a perplexed expression on her face.

"An Unidentified Flying Object, you know flying saucers," added the young man before launching into a brief explanation of the phenomenon for the benefit of an audience comprising of Elsie and a handful of fellow office workers.

Elsie's bizarre experience was about to become a Close Encounter of the office gossip kind.

Her missing time mystery was light years away from the usual tittle-tattle that broke up the hum-drum routine of office life. The story soon spread beyond the confines of the training centre and before long a reporter from the Northampton Chronicle and Echo turned up to interview Elsie.

Devoting 12 column inches to her sighting, the article in the Friday November 24 edition of the paper reported several more incidents in and around the area that week. A woman in Northampton claimed to have seen *a window in the sky with green flashing lights around it*. But there was no mention of the strange dumbbell shaped object with a green light in one end and a red one in the other.

British UFO Research Association investigators were soon on the case and took detailed notes of the Oakensen Case. Elsie, by now, was anxious to learn as much about what happened to her as possible and was more than happy to co-operate.

With the investigation almost complete there was only one further course open to them. Would Mrs Oakensen agree to hypnosis?

When she said *of course* the BUFORA team were delighted. They explained that hypnotic regression was a method which could take Elsie's mind back to that fateful evening enabling her to *re-live* the events, particularly during the period of her time loss.

A qualified hypnotherapist put Elsie into a hypnotic trance and led her mind back to those anxious moments in her car. During the hypnosis session, which took place nine months after her encounter, in August 1979, a detailed record of her recollections, and of her reactions were taken.

Elsie said: "My car engine has stalled, I feel hot. A band of pressure tightens around my head as it did at lunchtime. I am getting hotter and beginning to sweat. The pressure hurts . . . it hurts my head.

"A brilliant white light is shining in my eyes, a pure white light, very bright. Circles of very bright light radiate from it as it comes closer until I can only see the top of the semi circle . . . my body gets hotter . . . the pain in my head is intense.

"I feel as if I am sitting, I can't feel my legs, my arms are shaking. I am very frightened. The radiating semi circles of light seem to change to a small brilliant circle, obviously going away from me.

"It's still light, but hazy and through this haze materialise two shapes. The first is a long, thin shape that appears to the left and then disappears. The second is more rectangular and appears to the right - disappears - then both appear together. They shine through the haze, a silver glow outline both grey coloured shapes which have smooth rounded outlines, rather ghostlike. The bright light now shines as a small circle in the distance. I get hotter, my arms shake more, and my head hurts dreadfully. I am terrified."

At that stage Elsie's discomfort and distress was such that she was immediately taken out of the trance by the hypnotherapist. The investigators were disappointed that the regression had not revealed more clear detail of Elsie's encounter.

But the lack of any more vivid descriptions did not rule out the possibility of it being consistent with alien abduction.

The sighting of the UFO, the lights, the malfunctioning of her car and the missing time certainly make the episode a contender for Fourth Kind encounter status.

Was Elsie and her car taken up into a UFO? It has happened to some American abductees, if their reports are to be believed. Without filling in her missing time we'll probably never know the truth. But what does Elsie make of her experience? "I believe I was selected, scanned and rejected," she says. Selected by whom, scanned for what and why rejected? Elsie, now retired, says: "I cannot explain it but it has certainly left me with an open mind and an interest in this field."

Investigators agree that Elsie's experience is a classic of alien abduction phenomenon, but not so much because the events tie in with so many other abduction reports. What makes this case a gem in Ufology investigation terms is the quality of the witness.

She is undoubtedly a credible witness. A mature and responsible woman in a senior position in a professional career, Elsie is no crackpot, far from it.

Contamination doesn't come into this case at all. Elsie had never even heard of UFOs and had no interest in the subject. She had not been influenced by UFO literature, she hadn't ever seen any, and she was so ignorant of the flying saucer phenomenon that she could only liken the object she saw to an aeroplane.

Elsie's only regret about the incident was the reaction which she and her husband received from some people after she had agreed to give an interview to the reporter from the local newspaper.

Her husband John, a policeman, suffered some mockery from colleagues in the force and a few locals ridiculed Elsie's report. In fact on one occasion a man called at the front door of her home and when she opened it he simply stood there guffawing.

"I was furious," said Elsie. "What these people didn't seem to understand was that I was not making any claims about what had happened to me. I didn't describe that thing over the A5 as a UFO. I simply told people, as honestly as I could, what had gone on.

"Interestingly enough, when John retired from the force we had visits from other police officers who had since left. Some of them told me how bad they felt about the way John had been treated by some people. Then they went on to tell me they had seen strange things and heard reports that they dare not admit for fear of becoming victims of ridicule themselves."

Although there had been no corroborative sightings of the strange UFO seen by Elsie on that fateful November night in 1978, it later transpired that four Women's Institute members may well have seen the same object just two hours later.

The four ladies were travelling by car from Byfield via Woodford Halse towards Preston Capes - just a stone's throw from Elsie's home village of Church Stowe. They would have been passing through that area at sometime after 7 that same night.

First the driver of their car saw what she later described as a parallel sided beam of light shoot out from the clouds. Seconds later it disappeared. Then the beam appeared again, although this time only momentarily.

The direction of the beam? Ironically, it seemed to be aiming for Church Stowe.

Then as the driver turned into the Preston Capes road, she and her passengers could not help but notice a strange object in the sky. They described it as comprising *two lights, one red and one green* and the lights seemed to be about 12 inches apart, indicating that if it was the same dumbbell shaped object seen by Mrs Oakensen then it must have been some considerable distance away for its new observers.

Pressing on, the driver continued along her route trying to suppress the feeling that they were being followed. One look out of the window seemed to confirm their worst fears. The object was pacing their car. For one heart-stopping moment, the engine of the vehicle faltered, threatening to cut out as it swept along on the final leg of the journey to Preston Capes.

The driver knocked it into third gear and rammed her foot down on the accelerator. The motor responded energetically and the vehicle powered on. The lights moved off and out of sight in seconds enabling them to cover the remaining miles without interruption.

Had those ladies also been selected, as Elsie believes happened to her? And had the driver's quick reactions saved them from an encounter similar to that experienced by Mrs Oakensen? We will probably never find out.

Today, Elsie is still searching for answers to an experience which changed her life. Now retired, the mother of three and grandmother to four is still prepared to assist Ufologists in their work, in the hope that it might provide some answers, one day.

Privately, Elsie takes the view that her encounter was more spiritual in nature than an event caused by alien beings. This has been reinforced by the discovery that she has developed the 'gift' of healing, and has joined the National Federation of Spiritual Healers.

"It is something that came to me after my experience," said Elsie. "It is a gift I certainly didn't have before. Now I find that I can help others with my gift and I will certainly continue using it.

"I don't know for sure what happened to me that night.

All I do know is something very definitely did occur. In a way I'm a richer person for it."

David Thomas *(pseudonym)*
February 8, 1985
Pwllheli
North Wales

David Thomas knew the four and a half mile trek to his village down the Pwllheli road like the back of his hand. It didn't matter that it was three in the morning and black as hell, the starlight was all he needed to make his way home.

He was just grateful that the heavy snows that fell over much of Britain that day had missed the lovely Llyn Peninsula where the Irish Sea helps to temper the worst excesses of winter.

Although there was some snow on the ground and an arctic chill in the air David hardly felt it. He'd just enjoyed a hot night of music with his mates and the beat was still pounding in the head of this unemployed 19 year old.

About 20 minutes down the road David could have sworn that the music was still playing in his ears. He stopped, shook his head and then listened.

Silence, a deafening silence. An eerie stillness devoid of the night-time noises every country boy grows up with. No rustle in the grass, no owls' wing beats, not even a whispering wind.

Then yes, there it was. Not music but a humming. Faint, but humming nevertheless. It was like the low pitched thrum of an electricity generator, but David knew this part of the world well enough to be certain that there wasn't one in operation for many miles.

He peered through the darkness, across to the field where the noise seemed to be coming from. Turning his head first this way, then that way, he tried to get a bearing on the source of the sound. It was no good, he'd have to go and see what it was, he thought to himself as he left the road and padded over the frozen grass of the field.

As he made his way over the field the only noise to break into the insistent thrumming was that made by his feet crunching on the ice covered grass. The noise became louder, more distinct as David made progress across the field, his eyes scouring the dark horizon for a clue to its origin. Then he saw it. A large, dull, black thing that just hovered, hovering about two and a half feet above the centre of the field. He had only known it was there when he noticed something was obscuring the starlight. Moving closer, ever closer, David strained his eyes to take in as much detail as he could.

Domed and disc shaped, he estimated the object was about 25 feet across and 20 feet high. Antennae or stabilisers poked out from it and there was a drawbridge-like hatchway and windows at the top. He couldn't see any obvious lighting but the object seemed to have a dull, almost muted, fluorescent glow.

Standing there in the cold and darkness, peering at this strange, humming thing, floating above the ground and blocking out the starlight, David's attention was caught by a movement off to one side. Switching his gaze he saw a group of smaller shapes making their way across the field towards him.

A group of people, man-like shapes were making determined progress in his direction. He was overcome by the instinct to flee. But when he turned to do so he was too late. Another strange humanoid shape was blocking his only escape route. Frozen to the ground David felt a hand-like grip on his arm and suddenly he was being propelled forwards towards the strange floating object.

"They spoke to me, but not like a person speaking," recalled David later. "It was like they were talking to me in my head. They were saying *you're alright, you are OK.*" David was transported onwards, his feet not seeming to touch the ground. He is not sure how he entered the object but found himself in a large bare room where his captors left him alone.

As he waited there, his mind went over the detail he had

gathered on his abductors from close range. They were definitely humanoid in shape and were wearing what looked like octagonal helmets which were featureless apart from two dim lights in position where their eyes should have been.

They wore grey suits with gold coloured belts and straps that looked similar to braces. Black knee boots and gloves completed the picture.

Watching them as he had approached the craft David thought they reminded him of something he had seen in the past. Then the similarity struck him. They were like the robots that he had often seen in 50s Hollywood Sci-fi movies. Perhaps it was the way they moved their arms and legs in a rapid, stilted fashion.

David estimates he was kept alone in that bare room for some 15 minutes. He is convinced that he was under observation by his captors, whether this was assumed on his part, or telepathically communicated to him he is unsure. But throughout his experience he was constantly aware of voices in his head.

For reasons he still can't explain, David was not overcome by fear during his time on the craft, although he would certainly suffer terrors from it later.

After observation, David was led into what he describes as a control room. Three or four TV consoles were visible and a large screen was positioned on a wall. He believes the beings let him know that he was being decontaminated and then prepared for a time change. This information also seemed to be transmitted by some form of telepathy.

David was then aware of the craft taking off. "But there was no sense of motion at all," he said. "I was just sitting there watching this big screen showing planets passing by, Jupiter, Saturn and out to beyond Pluto where the craft docked with a mother ship."

On board the larger craft David remembers being taken for a medical examination. As he lay on the examination table, positioned in the centre of a room, one of his captors produced a long instrument which was pointed at one end.

He believes that instrument was responsible for burn marks which he claims he found on his body the following day. "It didn" feel like a burn at the time," David told investigators. "I didn't realise that is what they were doing until I saw the marks the next day."

David was confused by one aspect of the medical examination. He explained: "They checked me all over but they seemed to ponder over my private parts for a while. I don't know whether they were trying to work out whether I was male or female."

Probes were placed on David's head and chest and around his neck. He remembers his heart rate being increased and then decreased, as if on command from his abductors. He also recalls a bizarre telepathic request. Could they have permission to remove his eyes for further examination? He refused, of course.

A music tape cassette was removed from his pocket by one of the beings and apparently analysed in one of the consoles in the room. David recalls the irony of hearing a very earthy heavy rock anthem pounding out its beat across this most alien of scenes.

He is convinced that in a further telepathic conversation the aliens told him that they came from a planet beyond the constellation of Lyra, that they breathed oxygen and disliked the polluted atmosphere of the earth.

They had a temporary base in Greenland and had been forced to destroy a number of bases which had existed on the moon to avoid discovery by probes and visits from earth. They told David that their studies of our planet were conducted on the basis of non-interference.

How they reconciled abduction with a policy of non-interference was not volunteered. David told investigators that he was questioned about the USA and NASA and recalls being told that the aliens had captured a Voyager spacecraft for analysis. Their verdict: Very primitive.

David is not clear at what point he was taken back to the UFO from the mother ship, but he was aware that he was being taken back home. He suddenly found himself back in that lonely field in North Wales. His last recollection is of the UFO disappearing from view in the night sky.

He vividly recalls experiencing a feeling of dizziness after leaving the alien craft followed by a floating feeling which he assumed could have been caused by breathing a more oxygen rich atmosphere.

The young man was spotted reeling in the road by a passing police patrol car. The police officer stopped his vehicle and quizzed David, asking him if he'd been drinking or taking drugs. Satisfied that he was not breaking the law, the patrolman took David home where they arrived at 5.30 am.

The one hour fifteen minute journey on foot from his friend's home had taken twice as long, even with a lift from the police officer. But he had been with those unearthly visitors for what seemed hours.

As soon as he got home David was gripped by a terror, perhaps a delayed reaction from his traumatic encounter. Although now safe, in the bosom of his family, he was still in a state of shock.

After hearing his account, his mother agreed that they should seek help to try to find out exactly what had happened to him, to help fill in the gaps in his memory.

Two days later they tracked down the phone number of Contact International, the only UFO investigation group they could find.

Yes, Contact was interested in looking at the case, they were told, and they would be in touch.

The Thomas family waited just seven days before David's mum, worried by the violent nightmares her son was now suffering, decided to act. At one in the morning on February 17, 1985, she ushered the youngster into the family car for the long journey to the Oxfordshire HQ of Contact.

When they got to their destination they waited in their parked car for dawn to break before seeking out an investigator. David, described as pale, dishevelled and shaking with fear, had to be cajoled by his mother into relating his story. He did so reluctantly, reinforcing his wish for anonymity and refusing point blank to talk to the police or the media.

An ordinary young lad, David was bright and articulate, not prone to flights of fancy with nothing to gain by fabricating such a story. He had no abiding interest in UFOs and appeared not to have been contaminated by abduction literature.

He seemed stable and in no way an attention seeker, yet he was overcome by fear.

It took investigators several interviews to establish the reason for this terror that threatened to overshadow this young man's life.

Then during one interview session David confided the one telepathic conversation with his abductors that filled him with dread. They made it plain that they would return to earth again one day in the future and would seek him out.

"We will see you again," they told him.

"They have chosen me, they have instructed me and they are coming back for me," said David, his horror plainly etched on his face.

The investigators pointed out that it was highly unlikely he would have a second encounter and they pointed out the ambiguity of the words used by the beings. Perhaps it was merely a way of saying farewell.

It was impossible to placate the youth whose nightmares continued to plague him. His family were well used to him waking in the night in a cold sweat, his blood curdling screams rousing the whole household.

David's distress was such that his mother contacted a psychologist who decided that he should undergo hypnotherapy. After a course of such sessions David was able to come to terms with his encounter. He knew he had to pick up the pieces of his life and carry on. He could not live in fear for the rest of his days.

Today David is happily married and has put his abduction experience firmly behind him. So firmly that he refuses to discuss the incident under any circumstances. He also keeps to himself his views on UFOs and abduction phenomena.

But he can't deny that the experience has changed him, as he once said when being interviewed by investigators.

When they asked him what he had learned from his encounter, the then much younger David had said: "We humans are supposed to be big aren't we. But we're just very small. Insignificant.

And why do humans want to destroy everything that is good about our world? It makes you think. "The one time music-loving unemployed teenager is now an avid campaigner for Green issues - and he's also developed a talent for song writing and spontaneous poetry. One of the first poems he penned after his encounter had an intriguing title: *The Atom.*

Researchers who have investigated the Thomas case over the years unanimously agree that it is a classic. Not just because of the chain of events he reported experiencing, but because of the quality of the witness concerned.

An unemployed teenager a quality witness?

"As a rule of thumb the emotional content of a case is more important than the actual events experienced," said one investigator who had spent a great many hours interviewing the witness. "The emotional content of this case was compelling.

"I have interviewed David twice over the years, once shortly after the event and again some years later. The fear in this young man's face could not be faked.

"When I first went to North Wales to see him I could talk to him about any subject and he would respond quite happily. He was perfectly rational, totally at ease. Then as soon as I raised the subject of his experience his demeanour would change dramatically.

"He would fidget, chain smoke, and wring his hands. The body language was of a young man in total terror.

"I will never forget the fear in those eyes. I could almost see the beads of sweat break out on his forehead as I coaxed and sometimes bullied him into telling me the details. He was also very embarrassed about his new interest in poetry, so much so that he made me swear not to tell his friends about it."

David's reaction to the subject was just the same when he underwent a further interview some years after his encounter.

36

"By this time he had undergone hypnotherapy to help him overcome the nightmares and attacks of the terrors," recalled the investigator.

"He was older, more mature and had made a conscious decision to leave the incident in the past. He really did not want to talk about it. But when I began asking him about details of those past events he eyes, once again, filled with terror.

"He changed from a relaxed, self-assured young man into a total bag of nerves. David Thomas was not faking. He believes that those strange events that he described really did happen to him. The experience terrified him and probably still haunts him today."

Graham Allen
June 17, 1979
Newbury, Berkshire

Painter and decorator Graham Allen was just 20 years old when he had what he is now convinced was a Close Encounter of the Fourth Kind.

Back then, Graham was living in Staffordshire and his fiancée Charlotte, now his wife, was living in Maidenhead, Berks.

The long distance lovers had come to an arrangement to ensure that they could spend every precious weekend together. One weekend he would do the travelling and stay over at Charlotte's home, the next it would be her turn to make the trek and stay with him. This particular weekend it was Graham's turn to travel and as luck had it he had been working in Birmingham which meant he faced a slightly shorter drive than usual.

"It was the Friday before the longest day of 1979," recalls Graham. "Having checked the date on the calendar that makes it June 17. I'd been working in Birmingham, a place called Shirley, which was actually closer to Maidenhead for me because I was already on the A34, my usual route."

He knocked off at sometime after 4 pm that day, put away his work things and grabbed his weekend bag. As he stepped out into the open, the warmth of the afternoon hit him immediately. The sun had been baking down all day long and when he climbed into his car the interior was like a hot house.

Winding down the driver window for a bit of fresh air, he set off at about 4.30 on a route he knew well, he'd done it many times before and was looking forward to a smooth run. Sun shining, very warm and light traffic . . . perfect conditions to drive down to spend the weekend with the woman he loved.

Driving along with the radio going and a cooling draught from the open window Graham made good progress through Stratford-Upon-Avon despite the tourist traffic. He soon got down to the Oxford ring road, where after negotiating lighter than normal rush-hour traffic, he motored southwards into the open countryside, his normal turning to Maidenhead fast approaching.

I remember sitting at a traffic island and a sports car with some girls in it shot across in front of me. I remember going around the island with the radio going and the DJ saying *and now the time is five minutes to six.*"

A few minutes into the next record and the car radio began to play up. First it spluttered, then it crackled furiously and then it faded away completely.

"Must be passing under power cables," Graham said to himself. "It'll clear in a minute." But it didn't clear. Determined not to lose the company of his beloved car radio, Graham, one hand on the steering wheel, leaned over awkwardly, fingers groping for the control knobs that would hopefully enable him to re-tune the set.

It was no use. No matter which way he turned them the radio stayed, stubbornly silent. For a few short seconds he took his eyes of the road and glared at the radio as if he might spot the fault. The radio lights were on, he couldn't see any problem, but the speakers were dead.

When he looked up, gone were the blue skies and the sunshine of a few seconds ago. The sky was overcast and rain was teeming down.

Shaking his head in disbelief, he was forced to switch on his wipers to clear the huge splatters of rain that now obscured his vision through the windscreen. "Strange, I thought," said Graham later.

"I think I assumed it was some sort of a sun shower or something. I remember thinking those girls in the sports car would get wet.

But it was a very dramatic change, from a balmy afternoon to a grey, wet day."

It took him a few seconds to accustom himself to the change of scene, but slightly confused, he continued driving. Then gradually that confusion changed to a growing sense of unease. For some reason he didn't seem to recognise what should have been a very familiar route.

The landmarks he passed, the buildings, the churches, the cottages. None of them were ringing any bells. Yet he had travelled this route so often he must see something he recognised.

As he powered his car along the dual carriageway, he scanned the horizon for any clues to how close his turn off was.

Then suddenly, his worst fear was confirmed. A road sign he was approaching said it all: *Newbury 3 miles.*

"Blimey, I've missed my turning," he said to himself. How could he possibly have missed the road to Maidenhead? He'd never done it before, it was well signposted and he would have seen it coming up. Furious with himself he moved into the centre of the carriageway and turned right into the entrance to a farm.

The next thing Graham remembered was sitting in his car, the engine running, the radio working normally. The car was still in the farm entrance but now it was facing the dual carriageway.

The rain had stopped and the car and the road were completely dry.

Now Graham was confused. There was only one thing to

do; he would have to retrace his route to get to the correct turning for Maidenhead. Glancing at the car clock it was now five past six, ten minutes since the last time check by the DJ, and that was before his turning. He shouldn't have far to go to his turning, he thought.

Graham was stunned when he discovered that missed turning was 15 miles back along the road, and the spot where he had heard the first time check was a further five miles away.

Somehow he had driven 20 Miles in just 10 minutes.

The rest of his journey to Maidenhead was uneventful. He arrived at 7.15 pm although had been expected at 6.30.

"My fiancée was waiting for me when I got there," recalled Graham. "She came running out of the house. But I couldn't get out of the car. My legs were like blocks and they would not move. They were shaking. I felt sort of cold and clammy and Charlotte thought this was hilarious for some reason.

She helped me out of the car, laughing her head off, and I just said *You're not going to believe this.* I then told her the whole story over a cup of tea."

Over the next few weeks and months Graham's sleep was regularly interrupted by bizarre *flash-backs* of incidents and events which he could not place. Things that he seemed to know had happened to him, but didn't know when or where.

Mystified. he tried to put these *bad dreams,* as he called them, into the back of his mind, and to some extent succeeded until Christmas 1987. That was when the entire encounter of June 17, 1979 came back to haunt him with a vengeance.

Graham and Charlotte were now living at Rugeley, Staffs, with their four children. They had retired to bed at their normal time that night, but Graham was suddenly woken at 3 am.

"I was back in my car again on that summer day all those years ago," said Graham. "Suddenly it was surrounded by a golden light. The car had been stationary and I could hear a low humming all around.

"Then I saw a man with a dog on the opposite side of the road and that's when I started to panic. I shouted and called to the man to help me."

The humming became more intense and the golden light glowed more strongly as the car, slowly, but surely began to lift from the ground.

"I could feel the car rising and then everything went black," remembered Graham. "Next I can feel this high pitched noise in my head and then I find myself in a brightly lit room, lying on a smooth surface."

Graham was lying on his back and unable to move. He slowly opened his eyes to see three figures, alien figures, looking at him. Large eyes, smooth skinned, the beings, who Graham was unable to describe in great detail, seemed to be doing something to him . . . Suddenly Graham awoke to find himself in bed. From above there was a loud humming noise, loud enough to wake his wife and children.

Graham has been interviewed by a number of Ufologists who agree his case could be a CEIV. He has provided them with drawings of the beings he saw in his *dream* and has been happy to co-operate with researchers having developed a great interest in the subject. Now committed to the alien abduction theory Graham has had some odd after-effects following his experience. He claims to have received telepathic messages of various sorts on a number of occasions, including information on the construction of *anti-gravity* devices.

At the time of his 1979 experience there was no indication that Graham had been contaminated by UFO or other literature. The subject was then completely new to him. Today, his interest in Ufology is such that he liaises with other UFO *contacts* to exchange information.

CHAPTER 3
The Chase

Sightings of strange lights, slices of missing time and vague recollections of alien shapes and scenes? Are these really enough to point to Alien Abduction? Even when the credibility of the witness is beyond reproach couldn't their reports be explained by some sort of temporary mental condition?

Could the band of pressure felt by Elsie Oakensen around her head be a clue? Was there a physiological explanation for the events she thinks she experienced? Was that pain a symptom of something going on inside her head rather than in outer space?

She herself seems to favour a spiritual explanation. David Thomas was a young lad who had enjoyed a night out with his mates. Yet it is unlikely that he had the proverbial one drink too many, the jobless rarely have the money to spend on booze. But maybe he slipped in the dark on that lonely, icy road and cracked his head. That might account for his dreamlike encounter.

And Graham Allen's missing time could simply be put down to getting lost during a freak summer downpour. Was the dream of seven years later really that significant?

The cynic could argue that Graham's developing interest in Ufology could have caused the dream . . . a sort of wishful thinking. Of course it is possible to pick holes in every story. But an experienced investigator would have asked himself the very same questions that would occur to the cynic. And he would have answered them satisfactorily before going on with the investigation.

No, there was no evidence that Elsie Oakensen's bands of pressure were symptomatic of any illness. And what about the four Women's Institute ladies who sighted a similar object.

No, David Thomas did not fall and crack his head. His body bore no marks or scars, apart from the small burn mark on his left arm. His recurrent nightmares, which plagued him for some time after, surely indicated some traumatic experience.

No, Graham Allen was quite sure his missing time experience was more than just getting lost. He knew the route too well to have gone astray. And he believes the experience seven years later was significant. Hadn't his wife and children been awoken by the strange humming that night?

With so many question marks cropping up the seasoned investigator of Abduction Phenomenon often asks witnesses to undergo hypnosis. Hypnotic regression has been a favoured tool of Ufologists since the Betty and Barney Hill case in America in the sixties. It had been argued that testimony given under hypnosis could not be faked and that those accounts were a valuable piece of additional evidence.

However in 1977 American Alvin Lawson set up an experiment to test the reliability of hypnosis accounts. First he gathered together a group of people who claimed a genuine UFO abduction experience, had them hypnotically regressed and asked them to give an account of their experience.

At the same time he also gathered a second group of people who were given a basic outline of abduction and then asked to fake an account from their imagination. This second group were then hypnotically regressed and were asked for their account of abduction. Astonishingly much of the detail given by the imaginary abductees matched the detail of real reports and suggested, at the very least, that those who wish to fake reports under hypnosis had the capacity to do so.

The *fake* abductees accounts were interesting in that they produced a great deal of imaginary information which had not been input by the examiners.

Lawson's experiments were criticised on the basis that in the 1970s in California there would be few people who would not have knowledge of the UFO phenomenon. While this is true, the same applies to those who claim the genuine abduction experience.

The major difference between the recall of the genuine and the imaginary abductees: emotional response.

The genuine abductees displayed considerable emotion during recall, while the imaginary abductees related their account as if describing a TV programme they had seen.

However, said researchers, this merely indicates that those who claim genuine experience also genuinely believe it to have happened and are therefore potentially frightened of it, whereas those who do not claim the experience have nothing to fear. But the belief of an individual does not necessarily reflect the reality of the experience. Other studies have also cast considerable doubt on the reliability of accounts given by subjects while in hypnotic trance.

Hypnosis can be a dangerous tool in the wrong hands and if used on the wrong subject can cause problems. For that reason, and because of the doubts about the validity of the testimony gathered under this procedure, BUFORA imposed a moratorium on hypnotic regression a few years ago, and that ban remains today.

Experience had shown that it was not always easy to persuade witnesses or potential abductees to go through with what some can find a harrowing ordeal, and when they do the results can be disappointing. But in the case of Christine Smith the results were astounding.

Christine Smith (pseudonym)
March 4, 1982
Skipton, North Yorkshire

It was about 10.15 pm on the night of Thursday, March 4th, 1982 when the logical, rational workaday world that Christine Smith had become used to began to crumble and fall apart.

The thirty six year old mother of two and business woman had spent a pleasant day with her mum in Morecambe and was driving home to Skipton, North Yorkshire unaware that the strange events that were about to follow would force her to reappraise her view of life and her understanding of the universe.

Alone in her car apart from the family sheep dog which slept on the floor on the front passenger side, Christine bowled along the quiet country roads at a steady 50 miles per hour.

She hardly noticed the rugged moorland terrain that stretched for miles around her as she motored through the Lancashire and Yorkshire borderlands on this cold clear night. The moon shone brightly in a sky full of stars as her car coasted along the A65 to complete the final leg of the 50 mile journey she had undertaken many times before. But her mind was full of the household chores that needed attending to before she could get to bed and rest in preparation for the next day's work in the family business.

As she approached lonely Coniston Cutting, not far from Skipton, where the road slices through a large hill creating steep banks on either side of the carriageway, she was passed by a single car coming from the opposite direction. She watched through her rear view mirror as its lights slowly disappeared into the distance. Drivers through this vast expanse of moorland know that from Coniston Cutting one can see vehicle headlights for a considerable distance in both directions. And that night, at that moment, Christine felt as if her car was the only one in existence as it purred on through the night.

Suddenly, from the corner of her eye, she noticed a light coming from one side of her car. She turned and saw that the whole of the offside of her vehicle seemed illuminated with a soft bluish light.

It was then that she glanced in her offside wing mirror and saw the two lights. Two strange lights positioned behind and just above the height of her car.

About the same size as car headlamps one was royal blue and the other a vivid red. They seemed to be tailing her car, following in a side by side attitude with the red light on the outside. Noticing they were bright, yet somehow soft, Christine at times thought she could see a number of smaller lights behind them. She peered through her rear view mirror and all was blackness. Then she glanced again in the wing mirror and there they were.

She discarded the idea that they were odd headlights from a large lorry which had somehow caught up with her. They were too high, the wrong colour . . . God they were strange.

Whatever they were they didn't seem to bother the dog who slept on unaware of his mistress's growing sense of unease.

"Pull yourself together girl," she told herself, determined to concentrate on her driving. She only had a handful of miles to cover.

As her car emerged from the cutting, Christine's sense of relief was replaced by sheer terror. A beam of pure white light shot down from somewhere above and illuminated the road at the nearside of her vehicle.

A circle of light, more than 15 feet in diameter, first fell onto the fields, then moved onto the road. Suddenly the car was encircled by this girdle of bright energy.

"I suddenly felt very cold," she said later. "I knew that this in itself was strange because the car heater was on."

She also experienced the eerie silence that is often reported by close encounter witnesses. It was an unnatural absence of sound, except for the engine noise. It seemed to be revving far louder than it should have been.

Christine was determined to press on and drew on all her resources to keep driving, keep concentrating despite knowing that those lights, those damn lights were still behind her.

For what seemed like eternity she kept at bay the urge to slam on the brakes, scream and bury her head in her hands, yet later she realised the beam can only have paced her car for a distance of half a mile at most.

It was the sudden appearance of the headlights from an approaching large lorry in the distance that jerked her back to something more like reality. At the exact second that the heavy vehicle's headlamps appeared on the horizon, the beam flicked out and her red and blue pursuers vanished.

Still gripped by a terror that they would return Christine summoned up what strength she had left to complete the journey. The fear began to subside as her vehicle passed the familiar buildings and landmarks on the outskirts of Skipton that told her that home, and safety, were not far away.

As she parked up outside her home she was filled with a huge sense of relief, yet she felt mentally and physically drained from her ordeal. That feeling of complete exhaustion would stay with her for a further week, an indication of the traumatic effect her journey had on her.

Christine's husband Gerry shared a feeling of relief as he let his wife in. He had been worried for her safety. It was now after 11 pm . . . 1 hour and 35 minutes after Christine had left her mother's home.

The journey which normally took an hour had not been hampered by traffic and after seeing the disturbed state she was in he was anxious to hear her story.

Gerry had no problem accepting Christine's account. This well spoken, intelligent businesswoman had been visibly shaken by her experience; she was not a UFO freak and had never been prone to concocting fantastic stories.

Alarmingly the following day Christine found she had a rash on her back and chest, unusual for her, but it cleared up in a couple of days.

As word of the encounter spread among friends of the couple, one mentioned it to a colleague associated with UFO research. He immediately contacted Christine who agreed to relate her account on condition it was not publicised and that her identity be kept confidential.

Once this was agreed Christine and her husband went through the ritual detailed telling and re-telling of the experience as the investigator noted every single detail. Christine's version of events never wavered.

As time went on the Ufologist was convinced that he had an abductee. The lights, the malfunctioning of the car and the missing time pointed to a Close Encounter of the Fourth Kind.

Hypnotism was the obvious next step and the investigator was delighted when Christine agreed. But he had no idea how delighted he would be with the results of a series of hypnosis sessions which began on May 4, 1982.

Immediately after being put into a trance new material

began to emerge. Christine's account of events under hypnosis not only underlined the accuracy of her conscious recollections but brought to light aspects that she had either forgotten or buried away in her mind as unexplainable.

Hypnosis also enabled her to *remember* what can only be described as an apparent conversation with an alien being.

The hypnotherapist first put Christine into a deep trance and invited her to allow her mind to go back to that fateful night. For all intents and purposes Christine was back in the driver's seat of her car. She described in detail the appearance of lights . . . and some new and interesting details.

"Can your hear anything?" asked the hypnotist.

"A soft buzzing," said Christine.

The hypnotist: "How do you feel?"

"Very cold all over."

"How are you feeling?"

"I feel so very tired, I want to go to sleep," she answered, her head lolling over to one side as if asleep.

"How do you feel?"

"I can feel something soft and fluffy on my ankles and feet."

"Does it hurt?"

"No, it feels quite nice really. There's a tingling feeling going up my legs towards my knees."

When the hypnotist asked her if she was still in the car, Christine replied that she didn't know. She was unsure where she was, unaware of whether she was sitting or lying. But she could hear what sounded like heavy breathing and felt some sort of a veil before her eyes.

"Could it be a blindfold?" asked the hypnotist.

"It could be," she replied. "There is a bright light coming through the veil. It is going round and round."

At this point Christine began to gyrate her body from the waist upwards as if keeping time with a rotating light.

"Can you still feel the strange fluffy thing on your legs?" asked the hypnotherapist.

"Yes. It appears to be holding my legs down. I still feel very cold except for my legs. They are warm."

Christine didn't respond to a series of further questions then suddenly put her arms out in front of her, bent at the elbow.

Asked what she was doing she said: "I can't move them. Something is holding them. I can feel something touching my body . . . I can hear buzzing all around me."

The first session of hypnosis ended there. It was decided to give Christine a break to prepare her for the next session which took place on May 20, 1982.

Again she was taken back to the point where she spotted the lights and again new information was unearthed.

Under hypnosis she recalled feeling something being placed in the small of her back while she was still in the car. "Take it away, it hurts," she cried without identifying who she was speaking to.

Suddenly the *rotating lights* were back. Putting her hands over her head she called: "My cheeks are hot, my hands are hot. Whatever it is, it's above the car . . ."

Christine's mood changed suddenly. She began humming, then laughing. Her hands had begun tingling, she said, laughing out loud.

"It's funny, funny feeling creeping over me."

Could she feel anything in the small of her back? asked the hypnotherapist.

"No, not at the moment, I did have before. I've told them to take it away."

"Told who?"

"Don't know."

At this point Christine complained of a strange feeling in her head, a feeling of pressure. "It's a square there," she said, indicating a spot between her eyes.

A band of pressure around her head followed and now, after further questions about the lights and the beam Christine says her arms *feel funny*. With her hands out in front of her she makes as if feeling for something.

"What can you see?" asks the hypnotherapist.

"I don't know, it's very dark."

Then she reveals feeling as if she is lying down, she feels

something warm nearby, and says "They're wanting information".

"What kind of information?" asked the hypnotherapist.

"They can have all they want." Christine bursts into loud laughter. "They think that's funny."

"So they have a sense of humour then?"

"Oh yes. They don't trust us . . ."

At this point the investigator asked some pointed questions.

"Where are they from?"

"Distant galaxy" replied Christine.

"Where do they live?"

"Zircon, something like that."

"Will they show themselves?"

"They say they want to be like a friend . . ."

"Are you important to them?"

"Yes, yes, yes. Oh yes."

"Because you are a woman?"

"It helps."

"Why?"

"We can communicate better."

Christine describes how the *aliens* have many ways of communication, how they are so advanced, how they protect us. "They're just guardians, they're good," she said.

"How long have they been coming here?" asked the hypnotherapist.

"Centuries," replied Christine.

"Are they our Gods?"

"We call them such," replied Christine.

"We do?"

"Since time immemorial, we call them many names."

"What names?"

"Zeus, it's the first name, Akaber."

Christine then told how the *Guardians*, for want of a better name, had been visiting earth to offer help. She said they told her that they could give assistance through *special powers*.

"Who are they accountable to?" asked the investigator.

"A force greater than them."

"God?"

"Yes, we call him."

During the rest of this four hour session under hypnosis Christine spoke of good and evil forces at work, about the future of earth, and some vague threat to the planet.

Exhausted she was brought out of her trance state and immediately agreed to a further session. The third and final session began as the previous ones, taking Christine back to her night on the road. Suddenly she sat up with her head held high. Confused the investigator asked: "Are we talking to Christine?"

"I am Christine, you are talking to Zeus," she replied.

"Ask him how he travels from his distant galaxy?"

"By beam of light."

"Does he travel by machine?"

"Over long distances."

"How fast does his machine go?"

"As fast as he requires . . . the pressure is pushing down."

"Is it painful?"

"No, it's very heavy."

"Are you experiencing fear?"

"No."

"Is Zircon the name of their planet?"

"They say we do not know it."

"Ask them if life ends at death."

"No."

"If Zeus is a God should we worship him?"

"No."

"Can you name other Gods?"

"There are many Gods; they are an all-involved power."

"If Zeus has a name, the other Gods must have names?"

"Narcias is the name coming to me."

The investigator got a shock when he asked about reports of alien visitors to witnesses at other UFO incidents. Christine's response was almost vehement.

"They are not of this world. They are evil, evil, evil."

Asked for a demonstration of proof Christine replied: "In our own time."

"Are we speaking to one entity or more?"

"You are speaking to Zeus."

A reliable, credible witness, a bizarre series of events and an intriguing series of hypnosis sessions.

The events on that lonely night-time drive, the strange lights and the chase were odd enough in themselves. Combined with the missing time this case certainly had the ingredients of abduction.

Then the hypnotic regression led on to a bizarre question and answer session with an alien called Zeus.

Another classic in Abduction Phenomena? A rare insight into the unknown? Or is it another case of gobbledygook with about as much basis in fact as ghouls and goblins. Despite the reservations about hypnosis, serious researchers say there are some interesting details in this case. Again the quality of the witness, or abductee, means it is worthy of serious consideration.

It was tempting to suspect contamination in view of Christine's references to Gods and indeed Zeus. Had she read Erich von Daniken's Chariots of the Gods? If she had couldn't seeds of information about that theory have remained buried in her brain, lying dormant until being awakened by hypnosis?

Not according to Christine and her husband. She hadn't read *von Daniken* and his theories were completely unknown to her.

But the theory that advanced alien visitations could have explained the miracle-making Gods of ancient history has been put forward by a number of people in books, films and TV shows that Christine may have glimpsed over the years.

So if Christine's case was not manna from Heaven it must surely be food for thought. What do you think?

CHAPTER 4
Official Recognition

What on earth is going on out there? Even focusing on the alleged alien abduction material from the UK alone it is clear that something very strange is happening.

When you consider the many thousands of cases from around the world it seems incredible that there has been no concerted, authoritative, global scientific investigation into this phenomenon.

Ignore the millions of alleged UFO sightings and close encounters. What we are dealing with here are alleged abductions of human beings. People are reporting being carried off for examination and testing by beings that seem able to flout the law at will.

Even if you ignore the reports from Third World countries or far flung places where alleged alien abduction is regarded as having little consequence in a society which might be struggling to feed itself, there are enough cases in America and Europe to justify a real scientific examination.

But even in America, where UFO organisations have some big names and big money clout behind them, they have been unable to get their Government to launch a proper investigation.

Early in the spring of 1994 British cynics showed their true colours when they noisily debunked a European Community suggestion to set up a UFO research programme. With that level of cynicism, a research programme into Abduction Phenomenon is obviously a non-starter.

Yet abductions, if true. are far more serious than lights in the sky. We are talking about the alleged removal of people from their home environments, sometimes by force. Many of those people are damaged, psychologically if not physically. And it remains to be seen whether the reasons behind these events are sinister or otherwise.

Surely any Government is bound to act when its citizens are abducted and treated in this way? Unless of course these reports are not taken seriously. If a government fails to recognise a problem, then nothing will be done. Nothing is being done.

So why are our abductees not taken seriously? We have demonstrated in the few cases we have looked at so far, that the witnesses are credible. They have nothing to gain and much to lose by exposing themselves to ridicule. The circumstantial evidence is just not compelling enough for it to warrant a serious investigation.

Perhaps the major reason for the general reluctance to recognise Abduction Phenomenon is that in all the material available in a great many recorded cases world wide, one vital ingredient is missing . . . the stamp of authority.

Find a case with a credible witness, where an alleged alien visitation leaves some form of mark on the environment, where there is some physical evidence of an attempt at abduction and above all with some involvement by the authorities, i.e. the police, then you might make some people sit up and take notice, or so the theory goes. It is not always so, as Robert Taylor discovered.

Robert Taylor
November 9, 1979
Livingston
Scotland

Foreman forester Robert Taylor was 61 when he almost became the victim of a Close Encounter of the Fourth Kind. Only a combination of his Scottish stubbornness and luck meant he could claim to be *the one that got away.*

So credible a witness was he and so graphic his description of events that the police and other authorities launched a full investigation. Although the case did not go down in the annals of police history as *assault with a deadly UFO,* the official investigation provided a catalogue of evidence from a number of truly independent observers - the boys in blue. In fact 23 years on Robert has become such a local legend that a memorial has been erected on the site of his encounter with a UFO . . . the only such official commemoration of a flying saucer mystery in existence.

But Robert needs no help in recalling that fateful winter's morning in 1979.

To the married father of five grown up children it was just another working day with the forestry department of the Livingston New Town Development Corporation in Scotland. He had just enjoyed his usual breakfast break at the house he shared with his wife Mary at Deans, just outside Livingston, and climbed into his pick-up truck for the short drive to inspect some forest plantations at Dechmont Wood near the M8 motorway which links Glasgow to Edinburgh.

A punctual man, Robert left his home shortly after 10 am and headed off, knowing that he would have to make the last leg of his journey on foot as the rough forest track was impassable to vehicles.

At 10.15 he left the truck parked by the side of the road and, accompanied by his dog, set off through the rough woodland vegetation on the half mile trek that would take him to his destination.

Robert had worked on the land all his life and had been with the Livingston forestry department for the last 16 years, so there was not much he did not know about this patch of bonny Scotland for which he was responsible. But as he rounded a bend in the rough forest track Robert was totally unprepared for what would confront him in the clearing ahead.

A dome-shaped object, 30 feet high and grey in colour lay before him. Dominating the clearing, the strange mass, silent yet ominous caused him to stop in his tracks. Mesmerised, Robert noted how its surface seemed to become translucent and then change back to a dull grey, the same colour and apparent texture as emery paper, he thought. For some reason he found himself wondering whether this bizarre machine, if machine it was, was trying to camouflage itself.

What he later described as a *flange* girdled the strange structure, and antenna-like protrusions with what could have been rotors on top jutted out from the flange at regular intervals.

Transfixed to the ground at the end of the 30 yard wide clearing Robert's eyes scoured the surface of the massive object trying to make some sense of it. He noted several round porthole-type apertures in the top section of the dome.

It was while he was absorbed by the portholes when the *sea mines* appeared. That was how Robert described the two objects which suddenly came at him, apparently from thin air.

Spherical and with six or more legs or spikes protruding from them they rapidly rolled towards him. Measuring about a yard in diameter, and of the same colour and texture as the larger object, the sea mines made a sucking or popping sound as each spike or leg touched the ground, Robert recalled later.

Within seconds they had stationed themselves at either side of the now stunned forestry worker, each having a spike or leg attached to the material of his trousers.

Immediately Robert could feel himself being pulled forward, the spheres tugging him by his trousers, urging him in the direction of the large object.

He could see the material of his trousers, just below the pockets, straining under the powerful pull of the spikes or the legs. Robert stubbornly resisted them. He wasn't going to run away but he would certainly try to stand his ground against this damned invader. The spheres steadily increased their pull to such an extent that at one stage Robert could feel his Wellington boots dragging on the ground as he fought to keep his distance from the gloomy grey object.

A foul acrid smell that he had noticed as soon as the spheres approached now seemed to invade his nostrils. The intensity of the appalling stink increased as he struggled with his would be captors. Invisible choking fumes overwhelmed him as he summoned all his strength to resist the incessant pull of the spheres.

A strange pressure built up under his chin and he recalls a burning sensation in the same place.

Struggling for breath and exhausted from his battle with *sea mines* Robert lost consciousness and fell forward into the damp grass.

"The next thing I hear is a whooshing sound and my dog is racing round me barking loudly," remembers Robert. "But I'm not sure if that was before I lost consciousness or after I came round.

"When I did come round there was nothing there. The object had gone. I felt extremely weak and was unsteady on my feet. I dragged myself up and half crawled, half staggered to my vehicle."

On reaching his pick-up truck Robert automatically went to his two-way radio to report the incident to HQ. But as soon as they responded he found he could not utter a word. He could not speak.

But losing his voice was the least of his worries. After climbing, with some effort, into the driver's seat of his truck, Robert struggled to co-ordinate his hand and leg movements to enable him to drive.

After several attempts he managed to start the vehicle and steer it along the forest track for a few yards before it went veering into a muddy quagmire. Dazed and confused Robert made his way home on foot. Gradually his strength and his voice returned.

Mary, his wife, saw her husband walking up the road towards his home through the kitchen window. She noticed his face was dirty and his clothes disheveled.

Rushing out to meet him she cried: "What's happened. Have you had an accident?"

"No, I've been attacked," he replied.

"By men?"

"No, a spaceship thing."

"There's no such thing . . . I'll phone the doctor."

Robert stopped his wife calling the GP and asked her to run him a bath. He wanted to get rid of that awful smell that he said clung to him and his clothes.

Mary could not smell a thing but she did notice his jersey was dirty. And his trousers were torn on either side near to the pockets as well as being grubby at the front. He had obviously fallen.

Mary could see her husband was unwell. He was very pale. He seemed drained and exhausted and complained of grazes on his left leg and under his chin.

While he was in the bath, Mary telephoned her husband's boss, Malcolm Drummond, the forestry manager. When he arrived at the house Robert told his story, describing the domed object as like a large spinning top, accompanied by two smaller objects.

Mr. Drummond listened without interruption. He knew old Robert was a man of few words, not one for exaggeration. If this is what he said had happened then he was prepared to believe him.

Mr. Drummond said he was going to look at the site for himself and left. When he returned he brought Robert's truck and said that despite a cursory look around the location he had nothing to report. Robert insisted on returning to Dechmont Wood with his boss to see if the object had left any marks on the ground. There must be some sign of it having been there.

Indeed marks there were, and they were enough to convince Robert that he had not imagined his experience. Track-like marks and holes, three inches deep and at a slight angle into the ground. They suggested a heavy object had been sitting there. Mr. Drummond had to agree they were strange.

The police were immediately called in to investigate.

In his report on the incident PC William Douglas of Lothian and Borders Police at Livingston described the marks in detail.

"The central marks were similar to that of a caterpillar tractor and were uniform in size," he wrote. "They indicated that an object of several tons had stood there but there was nothing to show that it had been driven or towed away. I made a wide sweep of the area checking for fresh marks which might suggest a mobile crane but I found nothing. The central marks were surrounded by holes approximately

3.5 inches in diameter and the same in depth. Each hole had a toe which cut under the sod, in some cases by as much as four inches. There appeared to be no rational explanation for these marks."

PC Douglas's search for signs of a mobile crane implied that he thought the object, whatever it was, must have been lifted from the spot. An object, weighing several tons, according to his estimation, would certainly have left further marks when it moved off.

The official report by the Livingston Criminal Investigation Department concluded: "Despite extensive inquiries, no information has been gained which could indicate what, in fact, made the marks on the ground at the location. Mr. Taylor is a respected member of the community and is described as a conscientious and trustworthy person, not likely to invent a story.

The police investigation included a report from the Forensic Science Laboratory, where Robert's clothing had undergone testing. Nothing of significance was found. But the report confirmed that the tears in the hip area of the trousers he had been wearing, and in a corresponding area on the Long John underpants favoured by Robert, were "consistent with the material having been pulled up while the trousers were being worn."

The report from Robert's GP, Dr Gordon Adams, was equally inconclusive. He found no signs of a head injury or concussion. He had seen him earlier in the year when it was suspected that the headaches, from which he was suffering, could be the return of meningitis that struck him down some 14 years previously. However hospital tests ruled this out.

The flurry of press reports of Robert's experience were mostly the usual tongue in cheek Forestry Worker Meets Alien type, typical of a media which is unsure how to handle such stories.

Another observer at the scene at the time explained away the incident as an encounter with ball lightning. But Robert is hardly likely to have mistaken this natural phenomenon for the object he described in such detail and it certainly cannot account for the very physical effects of his encounter.

But the British UFO Research Association's own files throw up some interesting sightings from the same area and at about the same time as Robert's meeting with his *spinning top thing*.

The evening before, Peter Caldwell, a 35 year old clerk at a factory at nearby Uphall, saw a dull, white, round object travelling from west to east across the sky. Behind it was a large red patch *as if the air was on fire*.

That same evening postman James Forsyth saw two white lights pass in the sky above him. First they approached each other, then passed, then approached and passed yet again as James walked his dog through a park in the Craigmillar area of Edinburgh.

At 9.30 am, possibly on the same day as Robert's encounter, an Edinburgh woman reported a bright light in the sky travelling west, towards Livingston. She described it as a dull, white-grey colour with *neither wings nor tail*.

Mrs. Barbara Gerrard of Leslie in Fife saw three orange/pink lights in the sky on the afternoon of November 9, and at 10 am on the same day 35 year Violet Connor of nearby Bathgate saw a bright light in the sky to the west, over Armadale, which is just across the M8 from Livingston.

Robert Taylor's encounter baffled the Development Corporation of Livingston, the police, the medics, his wife and most of all himself. It still sparks fierce debate among Ufologists.

Were the occupants of the UFO trying to abduct Robert? He believes they were and fought back. Is he sure it was a UFO?

Robert is convinced, and neither the police nor the other authorities have been able to come up with an alternative explanation. And as far as other witnesses are concerned, couldn't at least one of those people making sighting reports to BUFORA over that period have seen the same object that Robert encountered?

Happily Robert has not faced the sneering ridicule that many witnesses have experienced. In fact he has achieved something of a celebrity status in his local community. So much so that local councillors voted to erect a Cairn or monument to the Close Encounter at Livingston. Erected in May 1992 the commemorative plaque and Cairn was the result of collaboration between the Livingston Development Corporation and the Scottish UFO research group Strange Phenomena Investigations.

CHAPTER 5
Multiple Abductions

The vast majority of Abduction Phenomena concern reports from individuals who have experienced strange events without witnesses. But couples and even groups of people have had Close Encounters of the Fourth Kind.

The advantage of the multiple witness experience from the point of view of the investigator is obvious. He has the accounts and descriptions of two or more observers to work on. He will interview all witnesses separately so that later he can examine, and compare their accounts to see if and where they differ.

Images and perceptions will differ to some extent with every individual but multiple witness case accounts will have a large area of common ground.

When two or more people claim to have been abducted, the investigator also has two or more points of reference for considering the authenticity of their report.

However good the lone witness, the critic can always argue that without any physical back-up his account is, by its very nature, subjective.

How do we know that the witness did not undergo some temporary mental impairment in the form of hallucinations? How do we know that he didn't just concoct the story for the hell of it? He could have made up the tale for a bet, or even for an alibi.

"No dear, I have not been in the pub all night, I've been abducted by aliens". . . not many wives would believe that one but anything is possible and some poor soul might think the excuse is worth a try.

The truth is single abduction reports are, for the most part, subjective. We cannot know with absolute certainty, that the truth is being told.

Multiple abduction reports on the other hand, are another matter. Of course two or more people can also concoct an abduction story for the same reasons as above, but it is more likely that their deceptions would be discovered, with two separate accounts of events to check and cross check.

Because more than one person is involved the accounts should become more objective, and, unless we blame mass hallucination, more believable. Most of these multiple alleged abduction reports come, as always, from the USA and the rest of the world. But here in Britain we have two of the most well-researched case histories known.

The first is known as the Aveley Case. The alleged abductees in this case were a whole family of five, John and Sue Day and their three young children. Their experience still baffles the experts nearly three decades later.

The second is known as the A70 case and concerns the abduction of Colin Wright and Garry Wood as they drove along a lonely highway in Scotland.

The Day Family,
October 27, 1974,
Aveley, Essex.

A quick glance around the car to make sure everyone was safely in was enough to tell John Day they were ready for off. He switched on the ignition of his Vauxhall Victor estate and began to pull away as his wife Sue leaned out of the front passenger window to say her goodbyes to her parents and sister.

John had been anxious to get on the move. It was still only 9.50 pm and the BBC 2 play he wanted to watch wouldn't start for another half an hour, he thought. If the traffic wasn't too bad they should do the trip home to Aveley in 20 minutes giving them just enough time to get the kids to bed and put on the kettle before settling down in front of the television.

"Hush," cooed Sue as she leaned awkwardly around to tend the two youngsters who had already fallen asleep on the back seat of the car. Karen, 11 and seven year old Stuart had been exhausted by their day at the home of Sue's mum and dad at Harold Hill.

They had only made the trip to welcome home Sue's sister Anne who had just returned from a week's trip to Belgium. But she was four hours late and John was cursing his bad luck in the way that only Cockneys can.

At least now he would have a chance to see that play he had been looking forward to, he told Sue as he leaned forward to switch on the car radio. It was a local station chat show. John was aware of ten-year-old Kevin standing behind him as he steered his car along the familiar route through Hornchurch.

"Not much traffic about, is there luv?" he said glancing over at his wife.

She didn't answer, content to enjoy the beautiful clear night. It was mild and dry. A lovely night for a drive.

About a mile from Hornchurch and heading south as they made their way along the section of the road which has terraced houses on one side and fields bordered with tall hedges on the other, Kevin asked: "What's that light."

Following Kevin's outstretched arm John and Sue spotted it immediately, just above the terraced houses on their left. It was an oval shape, a bluish iridescent light, like a big star. But it appeared to be no more than 50 yards away.

"Look, it's moving," said Kevin.

"Yeah, and it keeps stopping and starting," said his dad.

Sue asked her husband if he thought it could be a helicopter light, but he pointed out that they would have been able to hear the engine, and anyway it wouldn't move like that. Seconds later the light was obscured by a small wood which the car was passing. When it came into view again it was still travelling in the same direction and at the same speed.

Suddenly the UFO changed course and now approached the road they were travelling along. It picked up speed and zipped across them at a steep angle.

John pushed down on the brake, slowed the car and pressed his head close to the windscreen to try to get a better view of the strange object, but this time it was obscured by some high bushes.

The road then took them into a dip and, after a bend to the right, became Aveley Road. Pressing on for another mile or so they passed a gravel pit and several bungalows before approaching another curve. John checked his speed, 30 mph, no need to change down before negotiating the bend.

Suddenly he was gripped by a sense of panic. Something was terribly wrong. Sue looked across at her husband, fear in her eyes. The engine had stopped . . . no, it was just silent. They were still moving, the radio was playing normally, but they couldn't hear the sound of the engine.

As the car came out of the bend it plunged into a bank of fog or thick mist, although John remembers it seemed more like gas. Dense and green, the eerie fog bank was about eight or nine feet high, completely enveloping the car.

The swirling vapour seemed to start from a line of thick bushes that bordered the road on the left and swept down to the ground on the right in what looked like a perfect curve. Suddenly the car radio began crackling loudly and when John spotted smoke drifting up out of the apparatus he quickly leaned over and wrenched out a bunch of wires from the back of the set.

At that moment every light in the vehicle blinked out and the car began to jerk violently as the strange green mist curled around them, fingers of fog apparently exploring every square inch of the bodywork for some means of entry.

Windows tightly closed, John continued to drive, at least he kept his foot on the accelerator and gripped the steering wheel, watched by Sue and with little Kevin gripping his dad's shoulders for reassurance. Thankfully Karen and Stuart slept on peacefully through the unfolding drama.

Oddly John and Sue recall no sense of motion during those frightening seconds. However they do remember the car becoming much colder, as if the mist was drawing out every bit of heat from the vehicle.

Despite the fog it seemed light although hazy. Both later remarked on the total silence and experiencing a curious tingling sensation.

With a jolt, as if racing over a humpback bridge the car was now most definitely on the move. And the mist was gone.

In fact John estimated they emerged from the mist exactly half a mile along the road from the point they entered it.

John felt as if he was alone in the car until the vehicle had covered maybe another half mile or so when Sue sat up and asked: "Is everybody here?"

The cold had gone, the car was functioning normally, the interior lights were switched on, but the radio wires still hung disconnected from behind the dash board.

Nervous and frightened they spoke quietly about the mist until they reached their home. While Sue put the children to bed, John busied himself with rewiring the car radio and then checked the lights still worked.

Sue joined him, with a puzzled look on her face. She said, "John, what time do you think it is?"

"About 10.20?"

"No. It's one o'clock in the morning."

John cursed missing his TV play while Sue phoned the speaking clock to check the time. Three hours were missing from their lives and they hadn't a clue why.

John and Sue felt extremely tired the following day, so John decided not to go into work. Exhaustion apart they seemed to suffer no ill effects.

However some weeks later, in the run up to Christmas, John suffered a nervous breakdown. There was no apparent reason, no problems at home, and no difficulty at work.

Aged 32, John was forced to give up his carpentry job and remained out of work until September the following year when he began a new career, caring for the mentally handicapped.

He and Sue had not forgotten that night of October 27, 1974, but they hadn't approached any organisations for help in investigating the incident because they weren't aware of any and anyway they had enough on their plates with John's sudden illness.

Both, however, could not help but notice how their lives had changed since that night. John was more self confident, he was now apt to writing spur of the moment poems and yearned to begin a new career teaching arts and crafts.

Sue too enjoyed more self confidence and enrolled at a college for further education. Kevin, the only one of the three children to remain awake during the entire journey, also underwent a remarkable change. From being pronounced backward at reading by his school, he suddenly improved to a level ahead of his years.

In the weeks and months following their encounter the whole family turned vegetarian, John gave up smoking and they all took a fervent interest in Green issues.

Nearly three years after the incident John saw an article about UFOs in his local paper. He decided to contact the local research group mentioned to tell them of the strange object he, Sue and Kevin had seen that night.

Investigator Andy Collins came onto the scene in August 1977 and put the whole family through the process of re-calling every scrap of information about that night.

Although John and Sue managed to piece together a fairly detailed run down of events during their journey.

Andy wanted some clues to the missing three hours.

After quizzing them on dreams and flash backs they had both experienced Andy was convinced that there was a minefield of information buried in their heads. He asked them to consider hypnosis.

John and Sue were totally unaware that hypnosis could be used to delve for information. And John was so keen to get to the bottom of his experience that he immediately agreed to co-operate.

Sue did not feel ready for such an ordeal and all agreed that Kevin was too young for hypnosis.

Hypnotherapist Leonard Wilder agreed to conduct the hypnotic regression sessions although he had little knowl-edge of Abduction Phenomena at that time.

Andy was impatient for the therapy to go ahead. He had a feeling he was on the verge of tapping a wealth of abduction data from the Days. The interview sessions had prompted both John and Sue to volunteer snatches of information they had gleaned in their flashbacks, information they had previously *forgotten*.

In the first of three hypnosis sessions, Dr Wilder con-firmed that John was a good subject. The mass of informa-tion from all three bouts of regression combined with the data from other detailed interviews enabled Andy to piece together a remarkable account of events inside the green gas . . .

A white pillar of light cut through the greenness. John gauged it was just six feet ahead of his car. The weird fog completely engulfed the vehicle yet there was no mistaking it. That strange pillar of light, about four feet in diameter, was definitely moving towards them. The pillar seemed to *latch on* to the vehicle. Then a feeling of rising, of ascent, as if something was pulling the vehicle upwards.

John blacked out at that point but Sue recalls her head being thrown back and being conscious of Kevin, who had been standing at the rear, falling backwards onto the seat.

Now John was standing on a balcony with a railing in front of him. He was looking down on a large blue car which was apparently on a lower level. Inside he could see a man and a woman, both were unconscious. In the rear there were more bodies, but they were indistinct.

Despite a strong impression that he was looking down at himself and his own family he rationalised that he couldn't be. His car was white, a white Vauxhall Victor.

As he watched a ramp or a panel began to close in front of the car and he realised then that Sue and Kevin were standing beside him. Behind him was a tall person, an entity, standing perhaps six feet eight inches or so.

To his right, John saw an airshaft, in which, he is certain, he ascended to this level. It consisted of a cylindrical luminosity between the ground and the balcony. Down on the ground he saw the luminosity end at a hexagonal base.

John and the tall entity, moved together towards a blank wall when suddenly John experienced the ascending motion. A hole appeared in the wall and John walked through into a room containing a table with lights above. The tall being touched him on his shoulder and he was in blackness.

Sue too recalled being led away from the balcony towards a blank wall which similarly opened up to reveal an entrance to a room. Two small beings were waiting for her. A tall entity then approached and took hold of Kevin.

Angry that he seemed to want to separate a mother and her son Sue tightened her hold on the youngster's shoulders. Silently the entity drew the boy towards him, and then the child was guided wordlessly into another room.

John regained consciousness to find himself lying on an examination table. He felt as if he was being scanned by a bar which passed over his body. He could feel a tingling sensation and strange warmth in the area covered by the device.

Five figures stood around the table, three tall entities to the right and two *ugly looking beings* about four feet in height and wearing white gowns to the left.

He watched as one of the shorter beings, who he dubbed *examiners,* ran a pen like object, eight inches long, over his skin. Although it never actually touched his body, it emitted a light and caused a warm tingling sensation in those parts of the body over which it was held.

John scrutinised the examiner holding the pen-like object. The white gown he wore fell loosely to the ground; the long loose sleeves were drawn in at the cuffs. The being had no neck and appeared to be slightly hunched.

Bushy brain fur, or hair, covered its head and hands, its eyes were large and slanting, triangular in shape. A light brown nose or beak, a slit for a mouth and pointed ears which swept back completed the picture.

Large talons or nails protruded from the four digits on each of its two very large hands. Thickly set, the being walked awkwardly and occasionally made guttural chirps.

The examiners appeared almost reverential to the tall beings which towered a clear two and a half feet above them. They wore one piece seamless suits of a lurex type material. The material formed a balaclava shape over the heads of the beings. Their faces, being very different from the examiners', comprised two large eyes of a cream colour with pink irises. No visible nose or mouth suggested they were wearing masks.

John could clearly see their hands of three digits covered by a very pale, almost translucent skin.

Unable to move during the examination, when he felt they had completed their tests John asked if he could get up.

"Sit there for a while."

As he sat up and swung his legs over the side of the table John realised the reply had not been spoken. Some form of telepathy was involved because he seemed to get a mental impression of what they wanted to say.

From his new vantage point, John had a better view of the room he was in. It was about 20 feet in length by 12 feet wide. Vaguely oval in shape, there were no corners or seams. It was like sitting in a bubble. Apart from the table he was sitting on and the two lights above, the room was bare.

John found himself dressed in a one piece garment similar to those worn by the tall entities.

Now feeling bolder he began to ask questions. "What do you do when you're outside the ship?"

"We use a visor," came the reply. John saw one of the three entities holding out a hemispherical object with two head bands attached. It reminded him of a welder's visor. The tallest of the beings, the one who seemed to be doing the communicating said: "We find this unfortunate (the visor) because we see through your eyes for most purposes.

"There are occasions when we cannot find suitable eyes so we use the visor to change your light to match our optic nerves."

Encouraged by the response to his first question, John tried a second. "Why are there no colours on your craft?"

"For you there are not but for us there is colour," came the reply. "Because of the structure of our optic unit, the light we receive is interpreted differently. The conditions here are controlled in our favour and that is why you see what you see."

John then requested a tour of the craft. To his surprise a tall being immediately came forward to lead him to a wall where a hole appeared. Seven feet high and three feet across, the aperture closed as soon as John and the three tall entities passed through. They were in a connecting tunnel which led them to a room similar in size to the examination chamber. Containing couches and a single table upon which were some boxes, John felt this was used for leisure purposes.

Out into the tunnel again and on to the next room went John and the three tall entities. Now there was no doubting this room's purpose, thought John. Despite the strangeness of the design of the equipment he immediately thought *laboratory.*

"We use this area for research," said the voice in his head as if confirming his suspicions.

"Have you any microscopes?" he found himself asking.

At this, a tall entity led him to a large unit with a centre console on top of which were square translucent panels. He then placed a glass phial, filled with liquid, on one of the panels, passed his hands over the unit and another square panel slid out over the top of the phial. A bluish glow filled the space between the panels.

At this moment an enlarged hologram of the phial appeared over the centre of the console. Angles and magnifications altered as the entity made adjustments by touching the top panel.

"This apparatus performs the same function as a microscope," said the voice in John's head. "But this one is far superior."

John and his guides then moved out of the lab into a connecting tunnel and then into what the entities told him was a rest room.

Here four sets of couches, each slightly undulating and covered in a bubble-like material, were suspended one above the other. They were used for sleep periods and also for deep space travel for which each couch was equipped with its own mini-atmosphere, John was told.

Out again into the tunnels, through another room and up a vertical tube. John felt himself coming up through the floor into a large area. He immediately realised it must be the control room.

Four tall entities were seated at a crescent shaped unit which was covered in panes. Although they were facing away from him John could see they were busy passing their hands over the unit before them, obviously fully occupied with controlling the craft.

John was ushered over to a couch on which he lay down. A dish shaped object was placed a few inches above his head and as soon as he became settled pictures were projected onto the wall facing him. Short, sharp pictorial sequences, including maps and diagrams, flicked before his eyes at such a rapid pace that he could not take them all in.

From the dish at his head came a garbled commentary.

"It's going too fast," said John.

"Don't worry," said the voice in his head. "It is all being remembered by your mind."

Star maps, cross sections of the craft, scenes from the solar system flickered before him. *Phobos,* the name kept popping into his mind. *Phobos.*

He didn't discover until later that Phobos is the name of the smaller of the two moons of Mars.

After the bizarre picture show ended the entities led John to a darker section of the control room where he was asked to look in a certain direction. Instantly a hologram burst into life before his eyes.

He was looking at a planet, an alien planet. The closer the view, the stranger it seemed, yet John could make out metallic cone-like shapes, sprouting from the ground of this world in bizarre formation. Perhaps a city.

Behind the city he could see mountains. Bands of colour stretched across the sky. The atmosphere seemed dense. "This is what our own planet looked like in its last years," said the voice in John's head. "Ruined by pollution and natural problems . . ."

A figure appeared in the foreground of the hologram, dressed in a hooded robe. It was holding onto a glowing object with both hands. The round object glowed red and yellow. John was asked to touch it, which he did. As his finger made contact with the object a strange tingling sensation swept up his arm.

Overwhelmed by a feeling of having been honoured, as if he had been given the chance to glimpse the holiest of holy shrines, he tried to grasp what his hosts were trying to tell him.

"It is time to go," said the voice in his head. "We will meet again."

With a sudden judder, John was back behind the wheel of his moving car.

After seeing John led away from the balcony and after her forced separation from Kevin, Sue was filled with a sense of dread. The examination room she was led to contained two tables, one slightly concave and one flat. Behind them were arranged an array of instruments, leads and boxes.

Frightened and struggling, she was somehow lifted onto one of the tables. Straps were drawn across her arms and legs, tightened and she was unable to move.

Looking around her in a wild panic she saw two of the *ugly* creatures whose description matched exactly the two who examined her husband.

They set to work immediately, drawing a pen-like, glowing instrument across the whole of her body. Starting at her feet, the pen thing was moved slowly up her body to her head. The examiners seemed to enjoy their work, thought Sue as she listened to the humming, almost singing sounds coming from the pair.

Terrified and continuing with her vain struggle, Sue watched as one of the tall entities drew close. The examiner nearest to her immediately moved to make way for his obvious superior.

"We cannot do anything with you whilst you are like this," chided a voice in Sue's head. The tall entity looked down and placed the middle finger of his right hand on her forehead, the two outer fingers on her eyes.

Sue blacked out.

When she came round she was still on the table, but the straps had been removed. Still she could not move.

One of the tall beings came into view and Sue immediately knew she could leave the room.

When she was placed upon the table she could not recall having any clothes on, but now as she climbed off she saw she was wearing a long gown with a tight hood, similar to that worn by the aliens. The baggy sleeves were brought in at the cuffs. The material was opaque, but looked like crinkly cellophane.

Like John, Sue was then taken on walkabout by two of the tall beings. The first thing she noticed was that all the walls of the craft were covered by a honeycomb structure.

At one point on her journey she recalls seeing John in his one piece suit, moving in the opposite direction, accompanied by two entities. Neither acknowledged the other, apparently more engrossed in the wonders around them.

Sue then arrived in the craft's control room. Like her husband she found herself ascending into the large chamber and immediately guessed its purpose from the layout and from the level of activity.

One of the tall entities, seated in a chair, swivelled around to face her and took hold of her hand. As he helped her climb the step up to his level the words: "That wasn't so bad, was it?" formed in her brain. She knew he was communicating by telepathy.

Still uneasy, Sue sat in a moulded seat indicated by the alien. She felt as if she were floating as she glanced about the large room, noting the units and control panels.

A tray containing about a dozen pink discs was offered to her. She thought the discs looked like pink peppermint creams. They were obviously some kind of food.

I'm not going to take one, they could be drugged," she thought. The beings either read her mind or understood her apprehension. They removed the tray immediately.

The entity who was seated, Sue automatically thought of him as the leader, looked at one of those standing. Sue seemed to understand that he had been given an order.

The standing entity then began slowly moving his hands, his fingers tracing strange shapes in the air. Immediately the room was filled with strange harp like sounds. Somehow Sue knew that the soft strains that drifted through the air from the direction of the standing entity were meant to be relaxing. But she was still tense with fear and with concern for her husband and children.

The leader seemed to understand.

"Your children are safe," again the words entered her mind. "You value your children. We do not reproduce, we do not have children. We produce through you, you are our children."

Now Sue felt relaxed. The message was reassuring and now the music seemed to be having an effect. She looked over at the standing alien as his hands danced through the air.

"Everyone has a talent," came the leader's telepathic message. "This is a music man. This is his talent." When the music stopped Sue was ushered over to another seat nearer to the controls. Pointing at an array of squares the Leader ran through the operating procedure. *Touch this one and the craft will do that, touch this and it will bank.*

The Leader turned away to communicate with one of his colleagues, then turned back to Sue and asked: "Would you like to see where you live?"

"Yes," she cried excitedly. A rectangular screen materialised to her right. The scene was a mass of stars. The entity pointed to a tiny pinpoint of light in the bottom right hand corner.

"Here is where you live," came the words. The star grew larger until it became obvious it was the sun. Then the planet earth came into view, closer and closer until Europe and then Great Britain filled the screen.

Then the Thames Estuary came into view, roads, streets and street lights. It was Aveley in Essex. Sue could see her home; there was no doubt about it.

The screen went blank and Sue, stunned by the images, reeled as a feeling of intense homesickness passed over her. Whether those views of her home were real or not they made Sue wonder about John and the children. "Where were they? Were they safe?"

The Leader had said they were safe but she wanted her children now. She needed them, now.

Another of the tall beings interrupted her thoughts and led her to a darker area of the control room where he indicated she should lie down facing a screen above her head. Like John, she was shown a high-speed series of images accompanied by sounds. They seemed like old cinema newsreels and high speed TV documentaries. "It was like having the contents of an encyclopaedia pumped into your head all in one go," said Sue later.

Unlike her husband, Sue has a clear memory of only one piece of information imparted by the strange audio-visual show, a chart of our solar system.

She remembers being confused about the planetary scene. There was the sun; there was Saturn with its rings and the massive Jupiter.

She counted the planets that ringed the sun, and counted them again. There was no doubt about it, there were ELEVEN worlds whirling around the star Sol instead of the nine known to conventional knowledge.

The screen above Sue's head went blank and an entity helped her up from the couch and led her silently down a slope into what she describes as a black area.

John and Kevin were standing there when a hologram materialised before them. She saw the scene that had confronted John, the alien's home planet and she distinctly remembers an explanation of sorts forming in her mind.

"This is the seed of life, our past and your future, our whole existence". As before the words simply formed in her mind. "Accept this from us for yourself, your children and your fellow men."

As John and Kevin gazed at the figure holding the glowing orb, or ball, Sue recalls the command: "Touch the ball, touch the ball" filling her mind. John and Kevin were already reaching out to the figure in the hologram. Their hands were making contact with the glowing orb. Slowly Sue stepped forward and faced the figure that held the object.

The compelling urge to make contact overcame her and inch by inch she raised her right arm, reaching forward until she touched it. No feeling, no sensation, but as Sue turned away from the hologram more words were forming in her brain: "It is time to go, but we will see you again."

In the blink of an eye Sue's surroundings changed dramatically.

It was misty and vague and she was getting dressed. "Are you dressed yet, John?" she asked. "Give Kevin a hand," she added.

John said Kevin was already dressed.

"We'd better get a move on then," said Sue as she took a large gulp from a glass that was not a glass, some kind of drinking vessel. As she set the cup down the scene changed again.

Now she was standing on a catwalk looking down on the family car about six feet below. Steps led down to the vehicle which was parked facing downwards on a sharply sloping ramp. In front of it was a horse shoe shaped wall.

The Leader was standing by Sue and they were joined by the Music Maker whom the Leader addressed as *Ceres*. The Music Man now addressed the Leader as *Lyra*. The Goodbyes that were forming inside her head were from the entities, of that Sue was sure. Looking down she saw John climb into the car, the children were already in, and then slowly the vehicle began to dematerialise.

"It just seemed to *fizzle* out of existence," recalled Sue later as she described how the car seemed to pass through the horse-shoe shaped wall, front bumper and bonnet first. The whole area became very bright as the car silently passed through the wall until it eventually disappeared.

Concerned, Sue looked forlornly at the Leader. "Don't worry, you are going home," he said.

When she next looked down she saw the white Vauxhall Victor as it bowled along the country lane by the woods. She remembers effortlessly climbing into the moving car and closing the door behind her.

She noticed the interior light was on . . .then a jolt . . .

"Is everybody here?" she remembers asking as she found herself beside her husband in the family car. John's reassuring "Yes, of course" was enough to quell the sense of panic that threatened to engulf her.

John and Sue Day's Close Encounter of the Fourth Kind is probably one of the most complete records of such a case in the UK. Exhaustively investigated their account remains unchanged to this day.

One of the most unusual aspects of this case is the sheer volume of information gleaned from their abductors, much of which is omitted from the above account because it was not until much later that John and Sue realised how much data they had assimilated. Whether this detail was imparted telepathically or by some other means they do not know. Much of the information was volunteered by John while in a hypnotic trance. Other material came from John and Sue much later. The recalling of one or other fact during the regression seemed to bring back a further rush of forgotten detail.

John believes the beings told him that human evolution was only a part of the jigsaw of our development. The earth, he claimed, had been seeded by alien watchers for thousands of years. Seeding appeared to involve interbreeding.

But they also had the power to alter minds and physical structure to help the species become more aware and intelligent.

John said the *Watchers,* as he called them, had many contacts on earth. They could live for an indefinite period of time, but when their *shells* ceased to function they had to move on to a new *host.*

They also allegedly confirmed that they were the *Gods* of Greek mythology. At that time they were more involved in the affairs of our planet. But they greatly reduced their level of involvement when they discovered it was leading to stagnation of human society. Human development slowed down when denied control of its own destiny. They pulled back despite reservations that we could develop into a very violent and destructive life form, said John.

Did this mass of information really come from alien beings who abducted the Day family less than 20 miles from the City of London? Or was it a case mass hysteria - but on a smaller scale.

Contamination doesn't come into it. The Days' knowledge of the subject was minimal. The couple did not seek publicity or notoriety. They contacted Ufologists in a desperate attempt to discover more about their experience. They had absolutely nothing to gain by *coming out*.

They even provided detailed drawings and diagrams of what they believed they had seen. Investigator Andy Collins was impressed with the family. But he was astounded at the way John, a working class Cockney could speak articulately and without interruption about the most complex subjects for up to 20 minutes.

"I just switched on the tape and let him speak," said Andy who was then able to transcribe the tape to text verbatim, confident that it would always be in good, clear English.

If he asked John, a poorly educated man, to repeat aspects of the material he had dictated, he couldn't. In fact on one occasion, when told that he had been speaking authoritatively for 15 or 20 minutes on a particular subject, John could not believe it.

"It was as if someone had switched on a tape inside him", recalled Andy. Did whoever switches on that tape, also programme it with the abduction story he related? Cynics might find the reiteration of the Greek Mythology/Aliens line a little hard to swallow. They might also wonder why it took this family so long to realise what a treasure trove of information they had been bequeathed by their abductors.

Garry Wood & Colin Wright
17 August 1992
A70 near Harperrig Reservoir
Lothian District, Scotland

It was just after 11:30 pm when Garry Wood and his friend Colin Wright, left the city of Edinburgh for the half hour drive along the A70 to deliver a satellite system to a friend in Tarbrax, West Lothian.

Garry relaxed behind the wheel as he and Colin chatted

about the day's events and it wasn't long before they were well out of the city limits and speeding along the lonely stretch of road that winds its way through the sparsely populated countryside.

Colin glanced at the speedometer as their Vauxhall car approached Harperrig Reservoir. It read 40 mph. As the vehicle passed the huge body of water and began negotiating the blind bend that followed, something ahead caught his attention.

"What on earth is that . . . ?" he barked.

Saying nothing, Garry resisted the impulse to hit the brakes as he tried to make sense of the huge two tiered disc shaped object that hovered about 20 feet above the road ahead of them. It was far too big to be a plane or any type of helicopter he had ever seen or heard of.

Whatever it was, they were approaching it fast. Too late to take any evasive action Garry put his foot down hard on the accelerator and prayed that they could speed underneath the object without coming to any harm.

Hands tightening on the steering wheel, eyes focused firmly on the road ahead Garry used his right elbow to push down the door lock - just in case, while Colin stared mutely ahead.

As the vehicle approached the hovering giant Garry, a mechanic with the ambulance service, noticed that it was jet black in appearance and quite shiny. He felt it was metallic but had never seen any metal like it. There were no windows or exterior structures and furthermore the object spanned the entire width of the road.

With just a couple of hundred metres separating them, the object suddenly began to emit what Garry and Colin described as a *silver shimmering mist*.

"It was like the effect you see when a TV is tuned between channels. You don't get a picture, just a maze of hazy shimmering lines," explained Colin later.

As soon as the car made contact with the *mist* its two occupants were plunged into a total, inky blackness. Unable to see or hear each other or their surroundings, they were prisoners in a black void.

What seemed like seconds later, they were back in the car, their sight restored with their vehicle shuddering violently.

Suddenly Colin became aware that Garry was driving *like a bloody mad man* in an effort to get away from this scene. Fighting to control the car - at one point it was on the wrong side of the road - Garry sped away from the area and the pair continued on to their destination in silence.

As he reached down to unbuckle his seat belt after arriving at Tarbrax, a normally safety conscious Colin was startled to find that his seat belt was already unfastened. Perhaps he had unbuckled it during the strange episode in the car.

Both men were visibly shaken by events but decided to deliver the satellite system as promised. However, when they knocked at the door of their friend's home there was no answer for some time.

When their friend eventually opened the door he demanded to know where they had been.

For Garry and Colin were one and half-hours late.

The two friends were stunned. Their journey had only taken them about 30 to 35 minutes. That left almost one whole hour of unaccounted time.

The pair returned to Edinburgh later that night - but by a different route.

In the days and weeks that followed both Colin and Garry tried to put the events of that night behind them. Colin's memories began to fade but Garry suffered tiredness, sleeping problems and headaches.

He suffered from strange dreams and the headaches became so severe he took medical advice and underwent a CAT scan. The test showed nothing abnormal.

After numerous debates and arguments about the object they had seen on the A70, Garry decided to carry out some research of his own at the local library. He devoured every book he could find on UFOs and alien abductions in a desperate search for some answers to the questions that had been haunting him since that fateful night.

There were no straightforward answers to explain their experience. However, for the first time since their terrifying ordeal, Garry and Colin had to accept that there were undeniable similarities between what they had seen and other well-documented sightings of Unidentified Flying Objects.

Furthermore, aspects of their experience also pointed to a deeper mystery.

Garry's search for information had thrown up the name of respected UFO researcher Malcolm Robinson of the Strange Phenomena Investigations (SPI). He decided to make a call to find out if there was any form of help available to Colin and himself.

"I'll never forget the night Garry Wood telephoned me", recalled Malcolm Robinson. "I listened intently as his strange tale unfolded and I knew straight away that something very strange indeed had occurred to both men."

He arranged for Garry and Colin to visit his home in Alloa where he interviewed them at length.

"I was convinced these were honest, decent individuals who had suffered and were still suffering to some extent, from their experience. But it was also very clear to me that *something else* had happened that night and I was determined to help them find the answers to that mystery."

Malcolm discussed the possibility of using hypnotherapy with Garry and Colin to establish, once and for all, what exactly happened in that missing hour on the night of their UFO experience. He explained the controversy surrounding the use of this hypnotherapy but both men were equally determined to get to the bottom of their mystery and were prepared to try any means at their disposal.

Malcolm contacted hypnotherapist Helen Walters, someone he trusted implicitly. She agreed to conduct an exploratory hypnotherapy session with Garry and Colin and a date was set.

Garry and Colin responded very differently to that first session, the first of many. The experience was an emotional one for Garry who at one point burst into tears. On the other hand, Colin remained calm throughout with only the occasional movement of his head and body.

The following weeks saw more visits to Helen by both Garry and Colin.

Each session provided additional valuable data that enabled Malcolm to piece together an account of the events that took place during Garry and Colin's missing hour.

Under hypnosis, both men were able to relive the experience that turned out to be an encounter far stranger than they could ever have imagined.

Despite Garry's attempt at a headlong dash to their destination, under hypnosis both men remembered their car stopping on the road near to the floating UFO.

Three *small entities* appeared and opened both the driver and passenger doors.

Colin recalled seeing Garry being placed on what looked like a stretcher that appeared to silently hover above the ground. Garry, who remembers experiencing great pain in his abdomen at this point, also reported another entity, lurking or hiding behind part of the UFO.

Colin remembered being led, by the beings, up a ramp into the UFO. Once inside they led him around a winding corridor which eventually opened into a circular room that was completely empty apart from one unusual curved chair.

Here Colin was stripped naked and placed upon the chair. Although his recollection at this point was hazy, he was convinced that his captors conducted some form of clinical or medical examination.

Garry too, remembers being taken into a circular room devoid of any furnishings apart from a raised table. Garry also had his clothes removed before being placed upon the table at which point the entities informed him, seemingly telepathically, that he would come to no harm. This brought little relief, for by now Garry was terrified.

Unable to move, he saw a pool of dark liquid suddenly appear on the floor of the room. Seconds later a cylindrical object rose up and appeared to the right of his head. Roughly three and a half feet in length and 18 inches across, the object was slowly spinning in the air. Garry could hear the sound of a motor.

As he watched in disbelief, a flap in the object slowly opened. At this point the dark pool began to vibrate and Garry could make out a small, frail looking creature resembling a Grey, pulling itself free from the dark liquid. Almost skeletal in appearance, the creature seemed to be controlling the cylindrical object.

Garry later revealed he felt there were more creatures in the dark pool. What they were or why they were there remains a mystery.

Still paralysed, Garry later became aware of a black lens-shaped device floating in the centre of the featureless room. Measuring five or six feet by two and a half feet, the object seemed to twist and turn, as if it was trying to fold in on itself while an eerie *whooshing* noise emanated from it.

Eyes drawn towards the slowly moving object, Garry's concentration was suddenly shattered when a thin, translucent grey arm with long fingers came into his field of vision.

It was at this point that he snapped out of his hypnotic trance.

Garry is now convinced that in addition to observing the commonly reported *Greys* who feature in the majority of abduction reports, he also saw small brown beings with heavy folds of skin that obscured parts of their faces.

He admitted to being extremely frightened of one of these brown beings but doesn't know why as it never harmed him in any way.

Not all of the Greys observed by Garry were the four to four and a half feet in height as reported by most abductees. Some appeared to be a full six feet in stature yet retaining the smooth, grey coloured, almost child-like appearance of the stereotype.

Even stranger details of Garry's encounter were revealed during a series of follow-up hypnotherapy sessions.

At one point, while lying naked, he clearly saw two small creatures standing at the foot of the examination table. One was holding a bright, diamond shaped object which was pulsating with orange light. The creature began to move the device over Garry's body. Garry recalls being very frightened and very angry with his captors.

However, his feelings of anger and frustration were overtaken by sheer astonishment. For over to his left he could clearly see another human captive.

Stripped naked like him, this fellow victim, a young woman was sitting on the floor with her knees drawn up to her chin and arms clasped tightly around her legs.

She seemed to be crying softly and Garry thought she also seemed to be shivering slightly in the chill atmosphere of the alien room. Slowly and very gently, the woman turned her head towards Garry, her blonde hair framing a face full of despair. There was no mistaking the tears that streamed down her cheeks.

Silently, she looked away but Garry knew that her face, that image of sadness, had been etched on his brain for ever. If he ever came across that young woman again, there was no doubt in his mind that he would recognise her.

However, all Garry's conscious memories of events inside the UFO, had been erased from his mind by the time he found himself back at the wheel of his car.

Although the experiences of Garry's pal Colin Wright began in a similar fashion, there were striking differences that were revealed when he was hypnotically regressed.

After watching his friend being *stretchered* into the craft by a group of alien entities, Colin was escorted up a ramp, along a corridor and into a circular room where he was stripped and laid on an ultra-smooth curved chair. He strongly believes his captors then conducted some kind of medical examination but cannot remember any details.

Even under hypnosis, Colin could not reveal any details of a medical examination. However, he vividly remembers being extremely cold and recalls one of the smaller beings approaching him. Colin asked why they wanted him.

The response stunned him. "It is Garry we want," replied the entity before leaving the room. Colin was left shivering in the cold for some time. Eventually another being came into the room and touched him on the face. This touch felt extremely cold and gave Colin the impression that it was *cold blooded*. Again he was left alone.

Colin had a feeling that there was another room, out of his sight and behind him. He heard strange noises coming from that direction, sounds he had never heard before and could not explain.

Colin's next memory is of finding himself contained within a large glass or perspex chamber. Still naked, he was bound by straps attached to his wrists and ankles. However, there was little chance of his escaping for he found the only part of his body that he could move was his head.

And when he raised his head to look out through the transparent walls of his alien prison cell he saw that he was not alone. He was surrounded by countless other cells or chambers, each containing people, men and women.

Colin began to feel uneasy when a strange white mist began to rise up around the chamber. It reminded him of the clouds of vapour that pour from a dry ice machine. When the walls appeared to turn frosty Colin's discomfort turned to raw fear.

Were they trying to freeze him to death?

However, as if responding to his growing alarm, the frosting effect suddenly stopped and as the perspex walls of his chamber began to clear Colin watched as a strange looking device rose from the floor and floated before him at eye level.

The device, comprising a long rod connected to a triangular shaped object which had two red lights on its front, rotated soundlessly before descending out of sight.

Colin's next memory is of arriving back in the car with a jolt and watching a white-knuckled Garry manoeuvring their speeding car away from the UFO.

Like many abductees, Garry reported a number of post event incidents that gave him cause for concern. Were these further alien encounters or a symptom of a mind struggling to come to terms with a life changing trauma?

Garry recalls waking up in his bedroom two years after the A70 event to find a small Grey standing at the bottom of his bed.

He tried to wake his wife but no matter how much he shook her or called to her she remained inert and unconscious.

Anger welled up as Garry recalled the terrifying events of 1992. How dare they invade his home? He threw the covers back and raced over to confront the small being.

Garry told Malcolm later that he was sure there was a look of surprise on the being's face. But that didn't stop him drawing back his clenched fist and throwing the hardest punch he had ever delivered.

When fist and alien face made contact the being was sent crashing across the room ending in a heap on the floor. Almost immediately, the crumpled being climbed to its feet.

The Grey's eyes seemed to focus on its human assailant before going into a headlong rush towards him.

At this point Garry lost consciousness.

Three years on, Garry was again involved in another bizarre event. Driving in the countryside with his two young sons, the vehicle was suddenly and inexplicably filled with a fierce white light.

"It was like a magnesium flare," said Garry later.

The event was over within seconds but left Garry perplexed and his two sons very frightened.

Today Garry still feels that *they* are around, and that *something is going on.*

Hypnotherapist Helen Walters, is of the opinion that both men are telling the *truth* and are completely sincere. She was quoted by the Scotsman newspaper in September 1994, as saying, "There seems little doubt that they saw an Unidentified Flying Object. The question is what. There is no doubt that under hypnosis they appear to remember meeting aliens. The question is, are these memories or imaginings?"

Another hypnotherapist, a Dr Prem Misra from Glasgow, undertook further regressive hypnosis on Garry Wood for a BBC television documentary about this case entitled, *Cracking Stories.*

Dr Misra has no doubt that Garry Wood genuinely believes that he has had a close encounter and explained to

Garry that he should learn self hypnosis in order to alleviate his fears. It should be noted that under the influence of Dr Misra's hypnosis, Garry recounted exactly what he recounted under the hypnosis of Helen Walters, there was no detraction from the original story, no elaboration, just the straightforward recollections of a man that had experienced something out of the ordinary.

CHAPTER 6
The Ultimate Encounter

The British UFO researchers who have long argued that close encounter experiences are totally subjective and due to some kind of psychological or physiological process will rarely be moved even in the face of a multiple witnessing of an abduction.

Psychologists can always come up with psychological reasons for multiple events. The possible rational explanations for these events are many and largely based on hallucination.

So it does not matter how credible the witness, how detailed his account or how real his experience. The school of thought which favours a psychological approach to Ufology will not question the truth of the witness testimony, or its reality. They will question his perception of reality.

It's a heads I win, tails you lose philosophy based on the premise that flying saucers and aliens don't exist.

If the alleged abductees are not a fake, then there is something wrong in the old brain box.

So pity the poor investigator relying on the single abductees. His whole case is based on one individual's account of events. Back up might come from a good hypnosis session, but even that evidence is not regarded as sacrosanct.

He would count himself lucky to find additional evidence. Marks on the ground to support claims of a UFO landing, marks on the body of the abductees to support claims of physical and medical testing and a witness of impeccable character and credibility would make for a cast-iron case in Ufology terms. However in the real world, none of the above is sufficient proof of UFOs, aliens or alien abduction.

Let's face it, the serious hoaxer can fake the story, fake the marks and put on an Oscar winning performance under hypnosis if he really wants to.

So how does an investigator get sufficient proof to back up the Close Encounter he is probing?

Well, no investigator is ever likely to get enough proof to satisfy every cynic. They just have to live in hope that the next case is the BIG ONE.

Peter Hough, Chairman of the Manchester UFO Research

Association was convinced he'd got the big one a few years ago. The case that fell into his lap had all the right elements. A former Metropolitan police officer, a UFO, an alien entity sighting, a clear case of missing time . . . and a PHOTOGRAPH.

Yes, a photograph of an alien, a little green man. And it had been taken by a former bobby. How credible can you get?

Peter could not believe his luck when the witness, after being subjected to hours of interviews, further agreed to undergo hypnotic regression in an attempt to discover more about his particular encounter.

That session was also a success and this Close Encounter of the Fourth Kind had now become a classic case, one that would go down in the UFO history books.

Fellow investigators Arthur Tomlinson and Jenny Randles were also deeply involved in the case that was now being billed *The Ultimate Encounter.*

The witness had shunned all suggestions of publicity on the grounds that he wished to return to the police force, but agreed to hand over the photographic evidence for expert testing.

He was the perfect close encounter witness, intelligent, co-operative and disinterested in making any financial gain from his experience.

Surely this was this case that would wake up the world to the reality of alien abduction. A British bobby photographs the alien who space-napped him and lives to tell the tale. Sadly the big bad world outside the confines of Ufology did not bat an eyelid when the story was released.

The picture hadn't been faked, but the alien seen in it could have been a dummy. The policeman told his story, but no one wanted to listen.

For investigator Peter Hough it had been quite a trial. What's your verdict?

Philip Spencer (pseudonym)
December 1, 1987
Ilkely Moor
West Yorkshire.

The sun still hadn't risen when former police constable Philip Spencer set off from his home to cross the bleak moors over Ilkley, that dull, dark winter's morning.

A quick glance at his watch told him it was 7.15 am. He checked he had his compass and his camera and then trudged off in the direction of East Morton, the village where his father-in-law lived.

A methodical man Philip had already decided his route across Yorkshire's most famous moor. Instead of taking the tourist trek from East Morton, he would take the shorter, but much tougher, alternative up a steep hillside.

Even though he had made the five mile journey many times, Philip always took his compass along. He knew how easy it was to become disoriented up on the cold and misty moor. Even the most experienced walker could get lost up there when the weather turned. When the rain came down like stair rods, as it often did, you couldn't see your hands in front of your face. And in the depths of winter, a sudden heavy snowfall could turn the moor into a white wasteland, obliterating every landmark as far as the eye could see.

Still there was no sight grander than the view over Ilkley, seen from high up on the moor. And if the light improved he could get some good snaps of the town later, thought Philip, patting the pocket containing the camera that had served him so well for years.

A stiff wind began building up as Philip got stuck into the task of scaling the steep, grass covered hillside. Despite maintaining a steady pace he could still feel the biting cold through his sturdy hiking gear.

Careful to avoid rabbit holes and patches of slippery lichen, Philip made good progress. As the hill began to level out he spotted a path which ran alongside a row of trees.

Heading for the firmer footing of the track he was suddenly aware of a humming sound coming from above. He glanced at the lowering sky, assuming the mass of clouds was hiding an aircraft.

Then something caught his eye. Philip stopped and turned, peering into a large hollow, scooped out of the top of the hill. There, about 30 feet away, he saw what he later described as a *small green creature*.

"Hey", shouted Philip, as it scuttled off over the heather. Vaguely humanoid in shape, with a head, two legs and two long arms, the thing stopped when it was about 50 feet away, turned and waved.

With instinctive coolness, Philip reached into his pocket, pulled out his camera, brought it to eye level and clicked the shutter.

Then, shoving the camera back in his pocket, he jumped down the embankment and gave chase.

"I don't know why," he said later. "But I just ran after it."

Philip's running was reduced to a stumbling over the rough terrain, but when he saw his pursuer the creature darted around a huge outcrop and disappeared.

Using his hands to maintain his balance, Philip made his precarious way around the outcrop as quickly as he could.

Breathless and now sweating from his efforts, despite the cold, he worked his way around the mass of rock to find himself looking down into an even deeper hollow in the side of the hill.

The sight that met him nearly sent him careering back down the slope.

There, sitting at the base of the hollow was a strange something that almost defied description. The down-to-earth one time bobby saw what appeared to be two giant silver saucers, apparently stuck together edge to edge. A box shape protruded from the centre of the top saucer and was slowly descending into the object.

Philip found it impossible to gauge its dimensions from his vantage point, but the humming noise he had heard earlier was back and was gradually increasing in intensity. As the sound reached an almost deafening crescendo the object shot straight into the clouds.

Shaken and confused Philip decided to cut short his journey and slowly made his way back off the moor heading in the direction of Ilkley. His confusion became more acute as he walked into the town.

It was a hive of activity. Shops were open, pedestrians lined the streets and traffic was building up on roads that were normally quiet at this time of the day.

Philip looked up at the town hall clock . . . and then did a double take. There was no mistake. The clock said it was 10 am. Yet he estimated that it should have been no more than 8.15. Surely no more than an hour could have elapsed since he set off from home. "Am I going mad?" he asked himself as he mentally re-traced his steps from his home, up onto the moor and on into Ilkley. Philip was a man whose police training had honed his powers of observation. Estimating times, distances and speeds are all a part of the daily routine of a police officer so how come he had *lost* one and three quarter hours.

Then he remembered the photo. He knew a place in the nearby town of Keighley which operated a one hour photographic developing service.

He caught the next bus to the town and walked to the shop, taking a couple of pictures as he went. "I had felt guilty about wasting so much film," Philip recalled later.

He handed in his roll of film and then walked around the town to fill in time. His mind went over and over his route on the moor, searching for some rational explanation for the missing time. But there was not.

"What if the picture doesn't come out?" he said to himself. That would mean he had no evidence of something strange up on the moor . . . maybe that would prove that he was indeed going mad.

When he returned to the shop he accepted the prints nervously and marched straight into the street where he began tearing open the package and rifling through the contents desperate to find the picture that would show he wasn't crazy.

There it was. The quality was poor, but there was no

doubt about it. He had captured on film the thing he had seen with his own eyes.

That night, back at home, Philip went over the events of the day for the umpteenth time. The familiar walk to the moor, the slow ascent up the hillside, the encounter with the strange green creature. Yes the light had been poor and the creature had been green, a darker green than the grassy background. But there was no doubt about it. He had seen it. He still didn't know why he had given chase. It had been a sudden impulse. A hunter in pursuit of his quarry doesn't think before closing in. He had not thought before acting. Thank God he had taken that photograph first. If it hadn't been for that fuzzy colour print he would now be doubting his own sanity.

In bed later that night Philip tossed and turned. Flashes of the green creature and the strange craft kept sleep at bay. The questions kept coming. What was it? Where had it come from? Did it go into the saucer object? How could it have risen into the sky so rapidly?

Bleary-eyed after a fitful night Philip sat down to breakfast the next morning feeling a growing sense of determination. He was not mad, he had not imagined events, and he had seen something very strange on Ilkley Moor. Today he would go to the public library and look for some agency or organisation which could help him. He had heard of UFOs and all that nonsense. There must be someone out there who would be interested in hearing his story.

The letter from Philip that landed on the desk of UFO researcher Jenny Randles related his account in a matter-of-fact way. He briefly mentioned the photograph and pointed out that the compass he had carried that day was now totally useless. Its readings were inaccurate.

Because of his former links with the police force and his desire to rejoin the service Philip was very wary of attracting any publicity that might affect his chances of donning his uniform in the future. So instead of giving his address, the letter simply carried a PO Box number in Bristol, the city where his parents lived.

Jenny raised the case with the Manchester UFO Research Association where the reaction was muted. They had received many letters over the years containing the most astounding claims, most of which could not be supported with evidence. Jenny was encouraged to reply and ask for further details.

Meanwhile Philip was already regretting his clandestine approach. He simply wanted to report the matter to people who investigated such things and he wanted them to get to work now. He was desperate for someone else to confirm he wasn't mad and was not suffering from hallucinations.

He also needed to know that other people experienced similar disturbing events.

Even his wife Susan was having difficulty reconciling his story with his normally down-to-earth, no-nonsense nature. It was all just too fantastic to be true and that's what everybody would think even if they didn't say it, wouldn't they?

The sheer strangeness of his experience was infuriating for Philip, a man used to confronting problems and solving them.

Losing patience, Philip decided to telephone another name that he had dug up in his researches at the library. Arthur Tomlinson, a man who had studied UFOs for 30 years, took the call at the end of December.

Accompanied by flying saucer enthusiast Steve Balon, Arthur, who was also a leading light in the Manchester UFO group, immediately travelled to Ilkley to meet Philip and together the three men re-traced his steps to study the location.

Philip had no qualms about handing over the photographic print and the negatives for testing. In fact, he was heartened by the enthusiasm displayed by Arthur and Steve. They had listened with interest and indicated similarities between what he had seen and other incidents. They did not question his sanity, which was comforting to say the least.

In the following days Arthur liaised with Peter Hough,

Chairman of the Manchester UFO Research Association. He pointed out that in addition to the photograph Philip had a further piece of evidence, his compass.

Arthur had studied the instrument and decided it had reversed its polarity, pointing south instead of north.

Peter agreed to join Philip, Arthur and Steve on a further expedition to the site on January 3, 1988.

Before setting off for the moor the party met at Philip's home where Peter expressed some disappointment with the quality of the picture. It was grainy and lacking in detail. However he agreed that the entity appeared to have a long body, short legs and protuberances at the side of the head which could have been large ears.

The thin arms were long, the left one exceedingly so, because it appeared to be resting on the ground.

Philip recounted his story once again. It had not changed in any way since he first told it. Nevertheless, Investigator Peter Hough was unhappy at Philip's laid back attitude in view of the traumatic nature of such incidents.

He felt Philip was treating the entire affair with a degree of amusement. Was he making it up, had he built a dummy, taken it onto the moor and photographed it?

He decided to put those thoughts bluntly to the witness to test his reaction. If he didn't voice reservations now, someone else would when the story was eventually made public. Philip reacted instantly. Quite calmly he said: "I am not particularly interested in what other people think. I know what I saw and if people don't believe me that's up to them. I've got nothing to gain by doing that *(faking the picture)*. I don't see the sense; I've got better things to do with my time."

The investigators knew, in fact, that Philip had a great deal to lose by coming forward with his account. A police force would be loathed to take on a constable with a history of flying saucer spotting, much less a hoaxer.

As the four men made their way to the site, the swirling storm clouds and biting winds of Wuthering Heights country added a touch of irony. How odd that this bleak landscape which had spawned such a classic of literature might also be responsible for an entirely new chapter in the history books of Ufology.

After a 20 minute walk from their cars, the men reached the spot where Philip had taken his photograph. The distance from the camera to the approximate spot where the small figure had been seen standing measured 39 feet.

The terrain was much as Philip had described it. There were no markings in the depression where he had seen the strange object and no other clues at the site.

The men made their way back, a heavy storm was imminent. The investigation now centred on the photograph.

Examination of the camera, a 35mm Dixons own brand called a Prinz Mastermatic, revealed it to be a basic lightweight model, constructed largely of plastic, with a 45mm lens. An internal light meter had not worked for some years.

The camera, according to Philip, had been pre-set for low light conditions, and combined with the 400 ASA film being used should have taken a good picture. The dark and grainy picture it had produced was interesting. It should have been slightly over exposed rather than underexposed.

The investigators spotted another anomaly in the picture. Although Philip estimated he took the photo around 7.45 am, the sky above the horizon in the picture was light when it should have been dark at that time on December 1.

Extensive testing of the photograph by individual photographers, experts and Kodak in the UK came up with disappointingly inconclusive results.

All agreed that the picture was *NOT* a photograph of a photograph and the film had not been tampered with *after* processing.

The figure, whatever it was, was actually there at the site when photographed.

Meanwhile the University of Manchester Institute of Science and Technology devoted some of their substantial technical know-how to the mystery of the compass and its reversed polarity.

"Yes, it is a fascinating problem," said the boffin, who at that stage had no ready explanation for what had happened to the simple piece of equipment.

After some day's tests in the lab, the university's Total Technology Department came back. Yes, it was possible to reverse the polarity of the compass without expensive and complicated equipment.

Simply take a piece of wire, coil it, place the compass inside the coil and connect to the mains electricity supply. Switch on and the polarity is reversed.

The process would be accompanied by a very loud bang and some blown fuses, said the expert, but it could be done, albeit with a certain risk to life, limb and property.

Would Philip Spencer have known how to conduct such a potentially dangerous experiment when an expert in the field did not?

While these various tests were being carried out, Philip Spencer had a more down to earth problem.

On Friday January 15, 1988 an anxious Philip phoned investigator Peter Hough: "What do you know about two men from the Ministry of Defence who've just been to see me?" demanded the normally quietly spoken man.

"They have shown me their identity cards with their names on and they said they wanted to interview me about my UFO experience."

Peter assured Philip that his case was still entirely confidential and that no information had been passed onto anybody, including the MOD. Philip recalled the business-suited men identifying themselves as David Jefferson and Mr Davies.

Reluctantly, he had given them a brief run down of his experience without mentioning the photograph. But they specifically asked about photographic evidence, and when Philip admitted taking a snap they asked to examine it. Philip told them it was with a friend at which both men left.

"I'm worried that this situation is getting out of hand," Philip told Peter. "What if the media get hold of the story?

What if my picture gets lost? I'll have no proof of what happened."

Peter tried to reassure Philip and then immediately wrote to the MOD about the alleged visit. He never received a reply.

The following day Peter received another call from Philip. This time a national newspaper wanted to ask him about his UFO incident.

The former policeman had been adamant on no publicity. He was now withdrawing all co-operation and demanded the return of the picture and his compass.

Efforts to track down the reporter failed, but there were no press follow ups and Philip, after a great deal of persuasion, reluctantly agreed to allow the investigation to continue. His reaction to the possibility of publicity reinforced the view of the investigators that Philip was not a hoaxer. He had no motive. He had no interest in selling his story, or his picture, he valued his anonymity and was determined to resume his police career.

When the results of the test on the photograph and the compass came in, Philip was as disappointed as the investigators.

He had hoped that scientific examination would have found something that would have thrown some light on his missing one and three quarter hours, or would have helped provide some explanation for the green creature and the saucer like object.

The subject of hypnosis was broached. The investigators thought Philip would be a good case for hypnotic regression and explained that it was a process where the subject is regressed to the time of the incident in the hope that he can recall events that occurred during his lost time. Philip agreed to try the technique; after all, he had nothing to lose.

On March 6, 1988 Dr Jim Singleton, a consultant psychologist with no particular interest in UFO phenomenon met Philip and agreed to regress him. The doctor insisted that none of the investigators be present during the session but agreed to an independent witness *sitting in* to operate the tape recorders.

Once in a trance state Philip was told to cast his mind back and re-experience the events of that bleak December morning.

The following account is taken from a verbatim transcript of the tape recordings made during the hypnosis session. The words used are those of Philip Spencer:

"I'm walking along the moor. It's quite windy and there are a lot of clouds. Walking up to the tress, I can see this little something, can't tell, but he's green. Moving towards me. Oh. I can't move. I'm stuck. He's still coming towards me. I still can't move . . . I'm stuck and everything's gone fuzzy. I'm . . . I'm floating along in the air. I want to get down. And this green thing is walking ahead of me and I don't like it. I still can't move. I'm going round the corner and this green thing's in front of me. Oh God . . . want to get down."

After a long pause Philip continued, his breathing is much faster than before.

"There's a . . . There's a big silver saucer thing, and there's a door in it. I don't want to go in there . . . Everything's gone black now."

"You say its gone black?" asked Dr Singleton.

"Mmm . . . I can't see anything, like I'm asleep. Can't hear anything . . . Now there's a bright light, can't see where it's coming from. I'm in a funny sort of room. I can hear this voice saying don't be afraid. I don't feel afraid anymore. I can still see this green thing but I'm not frightened of it now . . ."

Philip continued: "I'm being put onto a table. I can move now if I want to but I don't feel frightened. And there is a beam-like pole, it's above me. It's moving up towards me. It's got a light in it. Like a fluorescent tube. It's coming up from my feet. I can hear that voice again, saying we don't mean to harm you and don't be afraid.

"Makes me feel warm as it's moving up me. It's coming up over my stomach, towards my head. Close my eyes, I don't want to look at it in case it hurts my eyes. It's gone."

"There's something . . . My nose feels uncomfortable," at this Philip wrinkles his nose. "That's gone as well. I'm standing up now; I don't know how I got stood up. I can see a door, there's one of these green creatures motioning for me to come with him.

"Don't really want to go with him. I'd rather stay in here. I don't feel afraid in here." After a long pause Philip continued:

"I'm walking towards the door. There's still a bright light. I can't see where it's coming from. There's light all around. Want to know where the light is. It's just bright, it's just light. Walking down a corridor. There's a hole opened in it so I can walk through. I'm in a big room, a big round room, I'm on a raised platform against the wall.

"My camera and my compass are trying to get away from me, going towards the ball. Its difficult to pull them back down again and this ball's moving around, with things around it. Looks strange. It's got some blocks on it.

"He says we cant stay in here long. He wants us to go out again. The hole's closed in the wall. It's gone strange. He says I've got nothing to fear, but I'd like to go home . . . It's got such big hands."

After another long pause Dr Singleton asked Philip:

"What's happening now?"

"Going down a corridor again. It's very bright still. I wish I knew where the light was coming from, and there's another door. I'm going through a door into an empty room.

Two of those green creatures have come with me. There's a picture. It's starting to move on the wall. Wonder how they get the pictures?"

Asked to explain Philip replied: "I'm looking at the pictures on the wall."

"Pictures on the wall?" asked the doctor.

"Mmm. Creatures seem concerned at the damage that it's doing. Pictures changing now, there's another picture, another film. He's asking me a question. He says *do you understand?* I said *yes*.

"It's time to go. Everything has gone black. I'm walking

up near some trees. Some movement. I can see something, a green creature. I've shouted to it.

"It's turned round. I don't know what it is. I'll photograph it. It's turned round now." Philip went on to describe his encounter with the saucer shaped object before his walk in Ilkley.

Still under hypnosis, he described the creature as about four feet tall - detailed examination of the photograph indicated it's height as between four feet and four feet six inches. He said it had large pointed ears, big dark eyes, no nose and a tiny mouth.

The hands were very large with three large fingers like *big sausages*. Its feet were V shaped with two large toe-like digits and it appeared to have difficulty walking.

He shuffles rather than walks," explained Philip. Of the two pictures, or films, he saw while on the craft Philip said the first involved scenes of destruction and starvation. He refused to discuss the second saying only: "I'm not supposed to tell anybody about the other film. It's not for them to know."

Philip's description of events matched the classic elements of abduction experience. Small creatures, couch in the centre of a room, physical examination, lights with no obvious source and ecological warnings matched similar accounts from around the world.

But was Philip really under hypnosis?

"Definitely," said Dr Singleton. "That's my opinion. To have faked it convincingly, Philip would have had to have studied hours of video taped sessions. Then he would have to be a very good actor to carry it off. I think the hypnosis was genuine. He was certainly recounting the incident as something which had actually happened.

"He described things typically as someone would recall a past event. He compares very well with other non-UFO subjects."

However the doctor added: "Experimental studies suggest that people can modify, or vary their recall. So obviously there is no certainty that what is recalled under hypnosis is

100 per cent. However, here I think I've helped Philip to recover memories that were hidden more deeply in his mind."

Why were those memories hidden?

"In terms of my clinical work, if people experience things which are unusual, traumatic or frightening, the mind protects itself by pushing them deep into the subconscious. Hypnosis seems to lower the threshold of this barrier".

Philip had been allowed to retain full conscious recall of his hypnotic narrative and when asked, after the session, how vivid was his recollection he replied: "It was very clear. I have no trouble remembering what I saw."

Through hypnosis it seemed clear that Philip had taken his photograph at the end of his experience rather than much earlier. This explained the missing time and the lightness of the sky in the photograph. When quizzed on his reference to a view through a window Philip explained: "It was the sort of view astronauts have during space missions. I could see the Earth. It was very beautiful."

Some weeks after the hypnosis experiment Peter Hough bumped into Philip. He had since applied to re-join the Police Force and had collected a character reference in the form of a letter from a serving police officer. He showed Peter the letter which spoke of Philip's good character and honesty.

Since that meeting Philip has been in touch with investigators to pass on further newly remembered details. This is not uncommon with abductees. Once their mental barrier has been broken down with hypnosis it is not unusual for additional details to be remembered at a later date.

Philip recalled: "The creatures seemed part of a team. They weren't acting as individuals, but more like bees, as if they were doing what they were programmed to do.

"I had a feeling of goodness about them. I don't think they would harm anybody. I would go so far, in retrospect, to say I actually liked them."

CHAPTER 7
The Nearly Files

One of the biggest files in the UFO investigators office is for the: *Possible Abductions,* the nearly cases that don't contain enough detail to be put down as classic Close Encounters of the Fourth Kind, yet which have factors which seem, to point in the right direction.

They are a million miles away from the graphically described cases that we have looked at so far. The witnesses, at least some, are perfectly credible but their recollections are sometimes confused and unclear.

"Maybe I dreamed it," is one way of explaining the fantastic images and events some find lodged in their brains. It's often easier to dismiss these monster memories as nightmares than try to trace their origins.

Brief snatches of events is all that some people's memories retain, as if their brain has already censored out the impossible. Being haunted by these flashbacks drives some to seek help from various therapists.

They seem instinctively to know that something strange has happened to them, but they can't put it into words.

Those who describe their encounter with perfect clarity, then say they have a vague notion of missing time, may or may not have had an abduction experience. They may not suffer from the dreams which for some provide clues as to what happened during those missing minutes. They may not respond to hypnosis.

Some simply don't want to delve into their minds for memories which were presumably locked away for good reason.

In these cases there is no way of knowing whether or not they were removed from their homes or familiar surroundings, whether they underwent the testing reported by others or whether they made contact with beings from elsewhere. Nevertheless their experiences are well worth recording . . .

George and Amanda Phillips (pseudonyms)
August 30, 1982
Cleveland
Tyne and Wear

It was a night like any other for George and Amanda Phillips. Baby Sarah put to bed, a couple of hours in front of the box and it was time to turn in. But that late summer's night took a sudden and dramatic turn for the worse at exactly 1.20 am.

Amanda remembers looking at the clock as a piercing scream from the baby's room left her shaking with panic. That was no ordinary scream, she said to George, as they both scrambled out of bed and headed for their ten month old tot. She sounded frightened or as if she was in pain.

George arrived in his tiny daughter's bedroom first and scooped her up into his arms. Amanda was close behind. She checked her child was physically alright before cradling her in her arms, a sense of relief washing over her.

At that moment both George and Amanda turned their heads towards the window. A bright, blinding light shone into the room from something in their back garden.

As they approached the window, George thought he could make out something, an object in the back.

"I had made the base for a shed and I could see something on the base," recalled George later. "It was oval in shape, and there was someone or something standing next to it."

Shocked, he told Amanda to take a look at it, and then headed out onto the landing. Something made him look over the banister to the bottom of the stairs. Two small figures were making their way up.

"I don't remember anything after that," said George during an interview with a UFO investigator some years later.

Relaxing at his semi-detached home in Redcar, Cleveland, the ICI factory worker seemed genuinely perplexed by the whole incident.

"It's so strange, I don't even remember waking up the next morning. The first thing I remember about the following day was opening up the door to the kitchen and saying

110

to Amanda: "I had a funny dream last night."

"She said, *well I had a funny dream as well.* Then we both, more or less speaking at the same time said *an alien sort of thing.*

"I asked her where she had seen it from and by this time Amanda was saying *Oh My God,* as if the remembering was frightening her. Then she said, *from Sarah's window.*"

The couple went up to the child's bedroom to look for clues, only to find a damp patch on the floor by the cot.

"We were pretty sure it was urine, but it couldn't have been Sarah's because she was still in nappies. We assumed one of us must have wet ourselves that night from the fright."

Under questioning by a UFO investigator, George and Amanda realised their *dreams* finished at different times. They both remember clearly being woken by their baby's cries and seeing the bright light at the window.

When pressed, George recalled the object in the back garden as being small and oval with a ring of lights around it. He described what could have been three landing legs and antenna like structures.

But his recollections stopped abruptly at the point when he left the child's bedroom to look over the landing at two creatures ascending the stairs.

During the interview Amanda took over the account at this stage. She remembered following George out of the bedroom onto the landing. But when she got out there, there was no sign of George. He had disappeared completely.

She looked down the stairs and saw the creatures which had confronted her husband. Amanda described them as small, almost child-like in size, with pale skin, no hair or nose and no clothing that she could ascertain.

Both George and Amanda agreed to go under hypnosis to discover the truth about that strange night. But it was Amanda's account of events that suggest a possible abduction.

Once in a hypnotic trance, Amanda was taken back to

moments before her baby's waking. Sarah's screams were the first thing she remembered, then the lights and then following George onto the landing.

She said: "I had Sarah and I went onto the landing after George and he wasn't there. I didnt know where he was. I shouted *George*, but he didn't reply.

Then there was a noise, someone downstairs. There's something on the stairs. Terrible . . . I don't know what it is.

"It's small, its skin is funny. It's like a child, pale, small, very small. Long face, very pale, no hair and I can't see any ears and I can't distinguish a nose. It's just standing there, still on the stairs. I see one behind, pale, I see two."

"Are you still on the landing?" asked the hypnotherapist.

"The stairs appear", she said.

"So you are going downstairs?"

"I can't see them any more, I can't see them."

Amanda then says she feels as if she is going outside, outside the house. Despite further questioning by the hypnotherapist Amanda can't say where she is. She hasn't a clue about her location.

"Where are you now?" asked the hypnotherapist.

"Outside," said Amanda.

"Are you happy there?"

"No".

"How do you feel?"

"Frightened."

"Of what?"

"I don't know where George is."

"Are you still outside the house?"

"I don't know."

"How about Sarah, where's she?"

"I don't know."

"What can you see?"

"Nothing. There is . . . nothing."

"How light is it?"

"Quite dark, I think. I'm not sure because I can't see anything."

"Are you dreaming?"

"No, I'm not acting."

"Where are you now?"

"Back in bed."

Amanda then recalls waking up with her husband and discussing their dreams.

Oddly, despite his graphic conscious account of the lights from the bedroom window and the creatures, George's version under hypnosis gave absolutely no indication of any unusual activity.

He described getting out of bed after being woken by his daughter's screams. Looking out of the window he thought he saw a movement in the back garden, went to investigate, saw nothing and returned to bed.

George and Amanda Phillips, although disturbed by the events of that night, did not seek explanations immediately. They had no knowledge of, or particular interest in UFOs, and were content to carry on their lives as normal.

There were no after effects that they could attribute to the lights or the creatures, no recurring dreams or flashbacks.

However George did become ill two months after the incident with a rare condition of the blood.

"It's a condition where your blood cells come under attack from your own immune system," explained George. "I was in hospital for about three months, couldn't walk, kidneys were being affected or something.

"Anyway, they treated me with steroids and it cleared up. The doctors said it was a condition that affected one in 100,000 people or something like that.

"Whether it had something to do with that night I don't know."

It was sometime later that the couple were put in touch with a UFO research group. They had been intrigued by what sounded like a missing time incident, hence the hypnotic regression.

The Phillips are just another ordinary couple who experienced a very extraordinary night of events.

Although the investigators who studied the case could never prove it, they said that it definitely had the feel of an abduction.

Amanda's feeling of leaving the house and then the sense of fear and the inability to describe her surroundings begged the question, *where was she?*

Douglas Tams
June 5, 1974
Staffordshire

Douglas Tams was driving the last bus from Kidsgrove to Burslem Depot near Stoke-on-Trent on that warm summer's night. After a busy shift it was nice not to have any passengers to worry about, he thought as he drove through Goldenhill, where the rows of houses on the right were in total darkness, not unusual at a quarter to one in the morning.

There was very little traffic on the road at that time of night and Douglas was enjoying the starlit view of the valley that swept away to his left as the draught from his open driver's window made up for the heat of a hectic day. Suddenly the engine, and all the lights in the vehicle cut out.

As the bus coasted to a halt Douglas looked down at the dash board hoping a warning light might be flashing to indicate a fault, but it was in blackness. Just his luck to breakdown at the end of a shift, he thought. It would take the breakdown crew ages to get out here and God knows what time he'd get home. He couldn't very well catch a bus. Wearily, he raised himself from the driver's seat, ready to climb out of the cab for a proper inspection of the bus when he was suddenly forced to duck.

Wedged between the seat and the dashboard Douglas couldn't believe what he had just seen. A massive object seemed to be falling out of the sky and heading straight for his bus.

He counted the seconds until he was sure that the thing

must have missed, otherwise he would have felt the impact by now.

Slowly pulling himself up, he steeled himself for another look through the windscreen. The thing was still there.

Ah, but now he could see that it hadn't really been on a collision course, it was now passing directly overhead.

"It's huge," he said to himself as his eyes followed the 300 feet wide oval shape move slowly and with deliberation.

The giant mystery machine, for machine it obviously was, followed an east-west flight path. It was difficult to estimate its height, but it couldn't have been very far above him, Douglas thought.

The underside of the object was illuminated by a green haze, less distinct than the bright ring of lights that defined its ovoid shape.

It probably took the UFO only a matter of two or three minutes to pass from one horizon to the other, finally disappearing from sight behind a line of houses, but to its sole witness it seemed an eternity.

"That's when the engine started and the lights came on, just like remote control," said Douglas later.

He climbed into the driver seat, put it into gear and headed off on the ten minute journey to his depot, his mind going over the events of the last few minutes.

"When I got to the depot I was *one hour* late," Douglas told a British UFO Research Association team. "I did not say anything to my colleagues for fear of them taking the mickey and laughing at me."

Despite being puzzled by the incident, especially the missing hour, Douglas declined the chance of becoming involved in a thorough investigation including possible hypnosis. This down-to-earth, working class witness had no wish to *dabble with the unknown,* as he put it.

BUFORA investigators were disappointed by his reluctance to take the matter further. They felt there was a good chance that hypnosis would at least throw some light on his lost sixty minutes.

They hoped that in time, they could persuade Douglas to have a rethink and co-operate with a fresh investigation.

Sadly they didn't have the chance. Some years after, Douglas died, taking the mystery of that missing hour to the grave.

Abduction? This case had all the makings of such. A UFO sighting, engine and electrical malfunction and a full missing hour.

Douglas had no motive for fabricating the story. The missing hour had caused him problems at work. His bosses wanted to know why he was so late back at the depot. The problem with the engine and the lights were the only aspects he dared report to his superiors. In fact he didn't reveal his full account to BUFORA investigators until *fourteen years later.*

James Millen
September 6, 1990
Fleet, Dorset

Retired landscape gardener James Millen and his wife Pam were on a camping holiday at West Farm, near Fleet in Dorset, when they became contenders for the *UFO nearly files.*

James was 54 at the time and he and Pam had driven down from their home in Putney, London, for a few days at the popular camp site which overlooks picturesque Chesil Beach.

West Farm camp site was less busy than usual. The peak camping season had just passed and the weather over the last few days had been a bit blowy, recalled James, not ideal for living under canvass.

The couple had enjoyed a day's walking and retired to their large tent not long after darkness fell.

James takes up his story: "I tend, at my age, to wake up in the middle of the night for the loo and that night was no exception. I made my way to the toilet block, which is in the same field, noting that there were only a few tents about, probably because of the weather.

"As I walked back, I gazed up at the stars. It was a clear

The 'entity' photograph *(enlarged)* taken by Philip Spencer
on Ilkley Moor, West Yorkshire, December 1st, 1987

Elsie Oakensen

Pauline Decour

Former P.C Allen Godfrey

Linda Jones—on site where her
experience took place

Rosalynd Reynolds   Rohan Hinton

John Day

Mik Burley

Robert Taylor

James Millen

William Barret being
interviewed on site by
overseas film crew

Graham Allen

night and I could make out the constellations beautifully. Over to the field on my left I could see an orange-golden glow - like sodium lamps. I thought the farmer must be working in the field, rounding up his cows for milking or something.

"Then I thought, that's funny. I hadn't noticed any poles in the field, so what had the farmer hung his sodium lamps on. I turned and looked again and there were several of these golden, orange balls of light, rising and falling in the sky.

"It was like someone was juggling with them. I stopped and tried to work out what they were. By now I was very close to our tent so I called for Pamela and she came out and watched them with me.

"I asked Pam what she thought they were and she just said *don't ask me what they are, I don't know. Whatever they are they're doing something they shouldn't be doing.*

"I remember saying to her that we were probably the only people in the South of England, standing outside watching a display like this and at this time of night. I looked at my watch and it was five to three in the morning.

Pam then said she was going back into the tent to make a cup of tea. I said I would watch the lights for a little while longer. Then I remembered my camera in the boot of my car and I thought I'll go and get my Praktica and get a picture of these things."

At this point James' recall becomes hazy and disjointed.

"The next thing I remember is being back in the tent with Pam, telling her *they've gone now. If we don't get to bed we won't get any sleep at all tonight.*

"Then Pam asked if I wanted a cup of tea and I said yes and then we sat down and just looked at each other without saying anything. It was as if we were stuck in time somehow. This *spell* was broken when Pam asked me the question, *what's that light coming through the tent?*

"I looked out and I told her it was the dawn breaking, The sun was just coming up."

James added "Pam remarked on how early it was for daylight, so we checked the time to find it was 5.35 am.

Somehow they had *lost* more than two hours of their lives.

"I looked at my wife and she looked at me, we were astonished," remembers James. "Then I noticed cigarette ends, down by our feet.

"There were about eight of them and we were not in the habit of leaving cigarette ends on the floor. Pam said she had the distinct impression that she had been sitting there waiting for me, waiting for some time. She didn't know why, except that she just knew she had been sitting, waiting and smoking until I came into the tent."

Tired and puzzled by their strange night, the couple decided to return home to London the next day. After packing up the tent and loading the car they agreed to make a detour so they could stop at Stonehenge in Wiltshire where James wanted to take some pictures of the ancient stones.

At the popular tourist site James took out his camera to find the lens covered in what he describes as a strange lime/mortar mixture.

"It was horrible stuff and difficult to remove," he said. "I couldn't understand where it had come from or whether it had any connection with the previous night's occurrence. I just chalked it up as another bizarre event."

Although he has never been hypnotically regressed, James has experienced strange flash-backs about that night in Dorset.

"I have had mental pictures of being in a strange room with lights on the walls, glowing lights. There is the impression of being surrounded by people, some tall, some short. I don't know how significant these dreams are but they are very odd.

"I can't explain any of this. I am not normally subject to illusions or hallucinations. But whatever happened it is surely worth researching properly."

Where did James Millen disappear to while his wife sat smoking nervously in their tent for more than two hours? Were the flashbacks of a strange room and strange people and indication of abduction?

His wife Pam had witnessed the lights which started off their experience, so we know they were not imagined, but sadly the missing time may always remain a mystery. Investigators felt James would not be suitable for hypnosis, however they hope, that in time, he will find other pieces of the jigsaw falling into place, other memories surfacing that may give him a clue to his seaside encounter.

Maxine Watkins
November 28, 1988
Holbury
Hampshire

Maxine Watkins was just 20 years old when she had an encounter with something more akin to the Hammer House of Horror than a UFO.

The youngster had just enjoyed an evening at her local working men's club and was walking home alone through the crisp November night. The time was approximately 11.20 pm and Maxine was probably no more than a couple of hundred yards away from home, and safety, when strange things began to happen.

As she turned into the avenue that would take her into the final stretch to her home she noticed the branches of the trees lining the road were waving furiously, as if in a gale. But there was no wind, not even a gentle breeze. Feeling frightened Maxine quickened her pace, anxious to get away from the spooky trees.

Suddenly a light appeared, a pulsating light. Maxine stopped and focused on the object she could see between the waving branches of the trees. Its was round, or oval with lights, strong pulsating lights.

"Then it came right over me," said Maxine later. "This light shot out and then I was in this place . . ."

She was in a strange room facing a man, a man with a bald head and wearing a flowing black cape with a high collar, *a Dracula cape* was the way Maxine described it.

The Dracula figure was holding both his hands out-stretched, cupped in them was a ball or orb with a cross at-tached.

"I had this really intense fear," said Maxine. "The man with the ball was holding it up in front of him. There were another two beings there, one either side of him."

Maxine then had the impression of movement which she found difficult to explain. "I was moving, but not walking, like hovering, going along. I was taken to this table and they put me on it and clamped my legs so I couldn't move. The clamps were so tight they left marks which I could see the following day.

"I was being told something, it was like something in my head. I just shouted to them to let me go, let me go, but they wouldn't.

"They were trying to reassure me but this had little ef-fect." Maxine described the room she was in as oval, "like a conference room."

As she was lying on what she assumes was an examina-tion table, Maxine remembers her captors pulling down a complicated apparatus and placing it over her head.

"That was it, the next thing I knew I was down in the road and I had no idea how I got there."

Maxine found herself in a crumpled heap on the pave-ment about 100 yards down the road from the point where she had first seen the UFO.

"When I found myself on the ground, I looked up and the object just went *Shisssh*. It shot up. It just disappeared in the sky."

Maxine, now suffering from a severe headache and eye irritation, realised at this point that the whole sequence of events had been in total silence. The swishing of the object disappearing in the sky was the first noise she had been aware of since finding herself in the strange oval room.

Disturbed by her experience, Maxine wrote to the British UFO Research Association and an interview was arranged.

The circumstances of her experience, the lights and the removal to a strange place, have links with Abduction Phenomena, but the descriptions given by Maxine sound more like the set of a vampire B-movie.

The first being she saw was dressed like Dracula and he was holding a cross of sorts. Perhaps this was the only way she could describe a scene so removed from her normal experience.

Maxine did not undergo hypnosis, so her encounter joins those in the *Nearly Files*.

CHAPTER 8
Anatomy Of An Abduction

Are all abductions the same or do they differ widely? The reason this question is often posed is obvious. If different people from different parts of the world report abductions which follow the same pattern this surely adds credibility to the theory that we are indeed the guinea pigs in an alien laboratory.

If the methods of capture, the details of examination and the mode of return are common then there is a greater chance of their being some truth in the experiences. If a selection of people from across the world make-up such stories, how come they are so similar? You would expect different folk from different backgrounds to imagine different tales.

Thomas E. Bullard, who holds a doctorate in folklore from Indiana University, researched and wrote a comparative study of Alien Abductions on behalf of the Fund for UFO Research in America, which was looking at the question of the link between the phenomenon and folklore.

Dr Bullard's scientific examination of about 300 abduction cases, most of them American, did not come up with any hard and fast conclusions on the abduction-folklore link. But it did offer a remarkable insight into the structure of Abduction Phenomena, breaking down a mass of abduction reports into their common denominators. Dr Bullard showed there was a sequential pattern of events in all abduction cases and many of the sequences he described in his paper can be identified in the British cases we highlight in this book.

From capture to return home, Dr Bullard identified each distinct stage of the abduction experience and quantified their frequency in the mass of reports he studied. But this was not merely a statistical exercise, it was a serious attempt to find a satisfactory explanation for why so many people were experiencing events which were so strange, yet so similar.

"The most remarkable thing about UFO abductions is that they happen at all," states the doctor. "The second most remarkable thing is that they happen so often. In quality and quantity, abductions best fulfil the meaning of the phrase, an embarrassment of riches." A striking but seldom noticed characteristic of abduction reports is the sequence of events that unfold."

Dr Bullard identified a maximum of eight stages through which abductees may pass. These include:

• Capture,
• Conference (where the abductee converses with his/her captors),
• Examination,
• Tour of the ship,
• Outworldly journey,
• Meeting with a divine or sacred being,
• Return and aftermath.

"Not every case contains every episode," explained the good doctor. "And some episodes are quite rare, but those that do appear follow this prescribed sequence. Out of 193 cases with two or more episodes, 163 show the correct order.

"Capture consists of four distinctive parts, intrusion, where a UFO appears and stalks the witness; zone of strangeness, where odd things seem to happen to the physical world; time lapse, when the witness suffers some form of mental impairment; and procurement, when the beings take the witness into custody.

"When two or more of these parts occur, they follow this order in 77 per cent of cases.

"Procurement has the complexity of a sub-episode unto itself, with a sequence of eight recurrent events: a beam of light may strike the witness, a force may draw him, beings appear and a conversation follows.

"The beings pacify him or otherwise control the witness, they escort him to the ship and float him on board. He enters with a momentary loss of memory or doorway amnesia.

"Again 77 per cent of the cases with two or more of these events arrange them in the prescribed sequence."

Dr Bullard also put the examination episode which many abductees report under his microscope.

"The examination episode breaks down into eight distinct activities: the beings prepare the witness by undressing, cleaning and positioning him on a table. Then the actual examination moves from the general to more specific concerns as the beings first subject the witness to a manual exploration, apparently to gauge external characteristics," says Dr Bullard.

"A scanning device, like an eye or light, next passes over the witness, followed by instrumental investigations aimed perhaps at internal structures and physiological functions.

"The beings then take specimens of skin, hair or body fluids and an examination of the reproductive areas comes next. At close examination, the beings show interest in the neurological system."

According to Dr Bullard, a total of 69 per cent of cases follow this pattern.

The way abductees report their return to the normal world also came under scrutiny in Dr Bullard's probe.

"The return episode begins with a farewell and thereafter reverses the capture," he points out. "The witness exits and experiences doorway amnesia once again as the beings float him outside.

"After watching the departure of the craft, the witness re-enters the normal world as he resumes his previous activities and memories of the abduction fade away. The four parts of this episode stay true to form in two thirds of the cases."

Dr Bullard adds: "What matters about the order of these events is that the pattern is not inevitable.

A conference could precede the examination or specimen taking, or the scan and the change would make no difference to the story. It would still make sense one way or the other.

"The fact that witness after witness sticks to one arbitrary order suggests that the experience itself is structured that way.

"The commonest sequence to the examination is a conference, a more or less formal period of conversation between the witness and his captors. Four topics characterise the conference: the beings may interrogate the witness about topics of interest to them; explanation of where the beings come from and why they are here are common; they make a request of the witness, often to forget the experience, but sometimes to learn or improve himself, or bring them information at a future date; they warn that certain aspects of human behaviour is dangerous and prophecies of coming events are also common.

"The prophecies usually predict coming disasters and even apocalyptic changes on Earth, events the aliens or an enlightened witness may mitigate. A few cases include a tour of the ship, apparently as a courtesy to the witness. This tour may include a glimpse of the engine room, where several witnesses report crystalline globes attached to a rotor device of sorts."

Dr Bullard's research also revealed a number of witnesses experience an other-worldly journey to, what some refer to, as another planet. Witnesses often reported seeing bustling cities and ample signs of alien civilisation.

Most rare is theophany, where the witness encounters a divine being or is introduced to something the beings regard as sacred in some way. After effects from abduction include nightmares, eye irritation, sunburned skin and cuts or puncture wounds.

Long term changes may involve new interests, a desire for learning, the development of extra-sensory powers. A change of personality, sometimes for the better and further encounters with aliens is not uncommon.

Paranormal experiences, visits by *Men in Black*, apparitional and poltergeist-like phenomena may follow.

Interestingly Dr Bullard points out: "Not all consistencies in abduction stories are limited to the form and content of the episodes.

"The craft has a discoidal shape in 136 out of 162 cases. In some cases the disc is thick, in others thin, sometimes a dome or projections differentiate the craft, and sizes vary so much that witnesses compare the ship to anything from a small car to a football field.

"The craft are clearly not carbon copies, but a few cigar or other shapes challenge the general discoidal pattern.

"Once inside, the witness usually finds himself within a circular, domed room without sharp corners. Lighting is uniform and diffused without a specific source being visible, the atmosphere is usually cold and clammy and the air difficult to breathe because of its heaviness, or less frequently, its noxiousness.

"The beings may be human, humanoid or monstrous," he says.

"Humanoids make up two thirds of the 203 cases where witnesses describe the beings, while humans appear in 52 cases. The standard humanoid is of short to average height, has a large rounded head and enormous, compelling eyes. The nose and ears are small and even vestigial, while the mouth is no more than a hole or a slit. No hair grows on the grey, ashen skin, and the beings dress in tight overall uniforms."

Some clues to the personality and the concerns of the beings emerge in abduction reports. Dr Bullard's report finds:

"Most crews have a leader who converses with the witnesses, using telepathy to address the humans but a rapid, mumbling verbal speech to communicate with others of his own kind.

"The beings are polite in speech and behaviour, but their courtesy often proves false, a mere front to manipulate the witness and win his co-operation. In fact the beings seem clinical and aloof, indifferent to and perhaps uncomprehending of human pain and fear."

Dr Bullard's dissection of every detail from a mountain of abduction reports also found interest in reproduction and fertility to be a common denominator for many.

"The beings interest in reproduction comes to the fore during the examination, but other hints reinforce the impression that matters of reproduction and fertility command a central place in their concern," he says.

"In their conversations the beings may state outright that they have trouble reproducing, desire to reinvigorate their stock by combining with humans, or come from a dying, infertile planet. Observations of the otherworld confirm this admission.

"A preference for youthful captives is striking in comparison of the ages of abductees, while the beings rejected one witness for being too old and another because of a vasectomy.

"These choices make sense if interest in fertility is what motivates them. The samples, tampering with the witness's genitalia, and the scale of the abduction programme suggest beings in serious biological trouble, exploiting human captives in an effort to survive.

"A number of strange phenomena associate with abductions, and these events can gather under the heading of *effects*.

"Some effects apply to the physical world and others to the mind. Physical effects include a vacuum like stillness surrounding the abduction site and influences on motor vehicles, some the traditional electromagnetic effects familiar in UFO reports, others a seemingly external control over the operation of the vehicle.

"The best known mental effect is time-lapse, a gap in the witness memory during the period of abduction. The phenomenon appears in 164 cases, while other forms of mental impairment such as unconsciousness or lethargy boost the total even higher.

"The witness may behave in uncharacteristic ways while under the being's influence, and they seem to have a number of mind control techniques by which they pacify the witness, relieve pain and induce compliance with their wishes.

"Other effects lie in the shadowland between the physical and mental. The witness floats to the ship, but does he defy gravity or only feel as if he floats? Evidence points both ways. Cases of passing ghost-like through a solid walls and an isolation effect, whereby the abduction takes place in an inhabited area in plain view, yet no one else intrudes, raise similar questions."

Dr Bullard says the mountain of data he piled up for analysis provided only a molehill of conclusions.

"The ultimate nature of abduction eludes the study because its real subject is not the experience itself but the abduction report," he says.

The conclusion was that three explanations could account for the similarities among abduction reports:

1. The reports may be alike because different people share the same kind of objective experience.
2. The reports may be alike because different people share the same kind of subjective experience. This assumed some kind of universal psychological phenomenon capable of generating the mental images and feelings of abduction.
3. The reports may be alike because different people share the same story tradition.

Narrators then merely repeat the form and contents of stories heard from other narrators, or more plausibly, a well publicised report influences the perceptions and descriptions of subsequent witnesses so that they distort their own experience to conform to their expectations.

Dr Bullard believes a case can be argued for each explanation but believes that his research has proved beyond a shadow of a doubt that "abduction reports as a body show far more similarities than accident, random hoaxes or purely fantasies can explain."

And he adds: "The consistencies in form and content down to numerous minute details demonstrates that abductions make up a coherent phenomenon, whatever its ultimate nature. Any sceptic who dismisses this unity relies on hope rather than evidence to support his case."

Dr Bullard's report was welcomed by abduction investigators and Ufologists who hope for more serious study and further scientific research.

However, the branch of Ufology that argues that abduction experiences are simply a part of modern folklore will point to this work as supporting their contention.

Is our modern culture so steeped in UFOs, aliens and abductions that it becomes a handy explanation to pull out of the bag when rational explanations fail us?

True we are surrounded by a host of books, films and TV on UFOs and aliens. Yes, even a top US soap opera used an alien abduction plot as a bizarre, yet entertaining audience puller.

But when confronted by the strange and odd events are we really going to opt for alien abduction theory unless it fits the bill?

As we have seen from our cases so far, most are more specific than lights in the sky and missing time.

Folklore surely can't explain away Philip Spencer's experience. He saw a green creature, and photographed it. He saw a craft and much more if we accept what he related under hypnosis.

What about Robert Taylor? He saw a craft and two further objects. He detected an acrid smell, he heard the noise of the spiked spheres approaching him.

He *felt* those objects pulling at his clothing and then he and the police found the marks that indicated something of several tons in weight had been sitting on the spot where he had seen the strange craft.

Robert Taylor had not used folklore to reconcile the irreconcilable. If he was having problems with his *perception* what was the thing that he saw, heard, smelled and felt?

Dr Bullard's extremely thorough comparison of all those cases could not hope to come up with any real answers, but it was interesting to note how many of the abduction sequences found in American cases are also found here in our British casebook.

His work has, at the very least, presented an at-a-glance guide to the anatomy of an abduction.

CHAPTER 9
The Vintage Visits

Now well into the 21st Century, with the 50th birthday of the term *Flying Saucer* behind us, it is safe to say that the UFO, and Ufology, has come of age.

As we said in the last chapter, with our cinema and TV screens full of aliens, space craft and sci-fi shows galore, flying saucers are as much a part of our culture as fish and chips.

Ask any youngster what an alien is and he'll be spoilt for choice. Darth Vader, Mr Spock of the Starship Enterprise or E.T, the cutest extraterrestrial ever to come out of Hollywood, all have an army of fans.

So as a piece of modern day folklore Alien Abduction is not as outrageous as it at first seems. The terminology, the descriptions of the craft and the aliens are available in abundance if we wish to construct our own piece of abduction fantasy.

Although the Abduction Phenomenon, as we pointed out earlier in this book, goes back a long time, possibly thousands of years, those tales used a completely different terminology, a different vocabulary. Fiery chariots, not flying saucers were ridden by angels or Gods, not, aliens.

However the following reports come from a generation who were not at all familiar with the UFOs and flying saucers that we now take in our stride.

In those far off days before the information technology revolution the great British public got their daily diet of news from the papers, the Home Service and cinema newsreels. The term Flying Saucer had only just been born, and would take a long time getting to these shores. The first alleged alien abduction had not yet been recorded. And the language of Ufology was unknown.

Yes, they may have had those early science fiction B movies. H.G.Wells' *War of the Worlds* was turned into a celluloid epic between the wars and science fiction, as a literary genre was beginning to make its mark in the States.

Dan Dare and Flash Gordon were beginning to appeal to the kids of the 40s and 50s.

But ordinary folk in those lean years after the Second

World War would not have a clue about Abduction Phenomenon. UFOs and flying saucers would have seemed absolutely ludicrous . . . as ludicrous as spaceflight and man landing on the moon.

So how do we explain the very descriptive cases which we have on record from way back then? We can't accuse them of being contaminated, can we? Considering that all the reports that follow came from senior citizens whose encounters took place either during or shortly after the last war gives them added credibility.

Like the rest of the reports in this volume, they had nothing to gain by recounting these events, they sought no reward. All three of the witnesses whose stories we recount, had no knowledge of the subject at the time of their experiences, but in the years that followed developed a keen interest in UFOs and abductions for obvious reasons.

Because of the many years that have elapsed since their experiences, and the age of the witnesses, the detail is sometimes lacking. Memories may fade with the passing of time, but investigators still maintain that the ring of truth can be clearly heard across the decades.

Commander Horatio Penrose, Royal Navy Rtd.
May 13, 1954
Burnaston,
Derbyshire

Commander Horatio Penrose, RN retired, glanced around his black Vauxhall Wyvern saloon, as he drove towards his Birmingham home and nodded with satisfaction. All shipshape and Bristol fashion, he thought, glad he had not agreed to sell the vehicle after all.

He had taken tea with a couple near Buxton who had expressed great interest in purchasing his one year old motor car and after chatting until 10.30 pm he told them he felt he wanted to keep the car after all and prepared for the drive home.

They were disappointed, but graciously accepted his decision not to see his handsome vehicle pass to someone else. The Commander said his farewells and stepped into the dark night.

He took the main Derby-Burton road heading in the direction of Birmingham. It was an uneventful drive initially with little traffic moving at that time of night. Then as he approached the Hilton Gravel Works near Burmanston he suddenly spotted a bright light ahead of him.

"It appeared to be coming towards me," wrote the Commander, who penned a full account of his experience shortly after.

At first he assumed the approaching light was an oncoming car travelling at high speed and he slowed down his vehicle in anticipation of a near miss.

As he braked, the light appeared to come to a sudden halt above him, causing his car to stop so abruptly that he was thrown forward in the driving seat, hitting his head on the windscreen.

"I thought I had been in a crash," said the Commander who then remembered a sensation of movement. The car felt as if it was rising, being lifted through the air by something magnetic. He could see the metal roof of the vehicle being distorted by the pull of whatever it was.

Craning his neck, he peered through the car window to see what was above the roof. He couldn't see any lifting gear, despite straining his eyes. But he thought he could see a very bright light positioned directly above the car.

At that point the Commander lost consciousness. He remembers waking in a hospital bed in Derbyshire Royal Infirmary where nursing staff told him he had received stitches to a cut on his forehead.

As he lay back, counting his lucky stars to have survived, he found he could clearly remember the chain of strange events that occurred immediately after the *crash*, so strange he dared not tell anyone of those memories, yet.

After his car had come to an abrupt halt and after it had somehow been lifted into the air it was then lowered onto the side of the road. A man, in a one piece suit, leaned in through the window and lifted the officer from his seat, apparently without effort, pulled him out into the air and up into a large circular object that was hovering directly overhead.

"The entrance was on the underside of this large round vehicle which was giving out a very bright light," he recalled at the time.

That light enabled him to look down upon the site of the *crash*. The car was now at the side of the road, but apart from that there was no sign that anything untoward had happened there.

Commander Penrose now found himself in a brightly lit room and was laid on a table. It was some kind of examination table, presumably used for giving medical attention. He looked around and saw the walls of the room were covered in what he took to be control mechanisms. The controls were being operated by a group of men and women, about five of them in all.

They did not appear unusual, apart from being of slightly shorter height than average, more like the Japanese, thought the Commander. They also had slightly almond shaped eyes and their hair was dark and worn short and straight. They all wore blue, one piece suits.

One of the female operators, attractive and shapely, seemed to *remember* the officer. She approached him and looked at his injuries. The Commander felt this woman, who was probably in her early 20s, looked sympathetic as she examined the injury on his forehead and his other minor cuts and bruises.

As she leaned over him he noticed her flawless white skin but before he could comment he realised she was speaking to him about his injuries. It was some form of telepathic communication. He seemed to know what *she* wanted to know and she seemed to know his answer before he spoke it.

The female gave him an injection and he saw that the syringe she used contained a green fluid of some sort.

"I asked questions about the mechanics of their vehicle," recalled the Commander later. "I was told it involved magnetic fields."

As he tried to make sense of the information communicated to him the female began to ask questions. What was his position, she asked?

The Commander replied cautiously. Could his benefactors be from some foreign power? She seemed terribly interested in his work with the Royal Navy, thought the seasoned serviceman only too aware that the last war had ended less than a decade ago.

Further questions followed about his naval experiences and his work with radar, then a relatively new technology.

He tried to steer the conversation away from himself and asked further questions about the craft and its engineering. But the female, similarly, avoided direct answers.

For some reason the female then volunteered a curious statement that left the Commander puzzled.

The words she put into his mind were clear: "We are not born in the same manner as you."

Around that point Commander Penrose remembered feeling drowsy. "That injection must have been a sedative," he thought before drifting off into unconsciousness.

When he came round he was back in his car and feeling groggy. The car had been moved. It was now perched on the gravel works railings.

It was just before midnight when a passing RAC patrolman spotted the wreckage and found the concussed Commandor sitting in the driver seat. He called the police who interviewed the officer about the incident. But Penrose declined to mention either the strange craft or its occupants.

Puzzled by the relentless questioning of the officers, he made inquiries and learned that they had been suspicious about the abnormally large amount of blood they found in the wreckage. It seemed far more than the amount one would expect to lose as the result of the relatively minor injuries sustained by the Commander. Some officers suspected he had not been alone.

After his discharge from hospital the officer returned to the scene of the accident in the hope that he might trace witnesses.

His only success was a railway signalman who said he had seen a *car* with an extremely bright light above it go past his signal box.

Commander Penrose remained silent about his encounter for a staggering 22 years. Then in 1976 he made contact with a Birmingham UFO research group and told his full story for the first time.

The Commander said he had avoided publicity because he feared the attendant ridicule. By 1976, he said, the climate regarding UFO research had improved sufficiently for him to *come out*.

Commander Penrose, was an *old salt* with an exemplary military record. Could the crash, or whatever happened that night, have put his mind off course? Investigators doubt it.

Furthermore his description of the craft, and its occupants are not too different from the many other reports that have followed since.

Horatio Penrose, officer and gentleman, grew up long before UFOs and flying saucers entered our language. Back in 1954, spaceflight was Sci-fi. UFOs and aliens were pure comic-strip fantasy.

Why would a Royal Navy commander concoct such a story?

Albert Lancashire
September 1942
Northumberland

Albert Lancashire shivered in the perishing cold. Winter must have come early thought the 27 year old sentry as he shoved his hands deeper into the pockets of his army issue overcoat. Still, guarding this secret radar base against the Luftwaffe was an important job, he mused gazing out over the North Sea. It wasn't as tough as what those poor Russians had to put up with.

"It's hard to believe it's only September," Albert said to himself, stamping his feet to get the circulation going. "Must be the flaming' wind coming off the sea."

He had no idea what time it was, but it was very dark. It was important to remember the standing order, he reminded himself, repeating the Captain's instructions out loud: "Do not fire at enemy aircraft as you will only give away the position of the base."

Firing at night would be worse, he thought. Jerry pilots would soon spot them and that would be the end of the installation.

Suddenly Albert spotted a light on the horizon, but within seconds a black cloud moved over and obscured it. Then another light moved into his field of view. A yellow light, this time, shining from the rim of a strange round object.

Now it was closer, a beam of yellow light, about a foot in diameter swung round straight into his face.

His jaw dropping, Albert instinctively threw his hands into the air.

"I don't remember putting my rifle down, but I must have because it was loaded and had a bayonet attached," recalled Albert. "I didn't use the rifle because we weren't allowed to. I just put my hands up."

A floating sensation overcame the young serviceman, then blackness.

Albert came to, shocked and dazed, lying only yards from the spot where he had been standing guard just a few minutes earlier.

"I lay there for five or ten minutes," said Albert. "I didn't know what had happened." Back then Albert didn't call the object he had seen a flying saucer. The term would not come into being for another five years. But he somehow knew that the object he had seen was unnatural, not of this world.

His conviction that something unusual occurred was reinforced by a series of dreams that disturbed his sleep in the following years. Often vague, he remembers looking down at the sea through a large window, a man in white telling him he had to carry him into the ship.

Then in another dream he is again on the ship and this time meets a woman in a calf length skirt. She seems to have red hair and she gives him some goggles.

It was not until the late 60s that Albert's story came to light. He had been reading about a spate of UFO sightings and wrote to BUFORA about his war time experience. Sadly the time gap between the event and his reporting of it made investigation difficult.

Albert was in his 70s and living in Denton, Manchester, when he last recalled that brief encounter. Having retired from British Rail and with more time on his hands he devoured every piece of UFO literature he could get hold of. He also developed a great interest in religious matters and all things psychic. Whether he really was Britain's first real abductee, we will never know, but it is significant that Albert felt that alien abduction was the only phenomenon that fits the bill . . . even after so many years.

June Rice
August 1956
Filey
Lancashire

Jovial granny June Rice dropped her paper in shock as she listened to the radio programme. It was a discussion about UFOs and alien abductions. They were talking about people who had claimed to have been abducted by strange beings who had taken them off.

June thought she was the only woman in the world to have been inside a spaceship. The only woman to have met visitors from other worlds.

She scurried off into the kitchen of her neat-as-a-pin home in Wallasey, Merseyside, and busied herself by making a cup of tea. Her head was spinning. Could there really be other people who had seen what she had seen? She had always been too afraid to talk openly about what happened to her all those years ago, afraid of the ridicule.

But if other people had experienced what she had seen then maybe she could find out more about those strange visitors. Maybe there was an organisation which could help.

Without revealing her reasons, June made inquiries about UFO organisations and soon got hold of the number for the Brirtish UFO Research Association. She picked up her phone and dialled the number.

The voice at the other end seemed friendly so she just blurted it out:

"I was abducted by aliens in 1956 . . ."

When two researchers, including Philip Mantle, visited June a few days later, they were struck by her friendly, bubbly nature. A doting mum and grandmother, her living room was full of family snaps and she was eager to point out the youngsters she was so proud of.

At first she seemed a little embarrassed about what she had experienced all those years ago when she was a young mum with an 18 month old son, but after some encouragement she agreed to tell her story.

It was during the warm summer of 1956 and June was staying at her mum's house in Filey in Lancashire.

"It must have been that August," she remembered. "A friend and I went out to the pictures one night and when we came out we decided to take the easy way home, which was across the fields.

"We walked together for some distance until we got near to where she lived. Her house was on one side of the fields and my mum's was on the other. We parted company and I set off for home on my own.

"It was quiet, unusually quiet that night. You could normally see lots of bats in those fields, but not that night.

"I was walking along, and it was quite dark by now, and these two men seemed to appear from nowhere. One minute there was nothing and the next these two men were there. They seemed to come towards me, stop and then stand there.

"They didn't say anything and I didn't. I wasn't frightened. I wasn't scared at all.

"They were quite tall and had whitish or silver suits on, like an all-in-one suit. It was a long time ago but I remember thinking they were very pale, very. They had lovely eyes, beautiful eyes and white hair.

"I don't know if they had any beards or anything, but I'll always remember the white hair and the beautiful eyes.

"Then they just turned and I knew they wanted me to go with them, so I just followed them and then I don't remember anything."

June can't explain the gap in her memory, but it is a classic case of entry amnesia, a condition reported by many abductees who rarely remember actually entering the UFO they see.

June found herself in a round room, again this ties is with many later accounts where witnesses often report alien rooms as rounded, seamless and without corners.

Although June never saw a UFO throughout her experience, she is convinced she was inside a craft belonging to the strangers she met.

"The room was completely circular with seats all around and there were people sitting on the seats. They sat me down on one and I remember that by that time I was getting a bit agitated. I had the baby at home, you see, and I said, *No I'm not staying, I want to go home.*

"They never spoke at all and I was saying, *No, no, no.* Then I realised I wasn't using my mouth to speak. It seemed as if we were communicating through our brains, you know, and I was upset about this.

"One of the people then just came up to me and put his hand on my head and I seemed to go backwards, the seat seemed to come upwards. All I remember from that part of things was a pain in my side.

"I cried out with the pain when this, this whatever it was did something to me. I don't know if something was piercing my skin or what but I was suddenly in my bed back at home.

"I just grabbed hold of my baby and hugged him and I thought *where have I been, where have I been?*

"I couldn't remember coming home or coming into the house and I had no idea what time it was."

The next morning June's mother pointed out that she had been out late the previous night.

June didn't say anything. She couldn't. She didn't have a clue of the time when she came in and climbed into bed. But she clearly remembered leaving the cinema at a reasonable time.

June put the incident at the back of her mind and got on with her life, what seemed to be her very normal life.

But when carefully questioned by BUFORA investigators it appeared that June may have had several sightings after that first incident.

Her recollections were often vague and therefore difficult to check, but it appeared she had experienced further missing time episodes.

June had not recorded dates or times in connection with the follow up episodes and although the investigators were convinced of her genuine sincerity there was insufficient data on them for any meaningful investigation.

Going back to that first experience the Ufologists asked June if the events of that night felt physically real.

"Oh yes, yes, it was real," she replied.

What did she think happened to her?

"I don't know. I think they examined me but I don't know what they did. I know when he put his hand on my head I felt very calm."

Taking her back to the room inside the craft, the investigators asked if June could describe any of the other people she said she had seen sitting in the seats around the room.

"I remember seeing a nurse sitting there and I remember an airman but there were four or five people in all," she said. "They were human beings, yes. They were just sitting there in a daze. They didn't speak to me at all.

"The ones in the nurses uniform and the RAF uniform stood out."

How had that event in the summer of 1956 affected her life?

"I believe in UFOs," said June. "I believe there's somewhere they're coming from, where I don't know. I never even thought about UFOs in those days. I don't think there were any then, were there?"

In the days after her encounter June became ill. Lethargy and nausea seemed to make her life a misery so she decided to see a doctor.

"I discovered I was pregnant," she said. "The whole pregnancy was a nightmare too. I felt terrible throughout and after giving birth I lost a lot of weight and continued to feel ill for some time.

"I used to think why me? I didn't know anyone else had been aboard a UFO."

It was nine months after her meeting with the strangers in the field that June gave birth to her daughter. She often jokes: "I don't know whether I was pregnant then or whether they impregnated me.

"My daughter says she always knew she didn't belong to this earth."

For some women that bizarre scenario is not a joke, as you will read later . . .

Gerry Armstrong
July 1953, Home Counties

Twelve years old Gerry Armstrong looked over his shoulder to make sure the coast was clear, then dug into his trouser pocket for the new pack of five Woodbines. Sitting in the shadow of a tree which gave him some welcome shade from the fierce afternoon sun, he fished out his matches, drew out a cigarette and lit-up, his first of the day.

"Who wants to play hide and seek with old Rice anyway?" he said to himself smiling . He thought it was quite smart of him to sneak away the way he did, right under his teacher's nose.

Gerry was one of a party of London school kids on a summer camp just outside the capital. His teacher, Mr Rice, had made sure he and his chums were kept fully occupied but the game of hide and seek was just too much for the independent minded Gerry. When his teacher had been looking the other way he simply sidled off in the direction of a wooded area.

Now he was far enough away he couldn't hear the shouts of his school pals so he stretched out on the grass, eyes fixed on the clear blue sky and enjoyed his smoke.

The heat of the day had taken its toll and Gerry was beginning to feel drowsy. He tried to stop himself nodding off, then suddenly he was in darkness.

"Get up Armstrong, where do you think you've been boy,"

Gerry opened his eyes with a start. A furious, red faced Mr Rice was bellowing in his face.

Why was he so angry, he'd only been away a few minutes?

Then he followed his teacher's gaze. He was staring at the half smoked cigarette which was still stuck between two fingers in his right hand.

"Get yourself up lad," screamed the teacher. "I want to know what you've been up to. We've been searching for you all afternoon and I want some answers."

Gerry was astonished to learn it was now after 8 pm. Mr Rice and parties of his school pals had been scouring the countryside for him for hours.

They had even searched the spot where he was now, but there had been no sign of him a little while ago.

Gerry tried to get up but his legs gave way under him. Helped by some of his classmates he managed to hobble back to camp where the he was checked over by a doctor.

The back of his neck was red and sore, his pupils were dilated and he was exhausted. Diagnosis: mild sunstroke. The youngster was packed off to bed.

Gerry Armstrong completely forgot about the fuss surrounding his mystery disappearance during that school camp until ten years later when he and his wife sighted a UFO near London.

The event triggered his memory of the seven hours that went missing from his life on that day, but he still couldn't recall where he was or what he had been doing for that period. Gerry's UFO encounters continued and became more frequent after he emigrated to the Lake Simcoe area of Ontario, Canada. And it was a hypnotherapist from Toronto who enabled him to recover the lost memories from that summer's day in 1953.

The fully qualified psychiatrist decided to put Gerry into regressive hypnosis in a series of sessions through 1978. The following account is a compilation of the memories that came back to him.

As he sat under the tree, enjoying his cigarette, Gerry's attention was caught by a bright light in the sky that seemed to descend to a point beyond a nearby clump of trees.

Within minutes the lad thought he could detect some movement through the foliage, and glancing in the direction where the bright light had appeared to land, he could make out two figures walking in his direction.

For some reason he could not explain, Gerry was frightened. The fear grew into terror when he discovered that he could not move. Time and again he tried to move his legs, to put out his arm, but his limbs just would not respond to the messages his brain was sending out to them.

Gerry began to cry. He didn't understand what was going on but he was very frightened. The figures were now very close. As they closed on him the youngster was aware of voices in his head. Voices that were telling him not to be afraid, that no harm would come to him. Now the strangers were with him, one positioned on either side of him. They picked him up and began carrying him away. "It was like floating through the air" thought the child, trying to laugh out loud to show he wasn't scared.

As he floated through the trees he could see a bright light in a clearing ahead of him, so bright it hurt his eyes. The object took on a vaguely rounded shape as he neared it although the intensity of the light made it difficult to work out what it was.

To rest his eyes from the assault of light Gerry turned to his captors. They were small, one was smaller than the boy who was probably about four and a half feet, and they had white-grey skins, small mouths and prominent eyes.

At last they reached the object. Gerry, who had now regained the use of his limbs, was instructed to climb the ladder which seemed to lead up to an entrance. As he began to do so felt a momentary severe pressure on the back of his neck, caused, he assumed, by something the strangers did.

Once inside the strange object he found himself alone and in a brightly lit room with no apparent source for the light. As he explored the chamber he felt a strange sensation and accompanying noise and seemed to know that the object, or craft, was now moving. After a while the beings returned and led Gerry along a semi circular corridor to another room where he met a being dressed in red. The youngster thought this person seemed older than the other two, and he was amused by the way the being addressed him as *My son*.

Gerry was instructed to look at a screen on the wall. He saw what he at first described as a *little ball*. But on closer examination he could see it was a planet.

"This is your home," said a voice in his head. The sudden realisation that he was looking back at earth was too much for young Gerry. Once again he was gripped by fear at the thought of being so far from home.

The being in red, seemingly realising the boy's distress, reached over and touched Gerry's forehead. Immediately the fear was replaced by calmness.

At that point he realised the noise that had started soon after entering the object had stopped. Had the craft landed somewhere?

The two strangers who had brought him on board, and the being in red indicated that Gerry should accompany them as they began to walk down a ramp.

An automatic door opened at the end of the ramp at which point the boy found himself looking out at the inside of a giant dome.

"It's full of children," said Gerry as he saw many youngsters walking this way and that before him. The voice in his head told him to be calm and to follow the being in red.

At which point the being put something into Gerry's hand. "It's like a ball," he said. But it was much more than a ball. On instruction from his captors Gerry looked at the spherical gadget and saw his life flash before him.

"Understand, be taught . . ." said the voices in his head. The lad now seemed to be alone, so set off to explore his new surroundings. He studied the building itself and noticed the dome was mauve, and transparent. Through it he could see strange craft travelling through the dark sky, craft that he thought might not be unlike the object he had travelled here in.

A woman approached him, breaking his reverie, and took hold of the silver cross that hung round his neck on a chain. He had taken it from his mother's jewellery box before leaving home for summer camp.

The woman passed the cross to the being in red and both studied it. Their words formed in Gerry's brain: "It is not right to worship."

They indicated he should study his screen, the ball like device, once more. The being in red touched the boy's head and he slept.

Gerry awoke to find himself being carried through the woodland area where he had first seen the strangers.

He was frightened again, but not of the strangers, of the reaction he would get from Mr Rice.

The beings set him down in the spot where they had found him. Gerry was surprised to see his cigarette was still there, burning although the sky was now getting dark.

The strangers said farewell leaving Gerry alone, once again.

Still tired, Gerry drifted off to sleep again . . . until,

"Get up Armstrong," roared Mr Rice.

CHAPTER 10
Is It All In The Mind?

Explanations for Abduction Phenomena are legion but the vast majority of the so-called rational theories fall under the umbrella of *psychological explanations*. And the numbers of papers written on the subject by psychologists from around the world with a whole range of theories must run into hundreds.

One research team actually said recently that abductees fell into a class of the population they labelled FPP, *fantasy-prone personalities*. This group of people, the researchers estimated, could account for up to four percent of the population, were categorized as excellent hypnotic subjects, prone to fantasising in both childhood and adulthood, regarded themselves as psychic or telepathic, experienced out of body experiences, had vivid dreams and often felt the ability to heal.

Yet these otherwise socially aware, normal, healthy individuals were also more likely to experience alien abduction. Now were this group of psychologists saying that alien abduction does not exist because the people who report these events were prone to fantasy anyway? Or were they saying alien abduction does exist, but it is more likely to happen to this group of normal, healthy, socially aware people who have a tendency to fantasise?

Well, like most psychological explanations for Abduction Phenomenon, you can read into it what you will.

Abductions are fair game for psychologists. They don't have to commit themselves one way or the other. The phenomenon is a fascinating one. Normal, rational, healthy individuals reporting the most abnormal, irrational events.

If a university will fund the research, the psychologist can spend many happy hours pondering whether the witness encountered a UFO complete with aliens, or merely perceived an encounter with a UFO and aliens. Then he will write his paper listing the various psychological options available and move onto the next project.

He does not have to put his professional neck on the line. He's not going to say human beings *are* being abducted by aliens in UFOs but then he doesn't have to commit himself and say people are *not* being *space-napped* by little green men.

Sadly that does not help poor Mr or Mrs X who may have had their worlds turned inside out by what to them is a real abduction. They may have seen a UFO, had an encounter with an alien, been taken into a strange craft.

If they are suffering from some type of psychological disorder then there are a lot of people like them out there.

We have already said that the numbers of alleged abductees that we know of are significant. The numbers may in reality be far greater. And new abduction reports are coming into UFO research organisations almost every day.

However the psychological link is tempting. Many abductees claim they have further encounters with UFOs or aliens after their initial abduction. A large proportion also claim to have had psychic experiences in the past and others, like Elsie Oakensen, say that they have developed powers, like healing, after their experience.

The fact that many abductees claim multiple abductions over a succession of years implies they are prone to the experience. And if they are prone to such events surely we should be studying them and not their experiences.

"Nonsense," says Budd Hopkins, New York artist and renowned UFO investigator, whose theory on alien genetic experimentation partially relies on the selection of various human individuals for regular genetic testing. He believes the fact that a number of witnesses report several abductions supports his theory.

The many similarities between abduction victims led British investigator Ken Phillips to launch the *Anamnesis Project*. The London maths teacher and researcher with the British UFO Research Association could not help but notice those similarities during his years interviewing possible abductees.

He had been struck by the number of individuals who had experienced psychic events or displayed extra sensory projection-type abilities. He had been impressed by the work of Dr Alex Keul, the psychologist and Austrian representative of the international research group the Mutual UFO Network. When Keul realised that vital data on UFO witnesses was virtually non existent, he devised a protocol called *Anamnesis - life memory.*

The anamnesis is a 60 plus page questionnaire which asks information about the witness's health, beliefs, dreams and previous anomalous experiences in order to gather a fuller picture of the individual. Only this way could one discover whether the same type of people were reporting the same type of incident.

As Ken Phillips puts it: "Instead of looking out of the window with the witness in the direction of whatever it was that had long since appeared and departed, we were now looking back through the window at the witness in order to profile who is doing the perceiving and reporting."

Ken began the daunting task of collecting the mass of information necessary for the Anamnesis Project.

One of the most interesting facts thrown up by early analysis of the data was that more people than were permitted by mere chance were dissatisfied with their treatment by society. This social dissatisfaction trend was also echoed in the number of encounter witnesses who tended to be loners.

However it was soon realised that the statistics being collected were relatively useless unless they could be compared to the results from a control group. The anamnesis reports were on people who had all had some sort of UFO encounter, otherwise they would not have come to the attention of BUFORA.

At present the project is on ice since Ken sadly passed away a few years ago.

One of the most exciting new approaches to the alien abduction engima comes from Albert Budden, a former member of the scientific civil service and science teacher. He joined a UFO research group as an investigator more than twenty years ago after certain *encounters* experienced by his wife led him to become interested.

"My wife had not been an abductee but had suffered a

number of hallucinations, figures appearing before her and so on," said Albert. "I wanted to know more and began to investigate other cases."

Like others before him, he was struck by the number of alleged abductees who had also had psychic experiences, out of body experiences and other anomalous effects.

But unlike others, he came up with a theory based on allergies and embarked on years of gruelling research, poring over scores of scientific papers and interviewing the experts until he was confidant that his idea was valid.

A recently published paper *Allergies and Aliens* maintains that abduction victims are a group of hypersensitives who react to certain conditions by hallucinating.

But the group of people he has identified are not simply allergic to certain foods or substances - but to a whole range of environmental conditions, including electro-magnetic radiation.

I believe some people are electromagnetic hypersensitives," he said recently speaking from his Brentford home.

"There is a great deal of electronic pollution in the world, from radio frequencies to emissions from aerials, mobile phones, emergency services communications networks and so on.

"People sensitive to these fields of electromagnetic energy can, in the most extreme cases experience hallucinations. These may be reported as UFO abductions or ghosts or other psychic events.

"I discovered during my days as an investigator that the people who reported UFO abductions were nearly always sensitives in one way or another. A great many suffered from various allergies and the chances are that they have a sensitivity to electromagnetic forces."

He believes that it is more than coincidental that UFO abduction reports did not start until the early 1960s, the beginning of the communications revolution. His theory would also go some way to explaining why the great majority of UFO and alien abduction reports come from sophisticated, technologically advanced western nations where electronic pollution would be at its greatest.

"The level of electro-magnetic activity depends on many things including geography," said Albert, who believes other forms of environmental pollution may also play its part. Albert also says exposure to a natural phenomenon known as earthlights, balls of electromagnetic energy, that can rise from the earth's crust via natural faults, can also have a major effect on people.

"The way people change after abduction experience is amazing," said Albert. "People can change their diet, become vegetarians, stop smoking.

"Take the Aveley case. The fog they went through was an electrical mist caused by the electrification of water beneath a line of pylons nearby.

"After that incident the husband and wife went through some great changes in lifestyle and the young son who went through with them found a dramatic improvement in his reading ability afterwards.

"It is my contention that the electro-magnetic energy has done something to the brain. This is where the neurologists come in because we don't know what happens inside the body to cause these changes."

Albert believes up to 20 per cent of the population could be hypersensitive to their environment. His book, *UFOs - The Electromagnetic Indictment* caused a flurry in academic circles as well as in the world of Ufology.

Even if Albert's theories prove correct and an incredible allergic reaction to the environment is responsible for alien abduction reports why do so many people see such similar things. Why don't we hallucinate about scoring the winning goal in the Cup Final, or being shipwrecked on a desert island or a million and one other things?

Is the influence of UFOs and flying saucer folklore so great on our society that our minds immediately latch onto it to explain bizarre hallucinations?

See if you can decide whether the following cases fall in with Albert's idea.

The first case that follows is probably one of the best known in British Ufology and has had a wide airing in the media.

PC Alan Godfrey
November 28, 1980
Todmorden
West Yorkshire

It was 5.15 am and PC Alan Godfrey was near to finishing his shift. In the past few hours he had been called to an estate in Burnley Road following reports that a herd of 30 cows had been roaming around. He hadn't found them so now he was returning for a final check before heading back to the station.

As he was about to turn off the A646, the main Burnley to Todmorden road, he caught a glimpse of a strange glow about 200 yards away. He drove on to investigate.

As he approached a huge almost diamond shaped object came into view. It was sitting in the road ahead. Astonished by the intensity of the light emanating from the object before him, he brought his Ford Escort panda car to a halt. The thing was now about one hundred feet away. The rain that had teemed down throughout the night had now stopped and PC Godfrey had a clear, uninterrupted view of the bizarre sight.

It was roughly dome shaped, with a top that was flatter than the base. Fluorescent light issued from the top and he could see a row of dark but square windows beneath the light. The top portion of the craft remained still while the bottom portion rotated as the puzzled policeman watched the headlights from his patrol car reflecting on its shiny white surface.

PC Godfrey resisted the temptation to climb out of his patrol car for a closer look on foot. He felt a sense of security in the familiar surroundings of his vehicle and although there was only a windscreen between him and the unknown, he was loathe to get any closer. Instead he used his trained policeman's eye to estimate the dimensions of the object.

About 20 feet in diameter, he judged, based on the way it spanned the road width. Hovering about five feet above the road surface it could not have been much more than twelve or fourteen feet high.

The officer noticed, to his further amazement, the leaves on some adjacent trees shaking wildly despite the fact that the dark morning air was completely still – not even a hint of a breeze.

"There was no doubt that what I was looking at was real," he said at the time. "It was no illusion. If I had got out of my car and thrown a brick at it, it would have gone bang."

The constable decided to report into the station. First he tried the car radio, but it was dead. Then he reached for his personal walky talky. Both VHF and UHF were silent, devoid even of the static that normally plagued the airwaves.

Determined to somehow record the sight before him the policeman grabbed his clipboard and sketched the object as best he could on an official police accident form.

Suddenly the officer looked up and the object was gone.

He was several hundred yards further down the road than where he had been - and he was driving!

He had no idea how he got there, no recollection of putting the car into gear and setting off. One minute he was sitting in his parked patrol car sketching the strange object before him. The next he was driving through a dark and empty night. But he did seem to remember hearing a voice in his head say: "You should not be seeing this . . . It is not for your eyes . . . You will forget it."

Seeing a colleague he stopped his car and gave him a brief run down of what he had seen. Together they drove back to the spot where he had seen the object. The place was deserted. However PC Godfrey and his colleague saw blotchy patches on the road surface over which the thing had hovered, in sharp contrast to the uniform wetness that covered the rest of the carriageway.

Looking down at his feet, the officer noticed a split in his boot, as if it had been dragged along the ground. That had not been there at the beginning of his shift, of that he was sure.

PC Godfrey decided to keep his astonishing encounter to

himself - until the following day when he discovered that three officers on the moors had reported a brilliant light heading towards Todmorden on the night of his own sighting.

Emboldened by the news he decided to file his report and it wasn't long before a team from the Manchester UFO Research Association became involved.

PC Godfrey's story attracted publicity in the local and national press and was followed by a book which detailed the results of Hypnotic regression on the 33 year old police officer.

During that session he recalled a meeting with a tall humanoid being by the name of Yoseph and a medical examination conducted by a group of smaller beings, less than four feet in height.

In a telepathic conversation his abductors revealed that they knew him indicating that there may be more to other previous periods of missing time which he could recall.

This was not PC Godfrey's first encounter with the strange beings. In the summer of that year he had been involved in another mystery when a body was discovered lying on top of a 20 foot high pile of coal in a railway goods yard in Todmordon.

The body was identified as that of 56 year old ex-patriot Polish miner Zygmund Adamski, who had disappeared from home five days earlier .

A post-mortem revealed that he had died of a heart attack, but could not find any reason for the burn marks on his head and back which had apparently been caused by some corrosive liquid.

The mystery led to wild claims about a mystery death with some so-called enthusiastic UFO watchers claiming Mr Adamski's body could only have been lowered onto the tip from above . . . presumably from a flying saucer.

Serious Ufologists have never claimed any significance in the Adamski death and have been embarrassed by the unfounded claims from some quarters.

PC Godfrey survived that investigation. But the publicity

surrounding his own encounter was too much for his employers who questioned his fitness for duty.

In the end Alan Godfrey was forced to retire from the force, with honour.

That would have been the end of the Godfrey story except for the fact that a witness came forward who claimed to have seen the police officer being escorted into an alien craft 11 months *before* the alleged abduction . . .

William Barrett
January 14, 1980
Heald Moor
Lancashire

Lorry driver William Barrett had a big job on that day. He had to pick up a large load of yarn from Courtauld's Mill at Hollingworth near Oldham, so he set off from his Burnley home well before 6 am to give himself plenty of time to negotiate the treacherous ice bound roads of the Yorkshire/Lancashire border.

William had to drop off a package at Todmorden en route so he took the A646 Burnley to Todmorden route which follows the River Calder as it winds its way through the windswept foothills of the Pennines. It was a bitterly cold morning with no moon or stars to relieve the darkness, only a mass of dark clouds overhead threatening snow.

The 55 year old former Royal Marine had only been on the road for 20 minutes when he crossed the railway bridge at Heald Moor which is approximately midway between Burnley and Pendle. It was at this point that he first heard the humming.

The deep thrumming, similar to the noise made by an electricity generator was quite clear. William could easily distinguish it from the not inconsiderable noise made by his engine despite the fact that the windows in the cab were fully closed.

But William didn't have time to worry about the strange

sound. Seconds after it began the beams of his vehicle's headlights picked out an odd shape in the lay-by ahead. "What's going on here?" William asked himself as he looked at what first reminded him of a giant toast rack. It was dark, metallic and had three *red rays* projecting from the top down to the ground. The whole thing was resting on the ground, not moving.

"I was quite relaxed about it," recalled William later. "There were people moving about and I took them to be workmen making an early start. I thought they might be getting a machine ready to lay tar on the road."

As the distance between the object and his truck closed, William's view improved. The machine, if that is what it was, looked more tortoise shell in shape and the three beams, now less red, were projected from holes about two third of the way up the side of the object.

On its top was a curved *pipe,* which led William to wonder if he was looking at a secret weapon.

He looked for the people he had seen earlier. The two figures, who he could only see as silhouettes against the background light from the object, were moving from side to side, and appeared to be looking at or inspecting the beams.

Reducing his speed to a crawl William peered through the darkness at the figures and saw one was wearing a peaked cap and a dark two piece uniform. His arms were at his side.

The second figure appeared to be wearing a one piece suit, grey or silver in colour, and he was stooping down, bending at his knees to look at the object "as if it had broken down," William recalled later.

At this point, the closest he got to the scene, William could see the beams were bright. They flickered or rotated, causing the silhouettes of the two figures to break-up as they moved in front of them. It reminded the driver of the scintillating effect he had noticed at laser shows. The beams cast a dim reflection on the surface of the object and also caused the bracken on the hillside immediately adjacent to glow an angry red.

As the lorry drew away from the lay-by William continued to glance behind him to see if he could see any further clue as to what was going on.

Suddenly he was plunged into darkness. His vehicle's headlights had gone out on the unlit road and he was forced to jam on his brakes to avoid running off the road. As the ten-ton truck ground to a halt William himself blacked out.

A sudden jolting sensation brought the witness back to consciousness. Still in his cab with the engine running he could see his lights were working again.

Scanning his surroundings he immediately knew he had moved. Looking over his shoulder William could see no sign of the lay-by or the object. Later he realised he had been a quarter mile further along the A646 when he came to.

"I just didn't know what had happened," said William later. "I didn't know where I was or whether I had been asleep. All I could think of was escape."

Feeling shaky and light-headed, he put the engine into gear and continued his journey into Todmorden where he now noticed that it was growing light.

He passed the police station but decided against making a report. He dropped off his parcel and continued onto Oldham without stopping.

When he arrived at his destination Williams was confused to see another delivery vehicle which should have arrived later. He asked one of the workmen for the time and was told it was 9.10 am.

He was stunned. A journey that should have taken him an hour and a quarter had taken three hours twenty five minutes. Where had he been during the missing two hours? William Barret drove home, nagged by a pain in his left leg. He found a bruise mark just behind and above the left knee but had no idea how he had got it. Extremely tired he went to bed and tried to forget about the day's strange events.

However the geography of the encounter came back to haunt him nearly two years later when he read a report of the PC Alan Godfrey incident in a national newspaper.

William was intrigued by a photograph in the newspaper

which showed the officer with Mons Mill, a Todmorden landmark in the background. He had passed that very mill after *waking up* following his own encounter.

Now feeling that he wanted to tell his own story, William wrote to various organisations including a national newspaper, but with no response. Then in 1984 his case landed on the desk of a British UFO Research Association investigator.

Researchers were astonished by William's clear belief that he had witnessed the abduction of PC Alan Godfrey. That would have been impossible as his episode took place nearly a year before the police officer's encounter.

William's interest in the subject had been sparked by press reports of the Godfrey case and he had noticed the vague similarities in geography. Both cases had occurred on the A646, but several miles, and eleven months apart.

Nevertheless his sighting was thoroughly investigated. And although no other sightings were reported in the area on that day a similar object was seen at Bradley, just across the border into North Yorkshire the following evening.

Two women reported observing a "rotating object with two slits down the side which gave off a red glow."

It would be difficult to come to any firm conclusions about the Barrett case. Reading about the Alan Godfrey abduction obviously coloured his testimony to the extent that he believed the uniformed figure he described was the police officer, a classic case of force-fitting erroneous detail.

The Godfrey case apart, William Barrett saw a strange object, experienced an apparently associated malfunction of his vehicle and reports two hours of missing time.

Rae Fountain
July 11, 1957
Leighton Buzzard
Bedfordshire

Nine year old Rae Fountain was playing hooky that glorious summer's afternoon. As long as he got back for the football match at 5 pm he would be OK, thought the young-ster, they wouldn't miss him.

But he had broken the cardinal rule of his boarding school: never leave the premises without prior permission. If his absence was discovered there would be hell to pay.

Rae found himself down a small, muddy track, bordered by hawthorn and other bushes. Idly scuffing the ground with his boots and regularly glancing at the gleaming new watch on his wrist, a gift on his ninth birthday, two days earlier, he spotted footprints in the drying mud.

The schoolboy typically tried to follow the trail by putting his own feet into the marks in the ground. After following the strangely closely spaced marks for a few yards, he looked at his watch again. It was 3.30 pm. When he looked up he saw two men ahead of him - possibly the men respon-sible for the footprints.

The child thought they looked odd, perhaps it was the grey all in-one boiler suits they wore, or the way they walked in unusually short steps.

Excited by the mystery Rae darted to the side of the track and tried to hide himself in the bushes. Peering at his quarry he saw one was about five feet seven inches tall and the other, who he assumed to be a woman was about a foot shorter.

The pair were completely oblivious of the boy as they carefully picked pieces of twig and berries from the bushes and placed them in a container before them.

Rae couldn't understand why they picked up lumps of mud, pebbles and weeds too. Stalking them, as children do, Rae darted from bush to bush, but he failed to get a look at their faces. All he could see was their closely cropped brown hair. He was confused by the small, narrow tubes which ran down one side of their heads and into their collars. A green liquid seem to run up and down the tubes as they walked awkwardly forward.

Rae had almost caught up with the two strangers when a blue tinged object suddenly appeared before them.

"It just swished into view across the track," recalled Rae much later.

It was metallic and roughly bell-shaped, about 30 to 35 feet across, and it just hovered a few feet above the ground.

A door in the rounded top slid open and a ladder was lowered to the ground.

Rae thought he spotted another figure through the open doorway. The two strangers climbed the ladder, entered the object and the door slid shut. The object then shot up vertically for several hundred feet before sweeping across the sky.

The boy's next memory is of a furious headmaster rousing him as he lay in a heap by the side of the road.

"Where have you been boy? Do you realise its 10.30 and we've had the whole school out searching for you?" Rae looked at his new watch. It still said 3.30.

After his dressing down by the headmaster, Rae's school chums pleaded with him for details of what he had been up to. The quiet, introverted lad kept his silence. Yet the boys were convinced he'd been somewhere exciting. They said he was *sunburned*.

Rae kept his experiences to himself until 1978 when he spoke to an investigator from Contact UK by which time he could relate two further encounters.

One was a sighting of three craft in Scotland and the other was a sighting of UFOs and occupants in Kent. On neither subsequent occasion did he experience missing time although his wrist watch again mysteriously stopped during the Kent encounter.

Was Rae's missing time an abduction?

"He seemed very sincere and pleased to get the encounter off his chest when he spoke," said the investigator. And the follow-up sightings tie in with many reports from abductees.

Rosalind Reynolds
September 1983
Sudbury
Suffolk

Citizen's Band radio fan Rosalind Reynolds and her then boyfriend Philip were on a late summer's drive through East Anglia when an encounter with a UFO changed her life. The couple had set off from Clacton, Essex to Corby in Northamptonshire where they were due to meet relatives, and they had given themselves two and a half hours to reach their destination so they could enjoy the journey.

They stopped off for a burger shortly after leaving Clacton, then continued on towards Sudbury through the warm bright evening with the windows of the car wound down and their radio tuned into their favourite station.

As they approached the outskirts of Sudbury they found themselves driving beneath some high tension cables strung between electricity pylons which march up the adjacent hillside.

Suddenly they were confronted by a strange configuration of lights as they emerged from underneath the power lines.

A horseshoe shaped set of lights was approaching them at high speed. The multi-coloured, mostly orange and red object seemed to swoop low over their car.

It was at that moment when Rosalind noticed the silence and strange stillness around her. As the UFO moved across the sky a lurid flash of blue electric light illuminated everything around her.

"It made everything look like a photo-negative," recalled Rosalind who will never forget the way huge electrical tendrils arced their way up the metal skeletons of the pylons in that heart stopping moment.

A strange, foul smell, almost like rotten eggs seemed to be coming from the object. The odour became stronger the closer it was.

Bemused by the strange light show the couple pressed on through Sudbury and at Long Milford joined the A604 to Haverhill.

As Philip concentrated on driving his Ford Cortina, Rosalind took in the surrounding countryside. Then her eye was caught by something in the distance.

"Look another one," she screamed, pointing to an oval shaped object that was heading towards the car. "It's coming towards us."

"It's probably just a plane, or a helicopter," grunted Philip, keeping his eyes on the road ahead.

"Why should a plane draw level with us?" she asked as she looked out at the opalescent ball that was now obviously pacing the car. Philip would have none of it, he simply continued to drive through the enfolding darkness of the late evening.

Rosalind tried to ignore the thing that followed them, but it was no good, she knew it was there. Philip refused to acknowledge its existence.

Later Rosalind said: "I don't know how long we drove on like that, it could have been twenty minutes, or two hours."

Suddenly they were plunged into darkness. The car's engine and electrics cut out simultaneously, and the disabled vehicle rolled to a stop.

"Philip was glued to the steering wheel, looking straight ahead as if he had blinkers on" remembers Rosalind. She assumed that, like she, he was shocked and scared by the presence of the UFO.

The thing was now so close they could not avoid looking at it.

Big, bright and round and sitting just sixty feet away from their now crippled car. "It was like a big ball of light with lots of little lights around it," Rosalind told an investigator later.

The couple reluctantly climbed out of their car and lifted the bonnet to see if they could find the trouble. The way the car had cut out it had seemed as if the battery had been suddenly drained.

As they stood looking into the engine compartment the Cortina's headlamps came on. The couple looked at each other and Philip jumped back in the drivers seat and tried the ignition. It started first time. Rosalind climbed in and they pulled away with the UFO still flashing nearby.

When they increased the distance between themselves and the strange object the pair seemed to relax. Then a few miles away from their encounter Rosalind saw what she believes was the same object shooting straight up into the sky with a pencil-thin blue light streaming out behind it.

Glad to be on their way they seemed to make good progress but when they got to Corby their host was not answering the knock at his door. After a while, a bedroom window opened, and a head popped out and asked: "What time do you call this? It's half past one in the morning."

Their two and a half hour journey had taken *five and a half hours.*

Rosalind and Philip were stunned by the events of that night, and by their missing hours. But the after effects of that encounter would be equally astonishing. Within months the couple broke up after six years together.

"He was a different person, not the Philip I knew," said Rosalind.

Rosalind had changed too. She dramatically lost weight, despite developing a craving for sweets, especially chocolate, and went down to just six stones.

She gave up drinking and smoking and suddenly became creative, speedily writing complicated scientific papers on such topics as: *How The Universe Was Formed* and *What Religion Really Is.*

But she was desperate to discover why she had three hours missing from her life. What had happened on that summer's evening which had changed her life so much?

Rosalind saw the chance to recover that lost time when she spotted an article in a local newspaper about an East Anglian UFO research group. She made contact and they arranged a hypnosis session at her home.

But the session went disastrously wrong. "A bright beam of light came into the room, the video recording was wiped out and all the clocks stopped," said Rosalind.

After the abandoned hypnosis session Rosalind was advised to see a psychic and was introduced to the man she would shortly marry, Mark Reynolds-Parnham who claims to have been psychic since birth.

Mark arranged a second hypnosis session in which Rosalind was taken back to her 1983 encounter. She recalled being approached by four or five small beings after their car had broken down.

The aliens, for that is what she assumed they were, forced her into their craft.

They took her to an examination room where she was undressed and laid on a clear perspex-like table for observation . . .

Rosalind became agitated, embarrassed and frightened during the hypnosis session. She described how the aliens undressed her and laid her on the table but then she became very quiet.

Suddenly Rosalind sat bolt upright in her chair and screamed:

"No I don't want any babies." So concerned were the hypnosis team by Rosalind's distress in trance, they decided to bring her back.

Rosalind is convinced she underwent some gynaecological procedure but she still prefers not to speak about her hypnosis session.

Since that night she has suffered irregular menstruation which she feels has cost her the chance to have children. Medical tests failed to find the cause for the problem.

She also reports an unexplained scar in the vaginal area, which she assumed is linked with her alleged abduction. Additionally she developed a *buzzing in her head* which troubles her to this day.

Rosalind says the after effects of that encounter were truly devastating for her. The initial weight loss left her friends and family worried that she might be anorexic and she was worried about her missing periods.

"I could not talk to anybody about these things because I thought they would think I was a freak," said Rosalind. "I just bottled it up. I became a recluse for a while worrying about what had happened."

Her husband Mark has helped her come to terms with her experience, but she now believes she may well have had UFO encounters in the past, short slices of missing time that she simply ignored.

Rohan Hinton
Summer 1988
Delaware
USA.

Twenty three year old Rohan Hinton was just seventeen when she had her first abduction experience. She had been having a holiday with her mother and her uncle and aunt at Chesapeake Bay on the east coast of the United States.

Rohan was familiar with UFO phenomena after both her uncle and her mother had separate experiences. But she was not prepared for what happened to her in her motel room that summer.

"We were staying at the beach for a few days," recalled Rohan. "My mum and my aunt and I checked into a hotel and we got a room with two double beds. My aunt and I were in one bed and my mother in the other.

"I couldn't sleep because I was feeling stressed. It was something that bothered me the previous summer when I was on holiday in the States, I had a UFO sighting and for some reason it stressed me out, it upset me.

"That night I was just lying there gazing at the ceiling of the motel room and then I heard the voice. It *said Don't worry, you are alright, we are not going to bother you because you cannot deal with it.*

"It was a voice in my head, more masculine than feminine saying, *We are going to leave you alone, you are not strong enough.*

I felt instantly calm and fell asleep. When I woke up, three hours later, it was dark but I could see because of the moonlight coming through the window. I realised I was floating . . ."

Rohan was several feet above the bed and could look down on the sleeping forms of her mother and aunt. She felt as if someone, some power was holding her aloft.

"The next thing I was in a bright, bright room and I said *Who put the lights on?*

"They were standing there, standing around me and I was lying on what felt like a sheet of metal. They were looking at me in an indulgent way, not hostile. Indulgent, as if looking at a child."

Rohan described her captors as light grey in colour with huge dark eyes.

"It was like looking at a black and white photograph because of their big black eyes and their skin colouring. They were definitely humanoid, hairless and with tapering heads."

Suddenly Rohan was back in the motel room, still floating and then crashed down onto her bed. "I hit the bed and sort of jerked up shouting *They lied, they lied.* They promised that they were going to leave me alone, but they didn't. They tricked me."

Rohan was convinced her experience was real, not a dream. The strange episodes have continued since. Now a personal assistant to a managing director, Rohan lives in a flat in Dulwich, East London, which has been the scene for further odd events.

Back in 1992 Rohan was sharing her home with a boyfriend, Andy, who was in the habit of leaving for work at five in the morning.

"It was about December or January and I woke up at about six in the morning. Someone was moving about in the hallway and I thought it must be Andy having come back to collect something he had forgotten.

"The light in the hall was on and I raised my head to look and then this thing just shuffled into the bedroom.

"It was thin with a thin face and very large eyes and it just shuffled over to the futon I was lying on and touched me with this incredibly long finger.

"I felt as if I was falling backwards, just like passing out."

Rohan awoke to find her mystery visitor had vanished. "I remember thinking at the moment that it touched me: *Oh my God, this is really happening.* There was no doubt that it was real."

Rohan has had a variety of anomalous experiences since early childhood when she would tell her parents she had seen a mysterious *grey lady.*

Further disturbed nights at her flat, followed by days of complete exhaustion caused her to wonder whether she had been taken somewhere during the night.

"I somehow know when I have had an experience the previous night because of the way I feel the next day."

Rohan has now come to terms with her UFO/Abduction experiences and she has turned what some contactees regard as a curse into a party trick.

She explained: "I was with my boyfriend and another girl the other week and we were standing on the roof of the house, having a drink and watching the stars and I said *I can bring a UFO here.*

"They said go on then, so I sort of sent a thought out, into the sky and a few minutes later . . . there it was. It was winking and flashing and it moved slowly across the sky."

Is Rohan Hinton a young woman whose multiple UFO/Abduction experiences mean she is of some special interest to extraterrestrials? Or is she an over-enthusiastic sky-watcher with a well developed imagination?

Theorists like Albert Budden might speculate that her wealth of psychic and UFO experiences could make her an electromagnetic hypersensitive.

Psychologists might say her UFO party trick was an indication that she is seeking attention.

Another case for debate.

Ernest Jones (pseudonym)
December 1972
Marlow
Buckinghamshire

Publican and ex-RAF man Ernest Jones was heading home on the A4155 Henley-on-Thames to Marlow road in Buckinghamshire sometime after midnight when he drove into a mystery that remains with him to this day.

It had been a totally uneventful journey through very light traffic on a bitterly cold night. As he motored along a half mile straight section of the road near Mill End he noticed a bright light ahead of him.

As he approached he could see the light was emanating from some farm buildings on his near side. Moving closer he saw the light was in fact some distance from the farm and coming from an object just ten yards from the roadside.

Hexagonal, or octagonal, the object was approximately the same size as a public telephone box with a conical top and strips of powerful fluorescent lighting running down it in a vertical pattern.

Mr Jones remembers pulling up alongside the object for a better view and tells that the UFO was in the process of landing. A high pitched whistling sound seemed to be coming from it.

Ernest Jones' next memory was driving through Marlow, about four miles further down the road and checking his watch . . . it was one and a half hours later.

Ten years earlier, while serving in the forces, Ernest Jones had another encounter while parked on moor land overlooking Holton Airfield in Berkshire.

Sitting in his car with his girlfriend, they watched in astonishment as a large white, revolving object dropped to the ground, disappearing behind some woodland.

The sudden appearance of the UFO sent his girlfriend into hysterics so Mr Jones agreed to move on.

He switched on the ignition, but the car's electrical system seemed dead. Finally he managed to shove the vehicle down the 400 yard incline towards the road, at the bottom of which the lights and the engine burst into life.

Typical of a great many less than dramatic cases, Ernest Jones makes no great claims or assumptions about what happened to him.

But Ufologists feel there are just too many such cases for them to be ignored.

Mik Burley
June 1978
Middlesborough
Cleveland

Mik Burley was in goal for his school on that hot and humid summer's day and the lads were kicking hard and fast, determined to score in this important junior fixture.

Mik hadn't been playing long when one of the opposing strikers raced down the field and kicked the old-fashioned leather ball high into the air.

He didn't see it coming, but Mik took the full force of the descending ball when it crashed into the side of his face knocking him sideways.

"It rattled my brain and made me feel dizzy," said Mik as he was escorted to the side of the pitch where he was laid down to recover.

"I put my head on my arm and then looked down and then I just seemed to black out. First there was a bright flash and I was out," he recalled later.

Mik assumed he was in hospital. He was lying on his back, a figure in a monk's cowl was standing to his right and through blurred vision he saw two or three other figures standing by his feet.

The closest figure looked busy, turning this way and that, handing things, perhaps implements.

"I felt naked at the time," recalled Mik. "I didn't feel cold, but I could feel a draught on the whole of my body. My head and my arms were restrained, so I couldn't move, my body felt numb.

"I seem to remember them cutting me and scraping and digging, but I didn't feel any pain."

Still groggy, Mik screwed up his eyes to try to make sense of the flashing colours that flickered on and off before him. He counted four rows of lights on what may have been a console.

The brightest light shone down from directly above him. "It was like being in the dentist's when they look in your mouth," recalled Mik. But this time he couldn't see who was doing to looking.

All he could see was the brown material of the cowl worn by the figures standing by his bed.

Then Mik was back . . . face down, lying at the side of the football pitch, a raging headache pounding relentlessly. Hauling himself to his feet he trudged over to his school pals who wanted to know what the gym teacher had said to him.

"I haven't been into school yet," said Mik. His pals didn't believe him. They had been looking for him for fifteen minutes. He had disappeared from the spot at the side of the pitch where they had left him.

Mik went to the changing room to get out of his football strip and immediately noticed a red mark on his side. That hadn't been there earlier . . . but it was a scar that would remain with him for the rest of his life.

Lorry driver Mik's entire life has been plagued with odd experiences.

As a four year old he would tell his parents about the strange little girl who would come to visit him in his bedroom.

The vision, a little girl with her ginger hair tied back, would appear behind the convector heater in a corner of his room.

The youngster would wake up in the middle of the night screaming.

"I remember I wasn't scared of the little girl," recalls Mik.

"I was scared by whatever it was that seemed to frighten her. You could tell she was scared by the look on her face."

An elderly neighbour solved the riddle of the midnight visitor. She said the description the boy gave was of a little girl who had lived and died at the house some years before. The child had been epileptic and was often locked out of the way in her bedroom by a cruel stepmother, according to the story. One day the little girl suffered a fit and choked to death. Her body was found by the heater.

Later in life Mik had another gloomy vision. But this time is was a bizarre case of precognition. He seemed to know that his marriage to his first wife would end in divorce and it did. Mik also complained of a head full of memories which should not, or could not have been there.

"It's left me wondering whether I've been reincarnated from the last war. I have had memories of being squeezed into an aircraft, a fighter and dog fighting. "I can feel four rounds hit my aircraft and four searing pains, like red hot pokers stabbing in my back from the left kidney to the right shoulder. Everything goes limp and I start to nosedive and I think *at least I'm not on fire . . .*"

On a further occasion Mik had what he calls a dream which seemed real involving his late grandfather.

"We had been very close," he said. "I was in a clearing in a wood, there was an area of neatly cut grass and a fence with a gate. I saw my grandfather walk round. He walked towards me, through the gate and spoke to me.

"He said *don't come through the gate, I'll come to you.* Then I actually remember putting my arms around him and he was exactly as I remembered him. I actually made physical contact."

Mik's most chilling experience of precognition concerned an horrific accident he was involved in which nearly cost him his life.

For two and a half years before the event he had been receiving baffling visions. "I seemed to be in the back of a church, dimly lit, lights at the front.

"There was something high to my right and a row of flashing lights. I could see a dim light ahead and walked along towards it. Then I saw somebody slumped over so I looked and he turned towards me. The right side of his face was missing . . . and the rest of the face was me."

That was similar to the sight that greeted a traffic policeman when he arrived at the scene of a collision between a lorry being driven by Mik and a huge crane. Explained Mik:

"The policeman pulled in behind my trailer and walked along the side on the grass verge. It would have been dark with the headlights of my lorry reflecting ahead like in my vision. The trailer would stand high at one side.

"The policeman would have walked up to the front and would have seen me hanging out of the front end of my cab. I turned to look at him and the right side of my face was hanging off. "It's the only way I can describe it. I saw what he saw, only I saw it two years before it happened."

Mik's case is not untypical. A UFO witness and possible abductee with a rich history of psychic and precognitive experiences. A down-to-earth Northerner he never tries to embellish his accounts and investigators who have spent some considerable time with him are convinced he is telling the truth.

Does this case support the school of thought that individuals who are sensitive to psychic events are often sensitive to UFO activity? Does this theory suggest that only a certain type of person will experience Abduction Phenomenon? And does that mean that Alien Abduction is nothing more than a psychological phenomenon?

CHAPTER 11
Close Encounters Of A Sexual Kind

Sex and Abduction Phenomenon may seem like odd companions in a book like this, but it is an aspect of the mystery that deserves close scrutiny. Remember when we pointed out the fact that strange abductions seem to have occurred throughout history with accounts abounding in ancient mythology and folk tales? Well, sex actually played a major part in many of those old stories, in fact in some cases it seemed to be the sole reason for the abduction.

Greek mythology tells of handsome Gods coupling with mortal maidens, sometimes inseminating them with their heavenly seed. Across the world similar stories can be found in plentiful supply. Lovely young virgin, stolen at the dead of night to be cruelly abused and defiled by a variety of villains from ghouls to goblins - the story is as old as the hills. Even the birth of Jesus Christ was the result of an immaculate conception. That story is literally as old as Christianity itself.

Human sexuality and reproduction is a central part of all human cultures, naturally. It is the reason humanity exists and continues to exist. Reproduction is a prime directive from Nature. The order to *go forth and multiply* was given to man, and maybe to others.

Having said that it could be argued that it is equally quite natural that the modern *folklore* of Alien Abduction should have borrowed one of the most compelling ingredients from religion and mythology, sex. After all, abductees and the people who investigate abductions are human. And sex is one of the most powerful of human drives. So where exactly does sex come in the abduction equation?

Right at the beginning.

The Betty and Barney Hill case, possibly the first recorded abduction, had strong indications of an alien interest in sex and reproduction. Betty underwent what can only be described as a gynaecological examination and was tested for pregnancy and Barney had sperm removed.

Indeed in the majority of cases that have followed there seems to be a strong interest by the *visitors* in the human reproductive system.

Female abductees often describe how *aliens* show inordinate interest in their sexual and reproductive organs when under examination. Males too also testify that their genitalia are often carefully scrutinised when being examined by their abductors. One South American abductee described how he was sexually aroused so his alien captors could gather samples of his semen.

Many female abduction victims report gynaecological problems following their encounters, the most common being an interruption in their menstruation. And some report rape or even sexual intercourse with their abductors.

Male abductees too have also gone on record saying that they had sexual intercourse with female aliens. But, once again, as we find with most abduction cases, the majority are from other parts of the world, largely the USA and South America.

As this book is concentrating on Abduction Phenomenon in Britain we will scrutinise four accounts from this country, three women and a man. These are not the only known British cases involving claims of sexual activity between alleged aliens and humans, but they are all accepted as possible abductees by the British UFO Research Association, their accounts have a very strong sexual-reproductive theme running through them - and above all they have been prepared to talk about this most sensitive of matters.

One of the women believes she had sex with an alien, another is convinced she was raped and the third had gynaecological problems which suggests that her reproductive system was tampered with. The male abductee clearly recalls the sex act with a female extraterrestrial.

The two women who claim that aliens had sex with them are unable to give graphic descriptions of those events because of the traumatic effect of their experiences. But reports like theirs has led researchers to ask whether abductions are carried out by different races of aliens .One of the reasons for this is that alleged pathology reports on the alien beings known as *Greys* - the slight grey skinned entities with large eyes, thin mouth and almost non-existent nose - have shown no evidence of external genitalia One pathology report read: "No apparent reproductive organs. Perhaps atrophied by evolutionary degeneration. No genitalia. In my judgement the absence of sexual organs suggests that some of the aliens, and perhaps all, do not produce as do the homo sapiens, or that perhaps some of the bodies studied are produced perhaps by a system of cloning."

So if the Greys were not responsible for our female victims of alien molestation, who was?

But before we look at these amazing cases in detail let us first consider some of the many theories that might provide some explanation for these *close encounters of a sexual kind*.

"A preoccupation with reproduction is a common theme from the earliest abductions onward, and a few stories describe rape, sexual activity and events that might be described as artificial insemination," said Dr. Thomas E. Bullard after looking at the available evidence recently.

One theory is that alien sexual activity with humans has been going on for thousands of years. It may be a way of introducing new genes and new traits into the human race, some sort of genetic control. This body of opinion states that a benign advanced alien culture could be using a form of super genetics to keep our race on the straight and narrow, ensuring a steady rate of development.

The other side of the coin portrays an alien Big Brother with a firm grip on our genetic reins ensuring we develop at the rate and level that suits them.

Another theory, popular in America, is that aliens are involved in the harvesting of genetic material for the continuation of their own kind. If an advanced extraterrestrial culture has evolved down some genetic cul-de-sac, is it not possible that they may need to reinvigorate their stock of genes? Some recent research suggested that the apparent absence of external genitalia, or other reproductive organs, in the many descriptions of aliens suggested that some aliens, if not all, did not produce in the same way as homo sapiens. Some other means, perhaps cloning, may be involved.

If they come across a race whose physical make-up is not so different from theirs might they take the opportunity of *borrowing* some new genetic material?

The *strange harvest* school of though points to the controversial mutilation of livestock in the USA and says that the removal of sex organs with surgical precision from these animals could be another sign of an alien search for answers to a genetic nightmare we can't imagine.

But why bother with genetic experimentation when the earth is full of women capable of being used as surrogates for the procreation of an alien race?

For a number of years many female abductees have complained of alleged *missing pregnancies* defined as *Missing Embryo/Foetus Syndrome*.

The women are pregnant, then after between six and twelve weeks their pregnancy simply stops. They have no sign of a miscarriage, have certainly not had an abortion, so where did their baby go?

A growing number of Ufologists in America believe these missing pregnancies are due to alien intervention. They believe suitable women are impregnated during abduction and then released only to be abducted again when the developing foetus can be removed.

New York Ufologist Budd Hopkins makes no bones about it. Some women, he alleges, are impregnated by aliens, have the resultant foetus removed to be brought to term elsewhere. He is convinced many women are being exploited as breeding stock.

He also points to the number of women who report *Wise Baby Dreams*. These women may have been through the missing pregnancy syndrome and follow up with dreams in which they see their babies intelligent . . . and alien.

So is the abduction of our race being used to overcome the inability of some alien race to procreate?

"Highly unlikely," is the response of many mainstream scientists. But how would they know the values and capabilities of a race so advanced that they have conquered star travel?

American psychotherapist Dr Jean Mundy is clear on alien genetic experimentation. She says: "We don't know the full scale of the programme, only that it exists.

"Around nine per cent of women with alien contact report medically confirmed pregnancies which disappear, usually in the fourth month. There was no evidence of miscarriage, they just were not pregnant any longer.

Some of these women wondered if the aliens were using them as surrogate mothers."

Could sperm be taken from male abductees and be used to fertilise alien eggs to provide a further supply of crossbreeds? The permutations are endless.

American Air Force pilot John Lear added to this debate when he claimed a secret US Government body had made an agreement with a species of aliens known as EBEs, *Extraterrestrial Biological Entities,* to ignore human abductions and mutilations of animals in return for high technology data.

Human and animal genetic material was essential for the EBEs survival, it was claimed.

There is a mass of so called evidence in the hands of Ufologists in the United States, some in the form of alleged top secret Government papers dictated for the information of the President. These documents, which are steeped in controversy, suggest contact between alien entities and Government bodies over a long period of time and contain pages of information on the visitors.

Interestingly one of these papers discusses alien manipulation of DNA - the genetic building blocks of life - in terrestrial primates over a period of 25,000 years.

Are we laboratory rats in a bizarre alien experiment? Does planet Earth offer a battery of surrogate mums to help top up an infertile race of ETs with a new supply of crossbreeds?

Or is the sexual aspect of Abduction Phenomenon simply a matter of Freudian theory surfacing in a psychotic experience?

The following cases should give you plenty to think about.

Lynda Jones
August 19, 1979
Didsbury
Greater Manchester

It should have been just another summer's day for 36 year old housewife and mother of two Lynda Jones. But it was a day which would change her life. The morning got off to a good start when a very old friend called at the comfortable semi-detached home she shared with husband Trevor and their two children Andrew, five and fifteen year old Dawn. Over a long, leisurely lunch they chatted about the good old days and long lost acquaintances until Trevor had to leave for work at a nearby factory.

Trevor was on a 2 pm till 10 pm shift and left his wife and their mutual pal to while away the afternoon in the sun-drenched garden watching the children at play.

The hours slipped by as Lynda and the family friend lounged in the baking heat of the day reminiscing about days gone by.

"Suddenly it was early evening and our friend reminded me he had to be on his way well before lighting up time," recalled Lynda. "He had cycled over to see us on an old bike which had no lights.

"I said we would show him a shortcut over the fields. It would be nice to take a walk with the children and I could indulge my passion for wild flowers.

"It was about 7.30 when Lynda, the family friend, pushing his bike, and the children set off over the fields that border the River Mersey which meanders through this southern part of the Greater Manchester conurbation.

They would accompany him as far as Simon's Bridge, a 15 minute walk across the high grassland, and then wander back home at their leisure.

After saying their goodbyes Lynda, clutching her copy of the *Oxford Dictionary Of Wildflowers*, began hunting for the colourful plants that were now her hobby.

The three ambled through the grass, Lynda and Dawn

often stopping to inspect an interesting looking flower or plant, while young Andrew raced this way and that, relishing the freedom of the open countryside. They were in no hurry.

Trevor would not be home for a couple of hours yet. So they could zig-zag back across the fields at their leisure.

Suddenly Dawn called: "Mum, the moon is coming towards us."

Lynda looked up to see a strange object racing across the sky, and apparently on a collision course with them.

"It was like a frisbee only a lot bigger," remembers Lynda.

"It had come into view from behind some trees on the golf course on the other side of the river and I could see a few golfers on the green as it came towards us. It was no optical illusion.

"The object had a spinning effect and it seemed to be coming at us at an angle.

"Get down, I said, *come on, get down in the grass."*

It was a natural instinct to hide in the tall grass.

For one fleeting instant Lynda thought the object might be a plane from nearby Manchester Airport, perhaps it was in trouble, or on fire. She feared it might crash.

As she crouched down in the undergrowth, an arm around each of her children, Lynda braced herself for an explosion, the sound of an aircraft coming to grief nearby.

But there was nothing, only silence.

Slowly raising her head above the grass Lynda saw the object pass overhead and then drop vertically and silently behind an embankment, part of the river's flooding defences.

That is when the total silence that now surrounded her hit home.

"It was more than just silence, it was a complete stillness," Lynda recalled later.

"There had been no noise from the object and then I realised there was no other noise either. No birdsong and no traffic noise from the nearby motorway.

"The traffic normally provides a constant background

noise day and night because it is so busy. But at that moment in time it had gone completely."

Pulling her children from the grass Lynda took a few steps towards the embankment behind which the object had landed. Maybe it had crashed and the embankment was hiding wreckage, maybe it was on fire.

Whatever, Lynda had a compelling urge to get closer to the object, and began walking and then running to the top of the embankment determined to see what it was hiding. As she reached the edge she had to catch her breath in shock at the sheer strangeness of the sight that greeted her eyes.

There, about 30 yards away on the bank of the river lay an object which she could only describe as *Biblical*.

"That was the first word that popped into my head when I looked at it," recalled Lynda. "It was just so weird. I did not know anything about UFOs, I just wasn't interested in that sort of thing, but looking back what I saw did not fit the standard description of a flying saucer or a UFO.

It was shaped like a crescent moon and coloured dark grey, but not metallic. It was made of a sort of latticework, an intricate design of latticework, but I could still see the field through it.

"It looked so, so old fashioned. It really did look like something out of the Bible."

With her children standing beside her Lynda stared at the object, almost unable to take her eyes away, as she took in every detail.

"I would say it was about 60 feet across and was hovering perhaps two feet off the ground," she said later.

"Some how, while we were watching it, it seemed to disappear, then appear and then disappear again.

"It had this light on the top of it, a bright white light that was separated from the structure beneath yet was still a part of it. I felt really drawn to it. As I stepped forward the light began to get brighter and brighter, the nearer I got."

As she edged her way towards the confusing shape before her Lynda saw an orange ball of light appear from the far side of the object and begin to move towards her, rotating slowly.

"As I walked on towards the object I thought that in a few minutes I would be looking in at them and what they were doing," said Lynda. "I don't know why I thought that but now it gives me the shivers."

Suddenly Dawn screamed: "Mum, come back. Come back".

The fear in her daughter's voice jolted Lynda back to a terrifying reality.

"I had this feeling of deja vu, really strongly. Then I took in everything around me and I thought *Oh my God. This is Judgement Day . . . I'm not ready for this. I've got no make-up on.*"

Lynda turned and fled. Grabbing her children by their hands, she charged back down the embankment, gripped with fear, heart pounding and eyes firmly focused on her escape route . . .

Running down the slope they quickly picked up speed. Only little Andrew faltered and struggled to keep up with the headlong pace of his panic stricken mum and older sister.

"It's there again, the thing is back at the side of us," screamed Dawn. Lynda's blood seemed to turn to ice in her veins. Too terrified to look back, she scooped up young Andrew before his tired five-year-old legs could give way under him, tightened her grip on her daughter's hand and drawing on every ounce of strength in her body she powered off through the grassland as if pursued by the devil himself.

As if in slow motion Lynda forced one exhausted leg before the other in long, loping strides that carried her and her little son across the grassy terrain at the same breakneck speed that her younger, fitter daughter had set.

"Mum, look. There are two of them now," Dawn called.

Breathless, sweating and on the very edge of exhaustion, Lynda suppressed the urge to turn to look at her pursuers, and with what seemed like superhuman strength increased the pounding rhythm of her legs. "Don't look back Dawn, just run," she yelled as she leapt onto the path that ran along the river, glad of a smoother surface on which she could increase the distance between the ominous object and her family.

Little Andrew, too frightened to speak, clung precariously to his mother as she ran side by side with her daughter on the final leg of their nightmare flight from fear.

And she held the youngster closer to her than ever as the odd presence had a bizarre effect on their surroundings.

"It was so strange," recalled Lynda. "The grass was folding down on itself, as if it was being pressed down from above. It happened as we reached the river path. The grass all along the side was just folding. It was the strangest sight I have ever seen."

Lynda and her daughter maintained their punishing pace even when they reached the edge of the housing estate where they lived.

"We didn't stop running until we got into the house," said Lynda. "Then we ran straight into Trevor who looked at me and said *What's wrong with your eyes?* I looked in the mirror and I could see my skin was red and scaley under both my eyes. Dawn and Andrew were both OK.

"I told Trevor what we had seen from start to finish. When I asked if he wanted to go back and look at it, he said *no* but he wanted us all to draw a picture of what we had seen."

Lynda's daughter had been so petrified by the experience that she had wet herself and needed to change. But later when Trevor studied the drawings of his wife and daughter he had to agree that they were similar.

Suddenly Lynda realised Trevor was home, yet he had been on a two till ten shift and would not normally get home until 10.30 pm.

"What time is it?" she asked her husband. "It's gone 10.30," he replied.

Lynda had *lost* at least an hour of her life. She and the children had left their home for the ten minute walk at

7.30. They had seen the strange object at about 9 pm and ran the equivalent of a ten-minute walk at breakneck speed. Yet they didn't get in until 10.30.

Lynda would have to wait another 18 months to discover more about her experience when she would go under hypnosis. In the meantime she and Trevor told very few people of her encounter.

One friend, who had been told, called the Air Traffic Control at Manchester Airport to see if they could throw any light on the mystery. All they could say was that they had no air traffic which would match the object's description.

In 1980 Lynda underwent a series of hypnotic regression sessions. Each session was recorded on video tape and produced ten hours of recordings in all. But Lynda found the entire experience disturbing and frightening and has refused to view the majority of the tapes.

She said: "It was very unsettling watching myself under hypnosis. At times I was becoming extremely upset by whatever I thought was happening to me. It was just too much."

However in the years since, Lynda has pieced together a vague, yet intriguing account of what may have happened to her during that missing hour or so, based partially on memories reawakened by hypnotic regression and other snatches of information that have surfaced over a period of time.

"I believe that at the point where the children and I turned to run away, I saw a person standing by the object. I was transfixed, unable to move, like what happens in a dream. Then I had a feeling of floating, as if I was moving unintentionally.

"Then I am in a room and six beings come in. They are humanoid, wearing dark suits, like motorbike suits with high necks.

"The beings, or whatever they were, seemed Oriental. They had slanted eyes, very dark hair and yellow/olive skins.

"I seemed to know one of them, as if I had seen him before.

"Then I felt as if I was being examined. I felt as if I was laid down on a table in this strange room and they were examining me. I distinctly remember them putting something on my legs, it felt like they were putting pieces of ice on me. Every time I turned my head to look at what they were doing bright lights were shone in my eyes."

Lynda still finds the memories of that evening's strange events frightening and refuses to speculate about what was being done to her on that examination table.

But the real-life medical side-effects she has suffered ever since her encounter make her quake with fear. Lynda, like many other female abduction victims, discovered that her menstrual cycle had been affected. Within a few weeks, she visited her GP to tell him her periods had stopped. He told her she had nothing to worry about, these things can happen.

"I knew I was too young to be on the change," said Lynda. "But I wasn't really worried." Lynda tried to get on with her life but suddenly found she was prone to strange marks appearing and then disappearing on her body.

"I'd get a mark, Trevor would see it but it would have gone by the time I got to the doctor's, it was really strange," said Lynda.

But the most mystifying after effect came some weeks after her encounter. She had been feeling tired and listless. Then one day she had what she describes as a *show*.

"I feel terrible talking about something as personal as this," she said. "But this waxy material came away. I was really worried and took it to my GP. He took one look at it and said *You've had a miscarriage*.

"But I had not been pregnant," said Lynda. "I was just stunned."

Lynda's menstruation did not return and was referred, by her GP, to a gynaecologist who embarked on a long series of tests and examinations to get to the bottom of the problem.

After a time Lynda was called into hospital to see her specialists. He had found something.

They had look at my fallopian tubes and found some scar

tissue on them. They said that type of scarring could only have been caused by an ectopic pregnancy, where the egg is fertilised and develops in the fallopian tube.

"But I had never had an ectopic pregnancy to my knowledge. I would have known because and ectopic pregnancy can be fatal."

Was Lynda conscripted into an alien genetic testing culture? Budd Hopkins would certainly consider Lynda's case as possibly supporting his worrying theories.

As he recently said: "What we get is an alien concentration on taking samples and working on the reproductive area without the abductee's will being involved."

But Lynda does not feel qualified to speculate. She said: "I don't know what happened to me, but something did. To be honest it frightens me. It has made me look at lots of other events in my life and wonder."

Immediately after her experience she noticed a strange mark on the jeans she had been wearing when she crossed the field. Amazingly it was in the shape of the object she saw and even matched the drawings she and her daughter had done of the object.

The jeans were tested at a university institute. They said that the image could have been done with printer's ink, but why in that shape?" asked Lynda.

Seven years later Lynda was working as a beauty consultant and was asked to wear a plastic name badge. Her name disappeared from the badge within hours. The same happened with a further two badges issued to her.

"The badges were again tested by a scientist, who said it could have something to do with radio waves," said a perplexed Lynda.

Her UFO encounter coupled with the strange after-effects made Lynda re-evaluate other odd events that she had buried away.

"Trevor and I experienced a missing time episode in 1972," said Lynda. "We went out for a spin in his E-type Jaguar. We took the country roads through Cheshire. It was early evening and we planned to go for a drink."

Trevor came to a halt by some traffic lights. He suggested he and Lynda call in for a drink at the pub at the next corner. It was about 9 pm. Suddenly the car began to spin.

"One minute we were sitting there, the next the car was going round and round. Trevor had the hand brake on and his foot jammed on the brake, but the car just spun as if on ice," remembered Lynda.

"Trevor asked me if I could see some bright lights behind us. Then the car stopped and he pulled away and turned left at the pub.

"We didn't get out of the car because we could see the pub was closed so we drove home.

"But when we got home it was 3 a.m. Somehow we had lost six hours."

Some observers would say that Lynda's experiences are similar to those of alleged abductees, particularly in America, whom, it is claimed are chosen for genetic experimentation by alien visitors.

Some Ufologists maintain these individuals are abducted and tested and re-abducted again and again to glean further information, like zoologists or biologists who capture and tag wild animals only to release them and recapture them to monitor their progress and development.

Lynda's view? "I don't understand what has happened to me. It is all very weird. I wish someone could explain it to me."

Gabriella Versacci, (pseudonym)
October 16,1973
Langford Budville,
Somerset

Gabriella Versacci was making spaghetti for her husband Alberto and their 14 year old daughter Maria when a sharp rap at the front door made her jump. The 33 year old housewife turned down the heat on the stove and padded out to the door to find the daughter of her friend on the doorstep.

"Hello Gabriella, my mum asked me to call to see if you could drive over to Wellington to see her, she's not very well at the moment," said the young woman.

"Of course, of course it is no problem," soothed Gabriella. In the ten years since she and her husband had landed in Britain from their native Turin she had made many friends. "In a new country we must make new friends," her husband Alberto always said and Gabriella's warm and helpful nature meant she was always in great demand.

"I'm in the middle of making the evening meal," she told her young visitor. "Give me half an hour and I'll drive over."

That promise was a little optimistic. Minutes after her friend's daughter had left there was someone else at the door.

A stream of visitors seemed to call at the Versacci's Taunton home that night and Gabriella didn't have the heart to turn anybody away, so it was well after 10.30 when Gabriella climbed into her 1967 mini saloon for the drive to Wellington.

Determined to make up for lost time, Gabriella decided to avoid Taunton town centre and took the A361 to Milverton where she would take the B3187 to Wellington itself. Despite the light traffic it was about 11.30 when she turned into the small, winding B-road which snaked across country to her destination.

As she passed the Langford Budville signpost, about three miles from Wellington, Gabriella could see the road was completely deserted.

Then as she wound along the country lane she thought she saw the glare of a single headlight ahead. As her car bowled along the clear road she realised the light ahead was too bright to be a headlight and it seemed stationary.

"Strange," she thought. "There are no buildings at that spot."

Concentrating on her driving, she pressed on hoping that her friend would not object to such a late visitor. She had promised her daughter that she would pay her sick friend a visit and a promise was a promise.

Suddenly the car seemed to lose power. The headlamps flickered, dimmed and then cut out. Next the engine faltered, spluttered and then fell silent. Panic-stricken, Gabriella pressed her face to the windscreen, struggling to steer the car to a halt in the almost complete blackness.

When the mini came to a standstill by the side of the road, Gabriella put on the handbrake, knocked the gear stick in to neutral and turned the ignition. Nothing. Nervously she glanced over to the bright light she had seen from the road earlier. Had that got anything to do with her breakdown? For some reason she felt sure it had. Pulling herself together Gabriella tried the ignition again. But the electrics were obviously dead.

Sitting alone in a silent car on a deserted country road and enveloped by complete darkness, the fear began to well up inside her. Gabriella decided she couldn't sit there and do nothing.

Even if she didn't know what she was doing she ought to look under the bonnet. It might be something simple like a loose wire, she told herself as she climbed out of the claustrophobic confines of her little car. At least she would be doing something.

Out in the night Gabriella fumbled with the bonnet catch and lifted it. In the gloom she peered at, what to her, was merely a jumble of oddly named parts. As she stood there, helplessly she noticed a humming sound, faint at first then seeming to grow stronger.

Raising her head from beneath the bonnet she glanced over at the strange bright light and became aware that the noise wasn't coming from any particular direction. It was the regular hum of an electricity generator and seemed to lie like a blanket over the whole area.

Closing the bonnet, Gabriella decided she would try the ignition once again. Whatever the fault was, maybe it was OK now, she thought as she tugged on the driver door.

A hand came down on her left shoulder. A heavy hand seemingly pushing her down into the ground. Turning slowly, trying to keep at bay the sense of panic that threatened to turn her into a gibbering wreck, Gabriella faced her assailant. He was tall, dark coloured and metallic.

Robot, the word crashed around her brain. Gabriella was being waylaid by a metal man. He was certainly more machine than man by the way the light from the bright object in the field was reflected off his metallic surface. Then more lights, flashing, coloured lights and then all was blackness for Gabriella Versacci.

When she came to from her fear-induced faint Gabriella was standing in a field. The robot was next to her and before them stood the strange, bright object. Half-moon shaped, it was rounded at the top and flat at the bottom.

Bright as an arc lamp, the object was some sort of machine. This impression became stronger as the brightness emitted by the object was reduced. It was silver-grey in colour, not unlike aluminium. It rested on thick legs, Gabriella saw two but there may have been more.

Transfixed to the spot, Gabriella's eyes explored the object for clues to its purpose. It was about 20 feet high and 40 feet across. Large, oblong windows punctuated its middle and from these a yellow light issued.

Now Gabriella realised it was the object that was emitting the humming sound. With that realisation the overwhelmed housewife blacked out for the second time that night. She awoke inside a strange room, which she took to be the interior of the object. She found herself in a circular room, strapped to a table in the centre. Naked, Gabriella wondered who had undressed her. She was grateful for the large light blue blanket that covered her embarrassment.

Gabriella tried in vain to raise herself for a better look at her *prison.* Her wrists were bound to the table by what she described as *large rubber bands.* Her spread-eagled legs were restrained in the same manner, with the bands holding her ankles to the cold surface of the table.

Gabriella shivered. The blue blanket was cold and the inside of the craft was freezing. She glanced over to a far wall where the *robot* stood inactive. The wall behind him was covered with an array of equipment. To Gabriella's right was a console covered in buttons and dials.

She looked down and saw the floor was covered in what looked like a black coloured rubber matting.

Although she couldn't see directly behind her Gabriella felt that was where the entrance to the room lay. She was proved right a few moments later when three men came into view. Two stood to the left of the table while the third went to the foot of the table and picked up some boxes, or cubes.

He placed three of the objects on a tubular rail which ran the length of the table, one by her head, one by her feet and one in the middle. As soon as the cubes were placed on the rail they began to glow.

Gabriella studied the three men, all of whom were about the same height, 5' 6" or 5' 8". Fair skinned and slim in build they wore the same garments. All wore a skull cap, tied at the back of the head and ending just above the eyes.

Face masks covered the nose and mouth, so only the eyes and facial parts around them were visible to Gabriella.

No hair was visible, but she could make out the hair bumps under the caps.

The eyes, more rounded than human eyes, seemed emotionless.

All three men wore a tunic with a grey coloured edging, long gloves that went to the elbows and very long aprons that fell as far as their ankles. Thick soled boots completed the picture. Every piece of clothing was the same colour - light blue. Throughout the episode, none of Gabriella's captors either spoke or made any other noise. They looked at each other frequently, and nodded occasionally. Furthermore they didn't appear to breathe, making no respiratory noises.

During the examination none of the three beings touched Gabriella. The examiner, the man at the bottom of the bed, took a number of grey coloured instruments, which he used one by one.

A small knife-like implement, was used to take a nail paring from her right hand index finger. A blood sample was taken with a small plastic-looking bottle with tubes and wires attached. A small device, which he held in the palm of his hand, was passed over the body and glowed with varying degrees of brightness depending on its location over Gabriella's form.

At one stage the examiner removed the blue blanket leaving her cold and embarrassed. A thin pencil-like device was used to prod and probe her and a large black rubber suction device was used on the area around her groin. Pushed firmly onto the skin and lifted again, this caused some discomfort for Gabriella, although the rest of the process was totally painless.

Gabriella's violent shivering attracted the attention of the examiner who then placed another blanket over her which provided badly needed extra warmth. She deemed the examination over when the man pulled the new black blanket over her entire body. Noticing her frequent glances towards the now inactive robot the examiner spoke to her in perfect English.

The robot was a trained retriever device, he said. It did all the manual work outside the ship. It brought specimens for examination and study. It was merely a non-thinking intelligence that was programmed to do certain tasks.

The examiner spoke with a deep male voice, although Gabriella could not see his mouth move beneath his mask. The examiner then removed the three glowing tubes from the rail. As he worked she noticed he had five digits on each hand, every movement looked practiced, deliberate and precise. His eyes never blinked, not even once.

When he completed his task all three men left the room together.

For several minutes Gabriella lay there. Further attempts to move were thwarted by the rubber bands at her wrists and ankles. When she tried to scream she found her throat too sore and painful and when she tried to vomit she couldn't.

She caught sight of the robot again. A flashing velvet coloured light flashed on it. It did not move but remained by the wall.

Gabriella's attention was caught by a movement behind her. One of the three men came into view from behind her and walked to the far end of the table.

He lifted the end of the blanket from the bottom and stared at her body. There was still no visible emotion in his eyes. The being stood, with the end of the blanket in one hand, his eyes boring into her.

Frightened, Gabriella sensed something horrible was about to happen. She struggled with her bonds frantically, but it was no good. The strong bands held her firmly to the table. The being took a small pin and placed it on her thigh. Gabriella stopped struggling immediately. The device caused a semi-paralysis, numbing everything apart from her head.

Rocking her head from side to side, Gabriella tried to scream, but her throat was too dry and sore. She tried to cry, but even that release was denied her.

The being climbed slowly onto the bottom of the bed. There was purpose in those cold emotionless eyes and she sensed there was evil in his heart.

"Oh my God," she thought. "He is raping me."

Gabriella didn't look, and couldn't move during the cold, calculating act of depravity. But she felt the being's every move. Praying to God for release, she felt sick at his cold alien touch.

But there was nothing she could do. The paralysis prevented her from fighting back. Feeling great discomfort, but no pain, Gabriella's mind drifted back to her sick friend in Wellington, her husband and her daughter. What would they think if they knew of this she thought to herself.

When the man had finished he slowly climbed off the tabled, pulled down the black blanket to totally cover her body and left the room.

Alone once again Gabriella became almost hysterical at the implications of what had just happened. Would she become pregnant? Would the child be a monster? How would she tell her husband?

The three men came into the room again, one removed the pin device from her thigh, while the other two lifted the blanket, folded it and placed it neatly on the floor by the console.

They removed the bands from her wrists and ankles and lifted her off the table. Gabriella looked down to see her clothes on the floor by the robot before passing out for the third time that night.

When she next gained consciousness Gabriella was standing, fully clothed, next to her car in the deserted country road. Dazed and shocked, she climbed in the vehicle, turned the ignition and to her surprise the engine started first time.

Gabriella did not remember the journey home. In a state of acute shock and looking ruffled and extremely upset she walked into her house at 2.30 am. An anxious Alberto held his distraught wife as she told him her sorry tale.

That night the Versacci's made a pact never to relate the story to anyone else. They would simply try to pick up the pieces and try to get on with their lives.

Four years later the Versacci's had managed to keep Gabriella's encounter out of the public eye, but hungry for knowledge she approached a UFO investigator who set about researching her case.

His verdict? Gabriella Versacci had nothing to gain and much to lose by seeking help over her encounter. She was found to be honest and trustworthy and her account consistent with many similar cases. In fact she was so concerned about the possible after-effects of the rape that she took a pregnancy test shortly afterwards. It proved negative.

Investigators noticed a series of amazing similarities between the Versacci case and that of police chief Jeff Greenhaw in the United States. His encounter came just one day after Gabriella's and the similarities between a *robot* he describes and the robot like figure which apprehended the British housewife appear too much for coincidence.

At about 10 pm on the night of October 17, 1973, 26 year old Greenhaw was the only full time police officer in the town of Falkville, Alabama.

He was off-duty and at home when a woman called in to say she had just seen a UFO with flashing lights land in a field to the west of the town. After a recent spate of sightings, Greenhaw picked up his camera and sped off in the direction of the reported sighting.

When he arrived at the location he made contact with the mystery intruder almost immediately. Standing in the middle of the road, it was wearing a silver suit, like tinfoil, said Greenhaw in his report.

He said the figure seemed tall and had something like an antenna on its head. After facing the entity for a few moments it began to approach him at which the police officer fired off four shots using a flash. The pictures, although blurred, show a figure moving towards the frightened officer.

Greenhaw raced to his patrol car and switched on the revolving light on its roof. The resulting flash of lights and noise of the siren caused the figure to turn and flee. Greenhaw claims to have given chase, but said the figure escaped at high speed over the rough gravelly road.

"He was running faster than any human I ever saw," said the policeman.

Greenhaw's much-publicised case may have given him instant fame. But it cost him his marriage, his wife abhorred the notoriety, his home which burned down mysteriously and his job. His police bosses thought his involvement with UFOs had damaged his credibility as a police officer.

The case was also tarnished by the suggestion that Greenhaw was involved in a hoax. However it would have been impossible for Mrs Versacci to have based her description of the robot in her encounter on the Greenhaw case.

She had no known links to Ufology outside of which the American case is virtually unknown. And she gave her description of the robot-like figure who *captured* her to her husband *before* the Greenhaw case occurred.

Investigators also agree that Mrs Versacci, a private woman, a respectable housewife and mother, would have no motive to concoct such an encounter story, particularly one in which she was the victim of a sexual assault of the most serious kind.

A religious woman, she was deeply affected by the alleged attack and to this day has refused to allow her real name to be connected to the report.

Jane Murphy (pseudonym)
March 1981
Birstall,
West Yorkshire.

Jane Murphy was asleep the minute her head hit the pillow. For the 22 year old housewife and mum of a baby daughter it had been another exhausting day. Husband Mick had climbed into bed as Jane tucked little Sharon cosily in her cot. She only just had the strength to get undressed and slip her nightie over her head before sliding between the covers.

But the sleep ended as quickly as it had come. Jane was awake but kept her eyes closed. For some reason she couldn't hear Mick's snores and the feel of the room was all wrong. When she opened her eyes Jane was standing in a field. She could feel the grass beneath her feet and looked up at a night sky heavy with cloud. It was cold but not uncomfortably so.

"I knew where I was," remembers Jane. "But I wasn't sure how I'd got there. I had the feeling that I had been led to this field near to where my mum lives. There was a farm I recognised but there was something over to one side that I hadn't seen before." The object hovering over the field was huge and metallic but Jane did not have time to study it. Her attention was caught by the movement of a group of figures, perhaps as many as ten.

The figures were vaguely humanoid, but for some reason

Jane could not focus on them. "They were just coming towards me," said Jane later. "One had a mask or a cloth in his hand and put it over my nose and mouth. I seemed to know they wanted to put me out so I pretended to be unconscious.

"But that didn't work. They seemed to know I was awake and two of them held me and one gave me some sort of injection. I assumed it was an injection because I felt the prick."

Jane blacked out.

When she came round the working class Yorkshire girl assumed she had been taken into the strange object by the *men* who had captured her.

"When I woke up I was on my hands and knees on this table in a strange room and I was really frightened. I just buried my head in my hands because I didn't want to look," recalled Jane. "I knew the figures were there but I didn't want to see them. Then they kept telling me to look at them. They weren't speaking, the words just came into my mind."

Fighting back the fear, Jane forced herself to look at her captors. The entity she faced was very tall, nearly seven feet, and human looking. Then Jane saw his eyes.

"They were black, totally black," she said. "Apart from that I would have said he was human. He didn't look like a monster, not by any means."

The young woman was then told she must bathe and they indicated a plastic looking object that looked nothing like a tub. Obediently Jane slipped off her nightie and sat in the *bath.*

"It just fitted around me, it was the same shape as my body, as if it was made for me," said Jane. "It didn't have any water in it but I went through the motions of washing and when I got out I was clean."

Jane was helped back on to the table in the centre of the room and now noticed that all but one of the humanoid figures had gone. The tall man who she had seen first remained with her.

Slowly the being moved towards Jane bringing his face close to hers.

"I just looked into his big black eyes and knew that it was going to happen," recalls Jane.

"Suddenly he was lying on the table and I was on top of him. We were sort of embracing, but lying very still. I remember noticing his smell. It wasn't very pleasant, not a human smell at all.

"Then we were having sex. It was the strangest sensation of all. We were lying together, not moving, but all the sensations of human sex were there. I looked at him, into his eyes and said *Why me?*

"The reply was strange because the idea came into my mind that he was saying *Because we love you,* but it was said coldly. There was no emotion there at all.

"I couldn't even tell you if he had any clothes on or not because I simply looked into his eyes. All I remember visually is those gigantic black eyes.

"I didn't think about it as a physical act. I can't say that I was conscious of his penis, because I wasn't, but inside, inside me it was all happening.

"I believe I came to a climax because at the time I felt it was the best sex that I had ever had. It seemed so strange lying on top of this stranger, not moving yet having sex and enjoying it."

After about five minutes Jane realised others had now entered the room. The newcomers included female humanoids. Her sex partner climbed off the table and left the room, while the remaining humanoids prepared Jane for an examination.

Some of the examiners appeared to use long instruments for what was obviously a gynaecological examination of the young human.

Jane felt no pain or major discomfort and after the examination was taken on a tour of the strange craft.

She was shown a table covered with a number of brightly coloured pills in geometric shapes. She was invited to try one and did so. But when she later tried to take a drink from a cup she had seen an alien using, a powerful tele-pathic message told her to stop.

"I don't remember much of my tour of the ship but I do remember seeing other humans," she recalls.

Jane's visit ended as abruptly as it had begun.

She suddenly found herself back in bed, the alarm clock said it was 6.28 pm, nearly time for Mick to set off for work.

Could it all have been a dream? Jane asked herself. Then she remembered the injection and looked at her arm. The skin was still slightly bruised around the tiny puncture mark made by the needle.

"I had a strong desire to bathe," recalls Jane. "I remember thinking I must wash otherwise I would have that bad smell clinging to me, the alien smell."

Then as she climbed into the bath Jane felt a heaviness in her stomach, the sort of heaviness she remembered from pregnancy.

That sensation was the beginning of a series of odd events that followed her encounter. First her menstrual cycle stopped completely, something which her doctor could not explain. Then she was referred to hospital for tests follow-ing her continued complaints about the heaviness in her stomach. Doctors gave her the all clear.

Finally she was plagued for three months with a vaginal complaint that doctors diagnosed as an *infection*. Fearful that it may have been associated with the alien she had sex with, Jane tried one course of antibiotics after another without success. Once again her GP referred her to a hospi-tal. This time a powerful course of tablets did the trick.

But although the medical after-effects of her encounter had now abated, Jane's life had changed beyond recogni-tion. Within months her alien captors were back.

"They were here in the house," explained Jane. "I don't know how they got in, but there was a man and a woman. They were just like the people I saw on the craft.

They began pumping the girl for information, data. She must tell them all she knew. "They wanted to know how babies were born," said Jane. "It was ridiculous. I told them. Everybody knew about babies I said. But they said their people didn't."

That was just the beginning of a series of visitations that drove Jane to the edge of a nervous breakdown. She would wake in the night to find one or more of the alien visitors standing by her bed or wake in the morning and somehow *know* she had been somewhere else in the night. Then the dreams started. Strange dreams about being pregnant and giving birth. All the dreams had an alien involvement and in one she dreamed of giving birth to a blond, black eyed alien hybrid.

"I don't know if I was on the spaceship," she said. "But I had the baby and it was blond and had its eyes closed. Then I looked again and he opened his eyes and they were black, like the aliens."

Jane's abduction and the stress of innumerable further visits put a strain on her relationship with her husband. He told her he did not believe that she had experienced these events.

"At one stage I thought I was going mad," said Jane. "I didn't want these things to happen to me, but they did. I just wanted to be normal."

In desperation Jane sought help from the family doctor. "Are you an LSD user?" he asked. Jane gave up. She did not believe she was hallucinating, yet a drug induced hallucination was the only explanation that occurred to her GP.

In July 1987 Jane's local paper carried an article about the British UFO Research Association's UFO Hotline, a 24 hour telephone service for witnesses to report sightings.

It was Jane's last chance, she thought, as she dialled the number and left her message on the answer phone.

Within days, the association's director of investigations, Philip Mantle became involved. The series of interviews that followed were enough to convince investigators that Jane was not a hoaxer. There was an element of contamination in view of the fact that she had read a number of abduction books after her encounter, but not enough to enable her to fabricate the entire episode.

What stunned investigators was the sheer number of alleged alien visits Jane recorded since her abduction encounter, which they estimated at more than 100.

In fact they worked out that Jane had her first UFO experience when she was just 16 years old. At the time Jane was living with her mother near Leeds. Lying in bed one night, she heard a loud whirring noise and watched as her room was flooded by a bright red light. The following day she heard radio reports about a spate of UFO sightings in the area and connected them with the strange experience in her bedroom.

But that was only a prelude to her alleged abduction and the many alleged follow up visits.

"I've been taken out many times by the aliens," recalls Jane. "Out into the fields or sometimes for examinations. Then other times I've had the dreams of being pregnant and once giving birth to this baby that had blond hair and alien eyes."

Jane's accounts were so close to those of one of the witnesses in the Budd Hopkins book *Intruders* that British investigators liaised with the American researcher. He was interested in gathering as much detail as possible.

Jane's dream about giving birth was also reminiscent of the *Wise Baby Dreams* that Hopkins refers to in his works.

Psychologist Dr John Shaw studied the Jane Murphy case and made the following observation: "The most predominant effect on Jane seems to be a strong feeling of incomprehension. As she says in the transcript, *I'd like to know what they want from me and why it's been happening for all these years.*

"The human drive to make sense of one's experiences is being greatly frustrated in Jane's case. This is not helped by the fact that she is a fairly unreflective individual, not given to close examination, it would appear, of her emotional and cognitive reactions.

"Trying to make sense of strange happenings is not all that unusual an occurrence. However this cannot usually be done without skilled help. This case underlines the need for a special kind of victim support system, either self-help groups, or one to one counselling or therapy.

"People like Jane have a desperate need to release their fears and be helped to develop a cognitive framework by which to understand what has happened to them.

"Victims need not stay victims. They can become wise as a result of their traumas."

Jane's visitations are less frequent today and she is less willing to talk about them. "I can't understand it so I try to put it behind me," she said.

Ted Johnson
September 27, 1985
Terling
Essex.

Part Romany, Ted Johnson has a lifetime full of strange experiences, precognition, UFO sightings and parapsychological events. But a bizarre episode in the countryside outside the village of Terling in Essex had investigators flocking to hear his account.

In his late 30s, Ted had reported many UFO sightings in and around his home in Witham, Essex, but nothing as outlandish as an encounter on a quiet country road.

Ted claimed that encounter led him to have sex with a female alien entity. As unlikely as it may sound, the experts soon had their files out to see if there were any comparisons to be found with Ufology's famous Antonio Villas Boas case in which a Brazilian cowboy claimed sex with a female alien.

Although the location was not as exotic as the South American one, Ted's claims were no less graphic.

"I saw a light in the distance and heard a low whistling sound," said Ted, who had been walking along a deserted section of country road at about 11 in the morning.

"The light became so bright it hurt my eyes and gave me a headache. The next thing I know, a green light hits me in the chest, knocking me to the ground and partly blinding me."

As he dragged himself up Ted noticed a strangely dressed woman approaching him. "She seemed to be signalling me to stay put, then she walked towards me. She was wearing a green-mesh garment and I could swear she seemed to glow."

Ted said the woman had large eyes with no apparent eyelids, a small nose and a slit instead of a mouth. Behind her he could see a strange object hovering in the field where other shapes were moving about.

"They seemed humanoid, but not human. They wore what looked like boxes over their stomachs," recalled Ted.

As the female neared him she told him to follow her. Ted did as he was told and was soon inside the strange craft he had seen hovering over the field. He then claimed he had sex with the female.

"She was naked and we had sexual intercourse. It was no different to human sex."

Two days later Ted claimed to be in the same area again. He saw what he described as a *UFO* landing in a field. Drawn to the object he was allowed to enter the craft where he again met the alien he had been intimate with two days previously.

"The spaceship took off and the female alien said *You have found your way back to me"*, recalled Ted. "We had sexual intercourse again and then I was allowed to return to my home."

Ted's story was picked up by renowned British investigator Ken Phillips who concluded: "This case is complicated and baffling. We have here a witness who has experienced a lifetime of phenomena, of which UFO incidents are merely a part.

"It would be easy to dismiss the whole case as nothing but the product of an over-active imagination. But there is the fact that some of his UFO experiences were shared by third parties, some of whom were independent of his domestic environment."

Considering all the information, Ken Phillips believed the phenomenon was *worthy of study*.

But was Ted's account one of abduction?

On the first occasion he willingly accompanied the female alien to her craft. He gave no indication that the craft moved. However on the second occasion he states quite clearly that the UFO took off.

What about the *Villas Boas* case? Back in 1957 the 23 year old cowhand was out late at night ploughing his own field near Sao Francisco de Sales.

After spotting a mysterious bright light in the sky Antonio's tractor broke down. The *light* he had seen descended to earth and landed in the shape of a UFO.

A group of small men disembarked and proceeded to capture Antonio and forced him aboard their craft.

The young man told investigators that once inside he was introduced to a red haired woman with high cheekbones and Oriental looking eyes. The woman made her intentions obvious and Antonio had sex with her.

Before parting the alien female looked at Antonio, then rubbed her stomach and then pointed to the sky. Back in 1957 the Antonio Villas Boas case was thought to be so outrageous that it was kept under wraps for a number of years.

Did Ted Johnson and Antonio Villas Boas enjoy the favours of women from the stars? Or were their stories pure fantasy concocted to keep the guys entertained at the bar?

Is this a case of sexism in Ufology? If a woman confesses to a night of passion with an alien visitor she risks being branded an intergalactic tart. While a man who boasts of his extra-terrestrial conquests is just one of the boys. But why would anyone expose themselves to the sort of ridicule these accounts would attract? Surely when ordinary people come forward with accounts like these they should be investigated.

CHAPTER 12
And Stranger Still . . .

Whatever the cause, whoever the victim, it is the strangeness of Alien Abduction phenomena which sets them apart from almost every other human experience. In fact, investigators give abduction reports a strangeness value ranging from low to high - the higher the strangeness value, the more difficult it is to explain the reported events.

As one investigator said: "If someone reports seeing a strange light in the sky you know that the likelihood is that he's seen a satellite, a planet or maybe even an aircraft. His strange light is unlikely to be strange to people who are familiar with the sky.

"On the other hand if someone reports seeing a UFO which beams them up inside the craft where they engage in telepathic conversation with a group of ETs then the strangeness value goes sky high. If the abductee is sane and credible, or if there was more than one witness the event is not easily explained away . . . unless you opt for mass hallucination which is a convenient, if unconvincing, explanation for the committed sceptic."

To any newcomer to Ufology and Abduction Phenomena the accounts recorded so far in this book will seem strange enough, but to Eric Morris of the British UFO Studies Centre in Winsford, Cheshire, High Strangeness abductions are becoming more common thanks to a growing army of amateur investigators willing to offer a sympathetic ear to victims of alien abductions.

"Abduction reports come in all the time and these days people are more willing to talk about their experiences than when I started my work more than 20 years ago, when folk were likely to become victims of ridicule," said Eric.

"Thanks to a more open minded attitude in society as a whole, abductees can now be persuaded to relate the detail of their experiences. However an investigator must possess a considerable level of social skills to first put the witness at ease and then win his or her trust. Once that trust is established you can then go forward together to analyse the details of abduction events providing a mass of new material for the cause of Ufology and at the same time enabling the abductee to come to terms with his or her experience."

Eric and his wife Linda are adept at dealing with people who find themselves in situations of crisis thanks to their mainstream careers as nurses. Perhaps that is why they have catalogued hundreds of cases including a great many abductions.

Abductees who go to the British UFO Studies Centre for counselling soon learn to trust Eric and Linda. They know that their meetings are totally confidential and they find that Eric's wealth of experience in dealing with abductees helps them to put their particular experience into some context.

Eric has provided us with the case-file on Suzanne Brown, one of his most outstanding abduction investigations, for consideration in this the final chapter of our book. Like the other two cases in this section, it is a *high strangeness abduction* which adds weight to the Genetic Harvesting theories of Budd Hopkins.

Linda was heavily involved in the Suzanne Brown investigation because of the intimate nature of the case.

She said: "The experiences Suzanne endured were truly traumatic and we felt that it was important for a woman to be involved when probing this sort of area.

"This would be a delicate subject for any woman to discuss so it made sense for me to take part. Suzanne knew that another woman would understand the emotional impact the events had on her."

Eric added: "Happily Suzanne's alien visitations have now stopped and the fact that they ceased as she approached the menopause seems to be far more than coincidence.

Could it be that her value to the alien visitors plummeted when she reached the end of her childbearing years?

High Strangeness, Genetic Harvesting and Alien Abduction!

Now read on and consider for yourselves the experiences of three remarkable women.

Suzanne Brown
Events between 1965 - 1989
Cheshire

Suzanne Brown felt Myriko's presence even before she opened her tired and heavy eyes to peer through the gloom to make out his slight five feet tall body standing by the side of her bed.

Even after all these years his pure beauty stunned her. Myriko smiled and gazed into Suzanne's eyes. As always he was perfectly groomed, with the flowing long blond hair which framed his slightly overlarge head sweeping down to his shoulders. He wore the same skin-tight membrane-like grey suit he always had, smooth and spotless.

Myriko's numerous night-time visits had begun when she was just a child of 12, so by now his effect on her was almost predictable. She felt warm and calm, no trace of fear . . . just love. Those feelings had never changed despite the years that had passed since he made his debut in the bedroom of her parent's home in rural north Cheshire close to the Welsh border.

Now a mature woman in her late 30s, with a successful career in a major department store and her own comfortable home, Suzanne still felt a tingle of anticipation. Even before his telepathic words formed in her mind, Suzanne knew that Myriko was taking her out again.

These night-time expeditions now followed a pattern, a routine which had begun years ago when she had followed her strange companion into the cold and darkness of the Cheshire countryside.

That first time she had been a teenager and had become excited at the discovery that she was floating inches above the ground as she followed Myriko across the fields near to her home. She would never forget her first sighting of the craft she saw floating perhaps two feet above the field.

Myriko had led the way through the entrance, along a seemingly endless dark corridor to a brightly-lit door. He seemed to be urging Suzanne to step forward to see what was inside. But the door seemed impassable. There were no handles, no hinges.

Suzanne felt confused as she floated inches above the floor, facing an implacable sheet of metal through which her companion was now insisting she should pass.

Suddenly she felt herself being propelled forward and passed through the portal into a massive room in which a group of three feet high, grey entities were gathered. They seemed to have been waiting for her.

One of the beings beckoned to her and led Suzanne to a small group of smaller entities whom she assumed were infants of the same race. The tiny grey figures gathered around her giving her the opportunity to note how they were simply miniature versions of the beings who had greeted her when she came through the portal.

Suzanne stretched out her right hand, to touch the infants and when her fingers made contact with the *alien skin* she was overwhelmed with a feeling of immense satisfaction. The beings were telling her she had done well.

Myriko was back at her side within minutes, urging her to follow him as he retraced their steps into the corridor, out into the fields and back to Suzanne's bedroom.

That was just the first of many expeditions with Myriko.

Over the following twenty years or so he returned twice, sometimes three times a year, to take her out to the craft. Each time he would lead her to a portal and almost challenge her to go through.

Sometimes she would find herself again with the curious little grey infants who never seemed to change or grow up. At other times she would be confronted by scenes which disturbed her, like the time she entered a room full of TV screens showing images of animals being mutilated.

The stories into the darkness even continued during the years when Suzanne was married and lived with her husband. Myriko would arrive as always and beckon her to follow him while her husband slept on.

Tonight though, Suzanne was alone following the failure of her marriage.

As she followed Myriko out of her home she pondered on the factors that contributed to their separation and eventual divorce.

Of course, their fruitless attempts to conceive a child played a part but what about her obsession with Myriko?

She admitted, to herself at least, that she had felt a stronger love for her mystery visitor than for the man she married. So much so that she had even fantasised about him while making love to her husband in the marital bed.

In fact, Myriko had started making his visits when Suzanne was in the throes of puberty and she had to concede that even then there had been a sexual element to her excitement at seeing him.

And now she was with him again.

"What is he going to show me this time?" she whispered the words to herself as the craft came into view.

As always the pair floated in through the entrance and along the never ending dark corridor until Myriko stopped at one of the illuminated portals. He looked into her eyes issuing the non-verbal challenge he always had and this time Suzanne did not hesitate to pass through.

The scene that greeted her was indeed different.

At the far end of a huge room, separated from her by what looked like a swimming pool filled with a green coloured liquid, were two people, a man and a woman.

They were definitely human. In fact the only thing alien about them was their apparent lifestyles.

The man looked like a vagrant: unwashed, unshaven and wearing filthy clothing. The woman looked like a prostitute. Bleached blonde hair, heavily made-up with a garish red lipstick and wearing a cheap and skimpy outfit that left little to the imagination.

"They looked shocked to see me," Suzanne told investigator Eric Morris months after the incident. "But then they began to kiss and fondle. I was horrified and disgusted."

Despite her revulsion, Suzanne felt compelled to watch the display.

Long minutes passed and gradually her disgust turned to

209

curiosity as her eyes and mind became focused on this overtly sexual performance.

Transfixed to the spot, Suzanne lost track of time as she took in the scene before her. The longer she looked at the couple the more engrossed she became in their activities until she reached the stage where she became engulfed in an atmosphere of lust.

Finding herself aroused, she responded immediately when the couple beckoned for her to join them. Suddenly realising that she was now naked, the night dress she had on when she left her house had disappeared, and she stepped into the pool and proceeded to wade through the thigh-deep liquid.

Half way across she completely immersed herself in the strange solution, obeying a telepathic instruction which told her she must.

By the time she reached the couple, any reservations about joining them in their debauchery had been replaced by an enthusiasm which was totally out of character for her.

Suzanne was aware of having sexual intercourse with the man and what's more she was enjoying it.

"It was me having sex with a stranger, but it wasn't the real me. I was there, getting involved with these two awful people. It was my body but not my mind.

"Calling it a nightmare would be the easy way out but the fact is that it was real, no dream." recalled Suzanne later.

By the time Myriko beckoned Suzanne to join him at the other side of the pool, the enormity of her actions were only just beginning to dawn on her. As she waded back through the green liquid her mind dwelled on the traumatic events that were over in moments, but which would stay with her for the rest of her life.

Those events were particularly traumatic for a woman who had been raised in a tradition of Middle Class morality and to whom promiscuity was merely a word in the dictionary.

When she reached Myriko he seemed normal, in no way upset at her behaviour which he must have witnessed.

Suzanne followed him as he led the way back along the corridor and out of the craft. They didn't communicate until she was safely back in her own bedroom.

Finally Myriko turned to her and smiled.

"You have done well," he said. "You have fulfilled my wishes."

Suzanne was too stunned by his reaction to say anything and watched in silence as her visitor took his leave.

She slept little that night, agonising over her actions. Throughout her life she had only one sexual partner, her husband. She was a normal decent woman who lived by a moral code which she believed in. Yet in a few short minutes she had abandoned her previous standards and behaved like a slut. Now she would have to learn to live with the shame.

When she woke the following morning, Suzanne remembered the previous night's events with renewed revulsion. Suddenly it dawned on her that neither she nor the man she had been intimate with had taken any contraceptive precautions.

Overwhelmed by a desire to cleanse herself she ran a bath, climbed into the steaming water and began to scrub her body from head to toe.

In the days that followed Suzanne's shame was replaced by the fear that she may have contracted a sexually transmitted disease from the stranger on the craft or worse, that he had made her pregnant. She spent hours in the bath tub examining herself, watching for any early signs of pregnancy.

Then when she began her next period a few days earlier than expected she breathed a huge sigh of relief.

Pregnancy would have been the worst possible scenario.

Life gradually began to return to normal for Suzanne. She went back to work at the department store and busied herself with the usual chores and tried not to think of her night of shame.

But the nightmare returned with a vengeance the following month. Suzanne missed her period.

"Maybe I'm just late", she told herself hopefully. But as

each day went by she knew the chances of her cycle being this late were slim.

The prospect of motherhood following a few moments of lust with a disgusting vagrant reinforced her feelings of revulsion. And they got worse as the first signs of pregnancy became evident.

Suzanne tried to get on with her life. She went to work, hoping none of her colleagues would notice the slight changes in her body and then raced home to the sanctuary of her own lounge where her mind would wrestle with the events of that night and the possible repercussions in the future.

What made matters worse was that she felt so isolated. The bizarre nature of her nocturnal expeditions with Myriko meant that she could not discuss them with anybody, not even her parents. So how was she going to explain her pregnancy to them when it became glaringly obvious that she was in the family way?

The loneliness of this nightmare was unbearable.

Where was Myriko when she needed him?

Weeks later Suzanne found herself trying to relax with a book on the settee in her lounge when she began to feel drowsy. The room seemed to darken as a heavy pressure bore down on her lower abdomen.

"The pressure was crushing and becoming very painful," said Suzanne later. "I opened my eyes and there was Myriko."

Myriko's telepathic words calmed and soothed Suzanne so much that the pain she had been resisting seemed to ebb away. He told her that she had completed the work she had been chosen to undertake and now his colleagues were carrying out the final task. They were merely taking away what was theirs, he said.

Suzanne then lost consciousness and when she came to, some hours later, found herself lying on her settee. She clutched at her stomach in reaction to the pain that gripped her abdomen. Slowly, she got to her feet and managed to make her way, unsteadily, to her bathroom where she began to undress.

Her clothes were soaking in blood and Suzanne could see she had very heavy vaginal bleeding, the type associated with miscarriage. Vicious cramping pains stabbed at her stomach but she resisted the temptation to call her doctor.

Instead she washed, swallowed some painkillers and went to bed.

Suzanne spent the following three days drifting in and out of sleep until the pain eventually subsided. On the fourth day she noticed bruising on her lower abdomen.

By the time she returned to work Suzanne was aware that the early signs of pregnancy she had discovered had ceased - another sign of termination of pregnancy. But she was unwilling to speculate on what really happened on the night of Myriko's last visit.

She threw herself back into her work routine and her life returned to normal.

Months later Myriko returned and invited Suzanne for another trip to the craft. Obediently she followed him out into the nearby fields where the craft was waiting.

But the similarity to previous adventures ended when they were met by a small group of excited grey entities who seemed intent on congratulating Suzanne.

Myriko led the way along the corridor to a portal through which Suzanne readily passed. Once inside she found herself in what she later described as *a nursery.* She could see infant entities of various sizes, and possibly ages, being cared for by a group of adult beings.

She suddenly stopped when she glimpsed a tiny, listless infant entity lying in a nearby cot and froze.

"Somehow I knew that thing had come from my body," explained Suzanne later. "I also knew that it had been removed from inside my body on the night of Myriko's last visit when I suffered heavy vaginal bleeding."

She resisted the impulse to pick up the infant and cradle it in her arms, fearing she might hurt it. The tiny creature, grey and silent, looked sick.

But an adult being nearby, recognising the mother-baby bond encouraged Suzanne to take the infant in her arms.

As she gently picked up the cold and rigid little body she felt it was responding to her warmth and as she looked into her alien baby's eyes tears began to stream down her cheeks.

The adult entity came closer and took the tiny bundle from Suzanne explaining that it was not at all sick and that this infant, whom she would see again, would live to a very great age.

Myriko returned to escort Suzanne back to her home. Before he disappeared he congratulated her, confirming that the infant was indeed her own.

That night Suzanne slept more peacefully than she had for years. She dreamed of babies and children and the following day the trauma of her sexual encounter with the vagrant and the pain she endured later somehow seemed worthwhile.

Suzanne Brown last saw her infant several years ago during Myriko's final visit when she was 39 years old. Since entering her menopausal years her nocturnal visitor has been conspicuous by his absence.

Investigator Eric Morris feels that the series of encounters experienced by Suzanne, stretching from puberty to menopause, supports the views of theorists like Budd Hopkins who are convinced that Genetic Harvesting is going on.

But Suzanne Brown is not interested in the Ufological arguments. She suffered a very personal trauma, and the memories of those events will stay with her for the rest of her life.

Today she continues with her career and lives with her new partner, content to live a life that at last is normal.

Sarah Ward
Bracknell,
Berks.
March 1993 - October 1995.

Sarah Ward had been reading until about 2 am that night
in early March 1993. Sleep had never come easily to her, so
when she put down her book and lay back in the bed of her
first floor flat she allowed her gaze to linger on the reflec-
tions of the orange street lights on her bedroom wall.

Suddenly she became conscious of a noise that seemed to
come from the street beyond her bedroom window. The
deep constant hum reminded her of the sound made by an
electricity substation transformer. Low and constant.

"It was the sort of low frequency humming you feel in
your body as well as hearing with your ears. It made me
feel sick, nauseous," said Sarah. "Everything seemed to be
vibrating, the structure of the building. The vibration affected my tummy, my middle body."

Sarah at first assumed somebody had left a vehicle engine running in the road outside. She wasn't sure how long
the sound had been there but hoped that whoever it was
would go away soon.

"It felt and sounded like a big lorry," she recalled. "I felt
really pissed off."

The vibration and the noise was making sleep impossible.
The thrum of what sounded like a big engine seemed to get
into Sarah's head. She had to do something. Exasperated
she climbed out of bed and crept to the window suddenly
aware of the chill in the air.

I think it was the cold that made me reluctant to get out
of bed, but the noise was so awful that I wanted to see who
was making it."

Sarah was naked and did not want to reveal herself to
whoever was out there so at first she stood away from the
window, peering out to see if she could spot the culprit. The
road was deserted.

"I moved up closer to the window," said Sarah. "There

was nothing there, nothing moving. I had this otherworldly sensation. This strange sense that everything all around was different. As if I was inside a high energy field. It was unreal, but I was not sleeping. I was wide awake."

Cautiously Sarah moved closer to the window pane. Looking down the road, illuminated only by the street lights, she could see it was deserted. No lorry, no vehicles of any kind and not a soul in sight.

"Suddenly something caught my eye," she remembered. "It was right above me. This massive structured disc-shaped object, directly above my apartment. Only one half was visible, the remainder being hidden behind the building. There are no words to describe how shocking this sight was, totally unexpected."

About 80 feet above the four-storey apartment block, the object hovered motionless, its mass obscuring a large section of the cloudy, starless sky.

Sarah, a qualified pilot, quickly gauged the dimensions of the UFO, her trained pilot's eyes taking in the form and geometry of the huge craft which she estimated must be similar in size to a Boeing 747, which measures 230 feet from nose to tail.

"I could only see the underside of the object from my vantage point but there was a central dome, convex, from which ribs or girders radiated out to the rim," said Sarah. "It was a work of art. I could not look away from it. It was stunning. It was the most beautiful thing I had ever seen. I wanted to run away yet was strangely drawn to it, compelled to look at its beauty. It was fantastically structured and detailed. I felt a sense of awe, tinged strongly with fear, that I may be seen by the occupants of the object and I felt an overwhelming awareness of my vulnerability as I stood at the window.

"I couldn't stop staring up at it. I didn't once doubt that I was seeing some huge alien craft. It seemed to be radiating light, mainly white and sparkling silver. I also saw a sort of electric blue hue surrounding the metallic-looking outer rim of the disc.

"I recall small areas of coloured light along the edge of the rim. The lights were not in any one place. They were blue and red and very vague. They seemed to pulse around the rim like coloured bits of mist. The sparkling silver effect of the surface gave it the appearance of being not quite solid, more like the surface of mercury. It was quite unlike the aluminium of an aircraft. It's shining surfaces did not reflect the street lights. Although it had an aura it did not throw light onto the ground. If I had not looked up, directly at it, I would not have known it was there.

"The low frequency humming was now quite loud and still making me feel sick. I couldn't understand how no one else was aware of it. I seemed to be the only one awake in the street and I felt so alone with this thing. There was an almost unnatural deadness about the street scene before me as if the street were under some sort of energy damping field. I must have looked out on that scene for about ten seconds, but it was the longest ten seconds you could imagine.

"I remember saying to myself: *Oh, shit. I just can't believe this.* I was very frightened. Standing there looking up at it awkwardly had left my neck hurting."

Sarah was then overcome by the impulse to flee. She wanted to run away from the window and hide under the kitchen table.

Terrified she began to back away from the window feeling as if *they* could somehow see her.

Suddenly a beam of light sprung from the underside of the craft and hit her head-on.

"I was paralysed instantly," said Sarah. "The beam of light, or maybe it was energy, was between one half and one metre in diameter. It shot out from the craft and hit me in my body. After that I could only move my eyes."

The coldness of the room she was standing in suddenly disappeared. Her terror began to subside.

"It was as if someone had reached in and tweaked a part of my brain," said Sarah. "All of a sudden my body was no longer responsive. I was physically restrained and emotionally gagged."

217

Sarah felt herself being slowly and inexorably lifted off the ground before being propelled towards the giant object.

"I passed through the windows as if they were not there, as if they were merely a mirage. My head was fixed so my eyes could only look forward, at my destination, the craft. Upwards I went, closer and closer. I could see where the beam had come from on the bottom of the craft and I remember thinking that unlike a spotlight, the beam had a constant diameter from the craft to my room. Soon I was passing through the underside of the object and I felt my feet in contact with a floor, which I believed was the other side of the point from where the beam had originated."

Still physically immobilised Sarah found herself standing on a metal-like floor in a large room.

"I was still naked so I thought I should feel the cold or at least feel the cold of the floor under my feet," said Sarah.

"But I didn't feel at all cold and hadn't since I had been hit by the beam. I was inside what I thought was the craft's control room. It was brightly lit but not dazzlingly so. There was no visible light source and no shadows either.

"Because of my immobility, my field of vision was limited. But ahead of me were what looked like technological control-type consoles along the two walls visible to me. Behind the console directly in front of me was a large curving wall with the curves convex in relation to my position. The wall and consoles were all a white or greyish white.

"To my left and just out of easy view was another console, slightly different to the one ahead of me. I felt that the curved wall may have been the inner part of the dome that I had seen in the centre lower area of the disc."

The four beings that confronted Sarah completed the alien picture.

"I saw several humanoids. Two were standing near the console ahead of me and they were watching me. This left me feeling ill at ease. One was standing by the console to the left and seemed to take no part in my experience. The fourth was standing within a metre of me and was looking at me and apparently waiting for something."

Sarah described the entities as small or childlike, similar in size to a ten year old youngster. They were slightly built, with large, balloon like heads. There were no features on the face apart from overlarge black eyes and a tiny slit-like mouth.

"I saw no ears or hair," recalled Sarah. "I saw no sign of a nose and their tiny mouths, if that is what they were, never moved or opened. The mouths were so small they could have been painted on. Their heads seemed too big for their torsos. They were balloon or pear shaped. The arms were overlong and very thin with no hands, as such, just three digits. The legs looked similar with tiny or non-existent feet. They were all dressed in what seemed like seamless one-piece overalls and the feet were part of the suit itself. The suits were of a silvery material which seemed like thin plastic or tin foil. They looked like they could have been sprayed on."

Sarah described the four feet tall creatures as having skins which were a light grey in colour.

The big black eyes of the bipeds dominated their smooth and featureless faces and had an almost hypnotic effect on Sarah.

"I was transfixed by the eyes of the entity closest to me," she said. "He never took his eyes off me for a moment. I call him a *he* yet the entities were sexless. There were no signs of any genitalia. The white-grey walls, the lights and everything, it could have been heaven-like if the entities had not looked like creatures from *hell*.

"I was feeling very disorientated, not frightened, but jumpy . . . like a horse that has been spooked. I was thinking *I've got to do something . . . but it's too late.* I kept asking myself *what the hell is happening?* I was inside some sort of discoid vehicle and I knew I was without any control over the situation."

Sarah snapped out of her brief reverie and concentrated on the proximity of the closest entity.

"This being was an arms length from me," she recalled. "Too damn close, invading my space but there was no aggression there. I don't think they have aggression in their make up. The threat was in my mind . . . but it also seemed to be in the creature's eyes. It wasn't just another life form trying to out-stare me. It was like all-knowing.

"The discomfort I felt was not because of the eyes themselves but a subliminal recognition that this creature was really inside my head and knew everything about me. It was invading my personality. It was like rape. You couldn't stop it. Your privacy had gone."

Drowning in the black depths of the strange creature's huge eyes Sarah suddenly knew it had opened up a line of communication.

"It was talking to me, not with its mouth, but with it's mind," she said. "I couldn't understand a word but I knew it was saying things, patronising things, as though it were talking to a child. Then I somehow knew it was telling me *don't worry*. I was still dazed, astonished by everything that had happened. I suppose I wasn't really taking in what it was communicating. Then it took a different tone. It was putting across what it intended for me. I was somehow understanding it in English although what it was putting across had nothing to do with the English language.

"I felt like a child being spoken to by a primary school teacher. It was telling me to pay attention and watch. As if it was going to tell me the serious stuff now. It wasn't asking for my attention, it was like a command."

At this point the two entities in the background who had been positioned by the console began moving their arms over the alien array. One passed one of his arms over the fascia which was devoid of the knobs, dials and protrusions that might be associated with a control board of terrestrial origins.

"I remember seeing that very thin arm move, the being was so thin I thought it looked anorexic in a big way," said Sarah. "The sudden burst of activity seemed to confirm my feeling that this was a control room, but controlling what, I don't know."

Suddenly the top section of the long console-like object burst into life. At first Sarah thought some TV screens had been switched on.

But they were not TV screens in any accepted sense. They each displayed a view, in sequence, but a view in three dimensions and in full colour.

"A fog developed several inches in front of the screen and images formed within it," explained Sarah. "I don't know if you would call it a hologram but it was in full three dimensional colour and the images had solidity and depth. One screen would show a series of images from my past then switch off, so to speak, and then another screen would take over.

"The scenes I saw were an aggregate of images from my life. The first one showed images of me as a small child when I went through a stage of having particularly bad waking nightmares. I would wake up and see small people coming into my room and taking me away. They used to frighten the life out of me. I would tell my mother and she would comfort me and tell me they were just dreams. I would feel hurt that my mother didn't believe what I had seen.

"The images I was seeing in that first screen were from that period and I felt that the entity closest to me was telling me that the images I would see were important in my development. The being was like a conductor, orchestrating the whole procedure and that the entities at the console were merely doing what they had been told to do.

"Somewhere at this point I had this overwhelming feeling that this being, the conductor, knew me. I was familiar to him as if I had been there before.

"The first screen finished and then the next screen carried on, displaying images from my past. The conductor-being seemed to be commentating on the images, pointing out what they all had in common. It was if he was lecturing me, his telepathy overlaying the visual images.

"I remember that seeing that first screen made me see how my mother's refusal to accept the reality of those bad dreams which I had as a three, four and five year old, destroyed my trust in the establishment. It was obvious that those *in charge* didn't have all the answers.

221

"That experience made me grow into a more self reliant person. The images shown to me in screens two to four were equally subtle but I remember thinking that I didn't want to look at scenes from my past life. I just wasn't interested. I think I was also quite frightened at seeing myself as a child being terrified by those night-time visitors. Floating little men with big heads that had a striking resemblance to the beings who had just taken me out of my bedroom."

Sarah wanted to turn away from the screens, but could not. Her captors were insistent she observed.

"I felt their attitude was *You are going to listen to this, pay attention, concentrate.*"

When the fourth screen went dark Sarah heard the being *speaking* to her again.

"He said *The next image we are going to show you is not of the past but of the future.* He was completely dispassionate to the point that I felt I was being treated brutally. He was riding roughshod over my feelings, as if I did not have any. As if my reaction was of no consequence."

Sarah then watched the images develop on the fifth and final screen above the console. She saw herself walking down a path which she recognised as being not far from her flat. She could see it was an early or late summer's day and she looked very much like her present self. If this was a scene from the future, then it must be the very near future.

"For the first time I took my eyes completely off the alien. I was swept into the image. I was not simply observing. I was now a part of the image and I was walking down the path and I could see a tall, thin man ahead of me, with a couple of kids. I remember thinking *I'm free, what the hell is going on?* I can feel the sun on my body yet I am actually inside a flying saucer that is hovering over my apartment.

"It was bizarre. I was inside a 3-D image yet I knew I was really inside a UFO. The irony of accepting the reality of a UFO and not a 3-D image is really quite striking. Yet for all intents and purposes I was very much a part of this image.

"I was walking down this path, getting closer to this un-shaven man in his 30s and wearing an old coat. I could see he was pulling a young boy by the arm. The child was about three. A young girl, older than the boy, was pulling the child's other arm. I realised she was trying to pull the boy away from the man, and seemed distressed.

"Suddenly I became irritated. I thought *this kid is being abducted.* I got closer then put my fingernails into this man's eyes and started to pull his head back. The boy needed help. He needed to get away and this was the only thing I could think of.

"The next thing, the man let go of the boy, wheeled around and grabbed me by the hair. He yanked my head back with some force and pulled me around in front of him. It was so realistic. I could feel my fingernails going into him and felt the pain of having my hair pulled so viciously.

"Then with his free hand, the man reached into his coat and pulled out a great knife and stabbed me in my stomach. He just plunged the knife deep into my stomach and sort of twisted the blade up. It was like an electric shock. Suddenly I couldn't feel my body and I just flopped to the ground. Next I was looking down at myself. My dress was torn and I was covered in blood. Then I saw the guy walk over to my lifeless body. He tore at my clothes and he raped me. Then he got up and ran away. All I could think was *how stupid to have given my life away for nothing.*"

The images dissolved and Sarah found herself standing beside the entity back in the control room.

"The conductor being seemed to be standing much closer to me. I was very uncomfortable. He was staring right into my eyes, right into my mind. I felt such a sense of coldness."

As Sarah returned his gaze she realised she was only aware of his huge black eyes. Then slowly she felt her body falling backwards. Her feet left the ground and she rotated back to a position of about 80 degrees.

"I seemed to be lying back on something," she recalled. "Something was supporting me off the ground, but I was not aware what it was. Some sort of table perhaps. The entity was positioned to my left. Then I became aware of someone else behind my right shoulder. I can't say if it was the same as the entity to my left. This new one was more shadowy, darker, thinner. They were both just looking at me."

Then Sarah noticed a movement behind her head. Something, like a piece of machinery had been moved into position over her head.

"It was shaped like a hairdryer and metallic. I assumed it had been rolled into position or had risen up out of the floor. I guess the part that was above my head was about eight inches long and was pointing down onto my head and chest."

The entity standing to her left continued to look down at her body.

Sarah felt that the being meant her no harm. In fact she had the distinct feeling that he was friendly.

The *hairdryer* machine was removed and another piece of equipment then rolled into view in the shape of a curved metallic-looking plate that was positioned over her abdomen and curved under her. What looked like a control panel was positioned on the top left hand side of the machine.

"The alien was looking down at the panel," recalled Sarah. "For some reason I felt left out. He wasn't looking at me any more. Without those deep eyes on me, capturing my mind, my sense of self-preservation started to return. For a moment I felt like I could get up and just run away but at the same time I knew I could not. The thought of the small aliens running after me and grabbing me was just too much.

"Then I felt a sensation of heat in my middle, as if the machine over my middle was looking into me. I felt a warming in my sides and then a heat right through my abdomen."

The entity that had been positioned behind her right shoulder now moved forward and another came into view from behind her left shoulder. Although similar to the being viewing the panel, they were different, smaller.

"They seemed to scurry, like insects. Then suddenly they

were touching me. They started by touching my jaw and looking into my mouth. They used their fingers to move my mouth making it open and close. It was like having your mouth inspected by a dentist. Then they began touching my face. They pulled my eyes down and up and looked into them. They weren't hurting me, but I was frightened of what they might do.

"Then they turned their attention to my arms, prodding and pinching the muscles. Their tiny little fingers were prodding and poking. I thought they were like children. Their actions seemed pointless and stupid. Then I thought they were like blind people feeling their way down my arms, looking for something. The one on the right was faster than the one on the left. He got to my hand and began pulling at each of my fingers, feeling them. Although the sensation was quite nice I kept telling myself I didn't want them to touch me because they do bad things."

The entities then moved to Sarah's legs and with their small fingers traced the line of her muscles, prodding and pinching and pushing downwards until they reached her feet. Here they separated and pulled at each of her toes before moving away from her prone body.

"I felt relieved," said Sarah. "I thought they had done what they wanted to do and that was that, the worst was over.

"Then I felt the first entity, the friendly one, just standing there and looking at me, like an adult looks at a child. He was smiling at me, not with his mouth but mind-smiling. He was pleased with my conduct. He was saying to me *you have done well,* but he was putting the words into my mind.

"He said I had done very well and I had been very good to him and hadn't given them a hard time. I felt good. I also felt strangely aroused, sexually aroused. I wanted him to touch me. I had done what he wanted me to and I was feeling really good.

"In the past I had been bad. I had asked questions, too many questions. But now he was pleased with me and I felt I loved him and wanted to please him. I wanted him to touch me, to make love to me. I had all the feelings, the sensations of arousal. I knew he was not human, not capable of that sort of love. I was like a child, happy. But I had the sexual feelings of an adult and I wanted him to touch me.

"While this sexual arousal occurred, the small entity on my right seemed to be doing something in the area of my groin, touching me or performing some physical test or invasive operation - I don't know exactly.

"Then he said it was time for me to go. I did not want to go. I wanted to stay. In a way I felt he was rejecting me. I felt a deep sense of frustration.

"The two smaller entities took me out through the underside of the disc, close to where the examination took place. As we left the craft I saw that it had moved from directly above my apartment and was now in a completely different position. This was obvious because unlike the near vertical departure path from my bedroom at the beginning of the experience, the arrival was in a gentle downward slope towards the apartment.

"We three entered the bedroom through the closed windows and came to rest standing on the floor. One of the entities telepathically instructed me to *put myself to bed* and I did as I was told. They left, one behind the other, out of the window area. I then came to full mental awareness and control. I was sitting in the bed and immediately went to the window to check that they were really gone. The sky was empty. No UFO, nothing. The feelings I had been left with were frightening," she said.

"The overwhelming feeling was that there was more to this than I consciously remembered. The events of that night convinced me that this was not a one off experience. There was more, much more buried away. And that frightened the life out of me. It still does."

Checking the clock, Sarah discovered it was now almost 4 am.

Sarah's experience had been vivid. She knew she had not dreamt it. It had been real. Yet her logical pilot's mind could not rationalise it.

"I knew what had happened, had really happened, yet because I could not explain it I could not come to terms with it," she said. "It was disturbing, frightening at times and left me feeling I was no longer in control of my life.

"I wasn't into UFOs and had read little about the subject, but now I wanted to know as much as I could in attempt to understand what had happened to me.

"What was really disturbing about the incident was the way it changed my outlook and my perception of my own personal history. Had those bad dreams I suffered as a child really been bad dreams or visitations by alien entities?

"I also thought back to a period of my life when I had experienced, even dabbled in OBEs - *Out of Body Experiences.* I had read how one can put oneself in a different state of consciousness which allows the mind to leave the body and I thought some weird experiences in my younger days were OBEs. Now I was asking myself whether those OBEs were in fact earlier encounters with these strange entities. There were certainly many similarities."

Sarah was reluctant to reveal her experience to anyone for fear of being branded a lunatic. Who would believe her anyway? UFOs and strange little beings from space were the stuff of science fiction.

Aliens don't just land in Bracknell, Berkshire and then wander into the bedroom of a woman in her late 30s. And any woman who says they do is bound for the psychiatrist's chair.

Yet Sarah knew she couldn't deny what had happened to her. The memory was crystal clear and in the following weeks and months her dread of another visitation was heightened by a series of dreams as alien as the encounter she had had.

When she eventually plucked up the courage to tell her boyfriend, a university academic, he listened to her account with an open mind. He knew Sarah was an intelligent, talented and perfectly sane woman and he was prepared to accept that she had experienced something very unusual.

He would like to become involved in investigating the phenomenon.

However Sarah knew that the reaction of others would not be so positive, especially those who did not know her well.

In the months that followed Sarah's terror subsided. But the anticipation never left her. She almost knew they would be back.

And when they did come back the effect of their visit was more terrifying than ever.

"It was one night in July 1994, more than a year later," recalled Sarah. It was dark in my bedroom and I suddenly sensed there was something at the bottom of my bed. It scurried and it was quite noisy. Then it stood by my bed. It was one of the entities, like the slightly smaller beings that had taken part in the examination of me. Slightly smaller than the other beings, slightly darker, it scurried like a great spider. But it was a biped.

"It climbed onto my bed and pushed me over onto my shoulder. I was paralysed. I couldn't move and I was in an awkward position. I was terrified. Out of the corner of my eye I could see it was holding a wand or a probe. It was like a car aerial, the size of a medium knitting needle, about eight inches long.

"I couldn't make out whether it was made of metal or not. It shimmered like the material that the craft had been made from."

The street lamps from the road below her apartment illuminated the bedroom enough for Sarah to see that the entity was preparing to push the wand thing into her ear.

"It was going to push it into the side of my head or my ear," said Sarah. "I was panic-stricken. I wanted to struggle but I couldn't. I think my arms started to shake. I was so very frightened. I thought they were going to hurt me."

When the entity pushed the probe into the side of Sarah's head she felt no pain, no sensation.

"I felt awful, sick with fear, but there was no pain and no sense of an object being put into my head. About thirty seconds went by and I felt that I could move. I wanted to put my hands up and cover my head but I was so frightened I did not want to turn to face the alien so I waited for another 20 seconds or so.

"When I looked around it was dark. I reached up and switched on the overhead light and they were gone."

Sarah's second conscious encounter with the entities underlined her conviction that they had absolutely no regard for the welfare of the humans whose lives they were invading.

"I felt like nothing more than a laboratory rat, something to be used or tested and then discarded," said Sarah. "Like the way they tweaked my brain so they could conduct experiments on me in the ship. They were not remotely interested in my fear, my terror and my loss of self-control."

Sarah concluded that the feelings of affection, or indeed love towards the entities, that she had reported experiencing during her first encounter, were merely implanted into her brain so that she would be more positive about the intimate examinations that took place.

Her cynical view about the visits of the entities was underlined on their third visit on the night of Boxing Day 1994.

The following detailed account was written by Sarah shortly after her return to the bedroom of her apartment.

"I feel more open and less afraid of the visitors this night and I can see the stars through the windows as I go to sleep. I am feeling fatalistic and think a thought to them: *Well, I'm here and ready for your visit.* I feel that something is going to happen tonight. I fall into a strange state of consciousness and cannot seem to move.

"After a little effort mentally I find I am getting lighter, lifting above the bed. I can see two children in the room, watching me. But they are not children at all, but aliens, three to four feet tall as I've seen before. They are attempting to appear to me as children but I can see them as they really are. But the attempt at illusion has kept me from freezing up in fear, which is quite a relief. To see them eye to eye is a deeply disturbing and frightening thing for me.

"They each take me by the hand and *float* me (literally)

through the windows. The night sky is breathtaking and I wish to be taken to some close celestial object. In fact I can see Mars above us and realising that everything else in the sky is many light-years away, I decide I'd like to go to Mars if it is possible.

"The *visitors* point out an irregular and fuzzy looking object to the Northwest and very low down, just above the horizon. Somehow they put the idea into my mind that this object is where I want to go. This duplicity is obvious, as my original desire to see a local planet still stays in my mind.

"We move toward to the object on the horizon, still unidentified. They telepathically inform me that they are my children - they (somehow) have come from me. I don't know if this is a lie or not. I don't trust them anyway.

"Strangely as we approach the object it seems to get no bigger, or maybe its details remain hazy and difficult to identify but it is a silvery-white colour with indistinct outlines. Then we are inside it.

"The entities float me through a huge grey-white metallic room until my feet gently touch the floor. I look about and see several human males standing about twenty feet to my left. They do not seem aware of me even though I am standing in front of them completely naked.

"To my right I see a man being floated up a strange beam of energy which slopes to an upper floor. On the upper floor is a small walkway in front of a glasslike wall of clear material behind which I can see coloured liquid - giving me the impression of a giant fish tank. As I take in my surroundings the two entities who had brought me here take my hands again and lead me to the energy ramp and we float to the upper level.

"The entities are putting thoughts in my mind, telling me that we are going for an underwater swim in the liquid. They lower me into the bluish liquid, which is thicker than water and my fear rises as it swamps over my body. It feels warm and, paradoxically, dry. Dry water!

"As they force my head below the surface of the liquid I begin to panic. I instinctively hold my breath but as my lungs seem about to burst they tell me I should breathe the liquid!

"Finally, I come to the point of no return and open my mouth to let the final bubbles of air exit my body. As I take the first mouthful of liquid into my lungs, death seems imminent. Thick and heavy the liquid enters my body as I inhale for the second and the third time. Strangely I feel no sensation of suffocating or lack of oxygen. I really am breathing liquid.

"The experiment ends as suddenly as it had started. Once they witness my breathing in the liquid the entities lift me from the tank and float me back to the lower area again. The transition from breathing the liquid to air is smooth. The liquid seems to run from my body like mercury, leaving it dry.

"Back in the *reception area,* the entities inform me it is time to go back. I step away from them, towards the three men I had seen earlier. I am not ready to go. I want to observe more.

"One of the entities tells me, in no uncertain terms, that they are in charge and after a minute or so they hold my hands and float me out of the craft into the night sky and towards my flat. They float me in through my bedroom window and lay me on my bed. One of the entities scurries around and across the bed while , presumably, his companions prepare to depart. I remember his face looking directly at me. I close my eyes until the sounds of their scampering around the room stop. When I open them again they are gone. I looked at my clock. The time was 05.45. The whole episode has taken an hour and 45 minutes, yet it seems more like half an hour. Was this missing time?

Sarah's experiences continued well into 1995 with a series of strange alien dreams and further abductions.

Very early in the New Year she dreamed that she was being forcibly controlled by alien entities for covert antihuman purposes. Transported into space to make a rendezvous with a hidden alien space station high in Earth orbit she was left with a feeling of frustration and helplessness.

Several nights later she woke in her darkened bedroom

aware that she was being watched by entities. Terrified she hid under her duvet until she felt they had gone. But she was left with a conviction that something extraordinary had happened that night.

Two nights later, January 8, 1995, she awoke surrounded by entities. She found herself lying on a table-like structure in a large room similar to the scene in previous abductions. She had the distinct feeling that she had undergone some sort of medical examination and caught glimpses of entities moving equipment out of her range of sight.

Physically immobile she was aware of one of six entities staring deeply into her eyes. She felt it was passing information to her, programming her with data in a telepathic monologue.

This programming session seemed to continue for one or two hours.

Later Sarah said: "I awoke in the dark of early morning with clear memory of being with the entities. I wondered how many other abductions had taken place in which I had but hazy memory of, or even no memory at all. When I went back over the recent times where I'd awoken to the presence of the entities it begged the question whether these were also fully fledged abductions with me only becoming aware of the entities as they were leaving the bedroom after returning me. I just didn't know."

The following night Sarah went to bed full of anxiety. She stared into the darkness unwilling to allow sleep to lower her defences against the intruders. Suddenly a sense of immobility spread over her body. She was aware of a small shape moving out of one corner of the room.

Unable to reach down to the bedside for a torch to probe the gloom in the corner of the room she stared into the darkness and watched as an entity seemed to materialise out of thin air!

The entity moved toward the left hand side of the bed and then climbed onto it, reaching out with a long, thin arm.

Sarah was frozen with horror as the alien's three long fingers gently touched her left arm. They felt moist and yet quite dry against her skin - like a kitten's paw-pads. As it touched her the being communicated a message: "Don't be afraid - don't worry."

Sarah's anxiety immediately began to subside leaving her with the suspicion that she was being emotionally controlled.

The entity's telepathic communication continued.

"I have been waiting for you," it said.

The statement suggested the being had not just arrived in her room so Sarah mentally asked how long it had been waiting.

"Sixteen hours, as you understand time," it replied.

At this point the entity squatted next to her pillow and transformed itself into an image of Sarah's mother.

It asked: "How do you know when they are coming?"

Sarah was fully aware that it wasn't really her mother asking the question. This amazing physical transformation confirmed that this visitor, like the previous ones, was prepared to use any subterfuge to ensure her co-operation.

Feeling confused and foolish, she replied: "I had a feeling they were coming, premonition-like."

The entity's gaze seemed to grow more intense and then suddenly she fell asleep. When she awoke, the visitor had gone.

Sarah's multiple abduction/visitation experiences were now beginning to take over her life. By day she dreaded the approach of evening when she might once again come face to face with her unwanted visitors, at night she slept fitfully listening out for any sound or any movement that would betray their presence.

At some point around this time her fear and apprehension was replaced by a fatalistic acceptance of her lot.

For some reason the Greys had a keen interest in her, an ordinary human being. There was nothing she could do to stop these visits and abductions so perhaps she should try to find out as much as she could about them.

On the night of January 16, 1995 she decided to try an experiment. As she settled into sleep she sent out a *mental* request for them to come and visit her. There were some

questions she wanted answers to. Who and what were they,
what did they want from her and other abductees?

Sarah awoke later in the night aware that she had received another visit.

She was left with a powerful impression of three of them
standing at the end of the bed watching as she passively
looked back. A *leader* entity stood in front of two other
Greys. She felt no fear and although she could recall no
other details she was aware that this had been the ending
of a more complex encounter.

In the early hours of January 23, 1995 Sarah was woken
from her sleep by the pounding of heavy rain against her
bedroom windows. Just before she had fallen asleep around
3 a.m. the night sky had been starry and cloudless.

She looked through the rain smeared windows and immediately noticed something was very wrong. The heavy
clouds above were illuminated by an intense bright light.

There was clearly something inside the cloud throwing off
an extremely powerful light.

Suddenly her curiosity turned to fear as her body was
taken over by the now familiar paralysis which often accompanied her alien encounters. A slightly altered sense of
consciousness confirmed her conviction that she was yet
again to enter the domain of the Greys.

Through the windows she could now see the source of the
strange light, a white egg shaped object. A beam of grey
light sloped from the egg-shaped craft and connected with
her bedroom windows as if providing a path to link the two.

Two entities came to her. But this time they were not
Greys - far from it.

They looked like Greek Gods, tall blond and attractive
human-like males with near perfect features and serene
expressions on their faces. They lifted her and began moving with her along the energy beam to the egg-shaped craft.

Sarah's relief that they were not Greys was tempered
with the knowledge that her more alien like abductors had
changed their appearance in the past even trying to fool her
into thinking they were her children.

As they traversed the beam, she noticed the heavy rain

had abruptly stopped, and realised they were heading for a circular opening in the base of the egg-shaped UFO straight ahead . . .

Once inside she immediately noticed how it was much smaller than the other alien *vehicles* she had been taken to.

Looking around she saw the two blond males who had accompanied her standing with a beautiful blond female. Along the wall of the room was a bank of instruments and controls and nearby she saw the inevitable examination table.

Silently one of the beings walked her to the table and helped her onto it. Feeling sleepy and dull in mind, Sarah realised there was little point in refusing to co-operate.

The following physical examination was conducted painlessly and in silence and after about ten minutes Sarah fell into a deep sleep despite her reluctance to lose both consciousness and what little control she had over the situation.

She awoke back in her bedroom and immediately went to her windows to see if she could locate the egg-shaped object. It was gone. The ground outside was wet but the storm had obviously been over for some time. She returned to her bed and fell into a deep sleep.

Some days later, after conducting her own research, Sarah discovered that her latest visitors fitted the description of a group of aliens known as *Nordics*. But her experiences with the Greys had taught her one lesson - never take anything about abduction events at face value.

February 5, 1995. It was 2.30 am and Sarah was roused from her sleep by a powerful sense of being watched by someone . . . or something.

Despite her drowsiness she could see a large object in the sky through her windows. She struggled to raise herself, but couldn't, as if drugged. Three small entities, once again the Greys, were coming into her bedroom.

When, finally, she came to her full state of alertness, she was still lying prone, but not in her bed. She was on a hard surface in a small dark room or cubicle. Around her stood the three entities whom she had seen entering her room what seemed like moments before. It slowly dawned on Sarah that she had been transported to this place from her apartment while unconscious.

While one entity stared deeply into her eyes, the other two performed a swift examination of her body. She felt their long, slender alien fingers probing her. Then she felt a strange sensation as a long, thin tube or flexible needle was inserted into her vagina and then removed.

Helped into a standing position by the entities and facing a brightly lit doorway, Sarah felt nauseous and weak. They helped her through the door into a huge circular room where she was allowed to flop down to the floor on all fours.

The aliens moved away, leaving her unsteady and disoriented. She sat back on her haunches and immediately saw two people - both young women - who sat or lay nearby. They were as disoriented and unwell as her, and appeared unaware of what was happening around them.

Sarah studied her neighbours. Nearest, maybe eight feet away, was a girl dressed only in a night dress. She lay motionless on the shiny but non-metallic floor. Beyond her was another woman - also in night attire.

As she took in her surroundings Sarah was aware of a telepathic command to *look up,* an order directed at all three women confined within an area surrounded by a circular wall.

Sarah looked up above the wall to a mezzanine-like walkway upon which three human males were standing. They were fully dressed, in contrast to herself and the women below. Sarah later recalled her overwhelming feeling of humiliation. Not simply because she was naked, but also because of her tangled hair and lack of make-up. She remembered her anger at being exposed to fellow humans in such a wretched and degrading way.

Seconds later the three men were floated down from the walkway and each one sat close to one of the women.

Sarah was aware of some mental communication between the entities and the men, as if the aliens were controlling the actions of the human males. The man who had been *paired* with her eyed her body and at first Sarah feared she would become a victim of rape.

She avoided eye contact with the man and looked up at the entities as if to plead for help.

But what happened next was more shocking that she could have imagined. Not because of the actions of the entities or their male human captives but because of her own.

Sarah, now on all fours, found herself involuntarily moving into what she later described as *sexually provocative posture.*

She said: "I was on all fours, like an animal, with my bottom raised up in a crude sexual way. The entities seemed to be studying what was happening to the men as I did this. I felt both threatened and humiliated and if I could have run away at that moment nothing would have stopped me. To my recollection, the man did not lay a finger on me. But that didn't lessen the feelings of outrage and humiliation."

As suddenly as it had started, the sexual experiment was brought to a swift conclusion. Under telepathic guidance from the entities all three women and three men were put through some sort of group-mind test where they had to solve a number of puzzles involving patterns and objects on the floor around them.

They were then instructed to try to find a solution to a hypothetical environmental catastrophe occurring in a South American rain forest due to human abuse of energies under its control.

Sarah remembers finding the gruelling tests taking their toll on her to such an extent that she begged to be allowed to go home.

Eventually she found herself lying on the bed back in her flat watching two Greys floating out through her bedroom windows. She remembers noticing that it was 5.30 am before she fell into a deep sleep.

The Greys returned a few nights later, on February 9, 1995. After retiring to her bed Sarah awoke to find herself lying on an examination table in a circular room, 20 feet in diameter, with three entities standing around her.

She felt no terror, just a deep curiosity about what was going on. Looking at the entity closest to her, whom she later described as the *leader entity*, Sarah formed a clear mental question in her mind and tried to project it at him.

"What are you doing to me and why are these things happening?"

To her astonishment the being answered her questions, not words, but in mental impressions which flooded into her brain.

"I can't recall the exact phrasing," Sarah said later. "But his answer seemed quite clear. The entities were attempting to genetically create new life-forms which would be able to exist in both their environment and in my human one. One of these new genetic life-forms was a micro-biological nutrition for the hybrid entities that were being genetically created from both our life-forms during abductions.

"They needed this nutrition as they didn't eat food in the way human life did and the hybrids needed sustenance for existence in both our world's environments."

As these messages were being communicated, Sarah felt the being was also *talking* to the other two entities.

The entity standing to her left moved forward and produced a silvery white probe-like instrument, about six inches in length. It seemed to emit a thin laser-like energy beam from its tip.

To her horror, the entity slowly drew the probe across her naked stomach opening the flesh and exposing her innards.

"It was terrifying, despite being painless," recalled Sarah. "The shock of seeing my innards exposed like that left me feeling sick. The entity first placed the probe below my navel and to the right and then drew it across to the left causing the flesh to part as it moved."

Somehow the entities projected images over Sarah's belly which she felt compelled to study. The first was a magnified view of what looked like millions of plant-like microscopic life-forms apparently living within her lower abdomen. A telepathic running commentary explained she was seeing the breeding of the nutritional life-forms they had told her of earlier.

Then that image was replaced with a view of a tiny foetus, seemingly growing inside her. Somehow she knew this represented one of the hybrid foetuses the entities were creating.

A third image then overlaid her open belly. This time she saw what she thought was a South American rain forest, the accompanying *narrative* informing her of the entities' attempts to help it survive the eco-damage from human technology.

As Sarah tried to take in the confusing series of images and the accompanying barrage of telepathic information, the entity with the laser-probe drew the instrument back along the slash across her body resealing the wound.

At that point Sarah awoke to find herself back in her bedroom, now flooded with daylight. In a panic she threw back the bedcovers and examined her stomach. The painless laser surgery had left no marks or scars.

The days that followed passed without further interruption from the entities. On the night of February 20 she feared another visit when, through her bedroom window, she saw two grey-silver discs fly across the sky.

During the following two weeks Sarah had a series of strange and frightening UFO dreams. But they were undoubtedly just dreams and she was thankful for that.

However the strain of this series of abductions and UFO events was beginning to take its toll on her mentally. She felt a deep sense of hopelessness about her lack of control of her life and admits she was in a near suicidal turmoil.

It was during one of these low points that the entities paid their next visit. She woke at about 2 a.m. on the night of March 3 immediately aware of the presence of two beings standing motionless beside her bed. They watched her intently.

One of them moved suddenly, partially lifting the duvet and putting its arms on her shoulder beneath, It then began the familiar *feeling* and *pinching* ritual, its soft spindly fingers tracing the muscles beneath her skin.

As the alien digits explored her body, Sarah looked at the

other entity whom she took to be the *leader* and sent out a mental plea: *Don't let him hurt me.*

At first the leader entity did not move or take his huge staring eyes from hers. Then it tilted its large pear shaped head to one side and chided her with the telepathic words: "You really should have learned to trust us by now."

At that moment Sarah's senses sharpened, her vision was suddenly much more acute. She stared at the leader entity standing three and half to four feet in height and for the first time noticed the texture of his skin . . . like wood yet leathery with vertical striations running from top to bottom.

She had the impression that this entity was much older than the helper who continued with his tactile exploration of her body.

Sarah mentally asked the leader entity: *Why are you here now?*

He replied: "We are here because of your deep pain. Only for this." He went on to reassure her that *nothing bad* would happen.

Sarah relaxed and fell into a deep sleep.

During the following months of that year Sarah continued to have abduction experiences in addition to dreams. And she is aware of a final visit by the Greys in October 1995. But the details remain hidden leaving only the recollection of the entities watching her in her bedroom.

Sarah Ward's alien abduction experiences are unique in that they are among the most thoroughly documented on record.

Sarah's pilot training combined with her observational talents enabled her to compile a personal record of bizarre events over a period of three years.

Times, dates, even weather conditions are noted in detail in her *Abduction Log*. Her descriptions of entities, alien craft and sequences of events in her many encounters provide one of the most comprehensive accounts of a series of abductions ever compiled, and one that will be studied by Ufologists for years to come.

Why Sarah? Why so many abductions of one woman?

Despite her gathering such a mass of observational data, Sarah is no closer to answering those questions than her fellow abductees.

However she has been struck by similarities between her abduction encounters and her Out of Body Experiences which she experimented with some years ago.

"It all seems to be connected with the nature of reality," says Sarah.

"The human arena of experience has always been multi-coloured and multi-dimensional. I remain open-minded about how these bizarre and outrageous events might finally be understood and fitted into our common understanding of reality."

Paulinne Delcour-Min,
May 16, 1996
West Didsbury, Manchester.

Paulinne Delcour-Min relaxed on the therapy couch in the consulting room at her Victorian terraced home in the busy Manchester suburb of West Didsbury and, with the help of the soothing words of her regression therapy student, allowed her consciousness to drift to another level.

An experienced past life therapist, with a wealth of first hand ET experiences which began at an early age, Paulinne, now in her forties, was determined to uncover the truth behind the tangle of emotions she felt for the most notorious of alien visitors - *the Greys.*

As the student therapist pulled the curtains to block out the bright early summer sun light and throw the small, but cosy consulting room into shade, Paulinne's mind flashed across the years during which she had experienced the fear and fascination of many encounters with the most celebrated of visiting alien life forms.

She snuggled deeper into the blanket covering her, as if trying to find comfort as she remembered the raw horror that almost froze her when she first saw and seemed instantly to recognise the cold, black eyes of a Grey staring

from the cover of Whitley Streiber's book *Communion*.
It was an image that was at once alien yet familiar. More
like déjà vu. In fact that emotional response was a factor in
the transformation of this intelligent High School teacher
and mother of three into one of Britain's most hardworking
investigators into the paranormal.

Her years of research into ET phenomena and past-life
regression, working alongside her husband Ye, had left her
open-minded, unshockable and *at one* with the universe
and its diversity of life forms.

Paulinne's mind latched onto the words of the student
therapist . . .

"Visualise yourself in a beautiful place . . ."

These were exactly the same words she had used herself,
countless times, when preparing clients for a past life regression. Deep relaxation without hypnosis was a means of
enabling the subject's consciousness to drift back in time
and to a previous existence.

Eager to know, comfortable with her surroundings and
unshockable, Paulinne Delcour-Min let go of reality ready
to explore a previous life - but unprepared for the revela-
tion that was to come.

"I am looking down at my feet," she told the therapist
when her mind had been taken back millions of years to a
strange place and an even stranger life.

"They are slender, grey with four toes that are a little
webbed. I have slender legs, body and arms. My hands have
three fingers and a little thumb. My fingers are long and
slightly webbed.

"I am a Grey . . . I am a mature adult male, my name is
Arkid."

Paulinne's detailed account, recorded during that two
hour regression session, throws new light on many of the
unanswered questions about abduction, involvement by the
Greys and their motives for their harvesting of terrestrial
genetic material. It also throws up many new questions.

Her account continues: "I am inside a craft and as I look
around I can see the blackness of space through the vision
apertures, but inside our craft is light.

"There are many others like me here and also machines that make a constant humming sound.

"Our machines are aware, they have a consciousness and intelligence and they run the craft.

"We give them commands, our mental power controls them, if we need to change direction, or dim the light for example.

"Random negative thoughts can be very destructive so we do not have individual thinking anymore, it would be too dangerous. Our collective thinking is so powerful it washes away individual deviations. The important thing is survival.

"There is a hierarchy in our society, the highest levels are not on the craft. They are in different places in the galaxy, on worlds and artificial worlds we have made. As a race we are in danger of disappearing from the face of the galaxy.

"We are having terrible troubles with our physical bodies, they don't work properly, we can't nourish them because of the digestive problems. We have so much pain and numbness: we exist on a soup type drink.

"It is all due to radiation damage. We destroyed our home world and those that escaped, escaped only with damage. How did it happen? Too much individual thinking led to greed. People forgot that at the deepest level we are all one, and with this illusion of separation people felt they could get away with things . . .

"We had already left our home world. We had bases on our moons and could travel through space.

"It all happened when I was a child - it was very, very shocking. I cannot express just how profoundly shocking it was. We were on one of the moon bases at the time. These were just staging posts, refuelling stops so we could not stay on. We had to find a new home.

"That is why we are cruising through space now. We took all the fuel we could and have crossed vast distances over the years, scanning for suitable worlds to support life in our form. Many other craft went in different directions on the same desperate mission. We have to find a new home.

"Time elapses. Then the scanners pick-up a possible world, the third planet out from a sun in a solar system. It is the Earth long before man has evolved. We evaluate the information. It does not seem tremendously suitable. It is not home, it is very bright and there is too much light so near to the sun. Its atmosphere does not filter out enough light; it would cause us severe pain, but we will be able to refuel and get supplies there.

"It makes us all long for home. There was water there too, and wonderful thick clouds. It was misty and damp and there were frequent soft, drizzly downpours. A gorgeous grey world with different landscape forms to this one.

"We land in an equatorial zone. There is desert behind us and we are in a green coastal area with the sea in front of us. In the sea there are fish and many life forms and on the land there are insects. It is so hot and bright that we stay on the craft if we can and send out robot sensors to search for minerals. It is very heavy gravity and we are not happy.

"We are consumed with grief for our home world. It feels like a very hostile galaxy out there. We have destroyed our perfect home and we all feel very down. It must never happen again is the collective decision.

"We use laser cutters to extract the minerals we need for our supplies. We take water and food stuff to make the easy-to-digest soup we live on: vegetation, minerals from the mud and rocks and some animal material. We make up the Earth soup and drink it. I can feel the life energy in my body now, raw vibrant life force.

"We all cry, weeping for our home. It makes us miss home all the more. It is so long since we felt life energy this strong, not since we left home. And we can never go home again. To live here we would have to genetically engineer our bodies. We see the beauty and the life force here, but it is not our type of beauty. It is a very fertile cradle for life though. We appreciate that very much.

"We live long lives and we used to reproduce sexually with the child growing inside the body of its mother. But since the destruction of our world our babies have been born terribly deformed and this way of reproducing has been abandoned.

"We are leaving now. We check out the single moon, not much of interest there, and go on to Mars. At this time there is water on this planet and lots of beings, humanoid, slightly simian types live on the surface of this world. They are friendly and helpful. They arrange a big meeting to discuss what help they can offer us.

"Because of our sensitivity to light we are offered the use of their massive underground caves. It is very kind, but not what we are looking for. What are we looking for? Home, and nowhere else will ever measure up to the home we destroyed.

"We feel very lonely, we feel consumed by our grief, we feel we are doomed to wander. We pass the other planets as we voyage through the solar system but our scanners deem none of them suitable. We are too frightened to think for ourselves. My job is in maintenance and I take orders from the taller Greys. They take their orders from the Machine Intelligence, the central computer on our craft which is linked to other craft.

"We pass out of this solar system and continue our search for home. Finally we get caught in a meteor shower, our craft is destroyed. We die. We are out of our bodies now, I feel free. There is no pain. The wreckage is scattered below us and we are now in our astral bodies. We look silvery-grey, a curious cross between a Grey and a tadpole. We are at a loss. We handed our power to the machines but they are gone. We are adrift in space. Our machines are just useless wreckage now.

"Time passes, then some angels appear and say: *We can help, come with us.* They take us to another dimension. It is very bright but not the kind of light that hurts. Now we are melting into the sun, passing through it, through the dimensions and into the pathways of light that link us to the Creator, the ultimate source of all being. What a relief!

"I am aware that I make a decision not to choose that incarnation again. When I emerge from the Divine Mind, I

245

shall choose another life form in which to express my consciousness."

When Paulinne came out of her marathon regression session she quickly discovered her fear of the Greys had been replaced by a profound sense of sadness. For she could now see the Greys were sad little creatures facing extinction and who can never go home.

The discovery that she had lived before as a Grey did not shock her. In previous past life regression sessions she had experienced other alien incarnations.

In fact it was simply an extension of the Reincarnation beliefs held by many including a number of terrestrial religions. If the soul can experience many lives over long periods of time why must those incarnations be Earthbound?

As time went by, Paulinne discovered her regression therapy had also left her mind full of an array of data on the Greys. She knew with conviction, for instance, that the Greys had overcome their reproduction problem by cloning. As one body became worn out, the consciousness would be transferred to a newly cloned shell.

"However, the more they cloned the weaker the life force in their cells and bodies became," explained Paulinne.

"That is why they have found the rich life force on our planet so attractive. Greys generally have lost their connection to Source and they fear surrender to the Divine Mind. They are resisting the evolutionary flow of the universe and after death they stay on board their craft in their astral bodies until they can incarnate into a newly cloned Grey or hybrid body. They literally put bodies on and off as we might a coat. This is a spiritual short circuit that cuts them off from higher guidance."

Paulinne believes the Greys fear that we may destroy our world as they did theirs. That is why they often show abductees pictures of the Earth exploding, as if to shock us into action to stop it.

She explained: "We are poised at a critical stage in our relationship with the planet. We need to change and stop poisoning her - or there is disaster on the cards."

But if Earth's fate is sealed, then the Greys have a sinister plan to repopulate the planet with hybrids - the hybrids they have been breeding using genetic material harvested from human abductees over very many years.

"The Greys plan to bring down the hybrids and reincarnate into them. It is quite simply their next, desperate, evolutionary step as they try to cheat destiny," added Paulinne.

"It is certainly not our next evolutionary step. It would be tantamount to being cloned with dinosaurs."

Paulinne and her husband Ye Min had been practising past life regression therapy long before they entered the world of Ufology. Circumstances, from regression clients reporting alien contact while they were in the womb, to full-blown abduction incidents affecting them both, conspired to cause them to change the direction of their research.

They both immersed themselves in the subject and discovered that the whole question of alien abduction and ET activity on earth could fit into a wider philosophy of life in a multidimensional and spiritual universe.

They formed AsSERT, the Association for the Support of Experiencers through Research and Therapy which offered abductees an ongoing support structure using regression therapy without hypnosis. The steady stream of clients who came to use their services to try to find their own answers to a wide range of strange experiences soon provided a data-base of encyclopaedic proportions. Paulinne and Ye examined these case histories to help them piece together a cosmic-cum-spiritual jigsaw puzzle.

In fact it was regression therapy which led them both into Ufology and helped Paulinne understand an event during her teenage years which had always mystified her.

Back in July 1964 Paulinne, then 16 years old was enjoying a summer's evening stroll through the countryside with her best friend. At the time Paulinne lived in the sleepy Cheshire village of Frodsham near the flat, lush countryside around the estuary of the River Mersey.

Absorbed in girl talk the two friends ambled along deserted country lanes unaware of the time and simply enjoying the balmy evening air.

Suddenly they were in a field and Paulinne found herself on her hands and knees as if she'd just fallen. Strangely she couldn't remember any mishap and scrambled to her feet to see her companion looking equally confused.

The pair decided to head for home and began retracing their steps in silence as the sun began to slip towards the horizon. On the return journey, Paulinne recalls a woman rushing up from behind her saying: "Good God, child, what have you done to your leg?"

She looked down and saw that the white ankle sock on her right foot was covered in blood. Astonished, she examined her leg and found a long cut down the back of her calf, blood still oozing from the wound.

"I was shocked and my leg felt numb, icy and frozen but it didn't hurt," said Paulinne.

The teenager returned home and the four inch wound healed remarkably quickly. She never did remember how she had received her injury but the resulting scar, so noticeable that friends often mistake it for a ladder in her tights, is a constant reminder of the mystery.

More than a quarter of a century later, in 1992, the question of the scar came up again when Ye had been reading the book *Missing Time* by Budd Hopkins. He recounted the case of Virginia Horton.

"I suddenly realised my scar sounded like hers," said Paulinne.

"As I looked back at my life, there were other things which left me wondering if I had been in contact with aliens."

As a child she had experienced a missing time episode and had recurrent dreams of UFOs disguised in clouds and *watching* her.

"Insomnia, panic attacks, my reaction to the face of the Grey on the cover of *Communion,* the compulsion to constantly scan the sky if we were driving out at night and the way my body would respond whenever I'd talk about aliens," added Paulinne.

"My heart would beat faster and the *fight or flight* response would activate, with adrenaline rushes. My body clearly remembered something I had forgotten."

At this stage in her life Paulinne had become an established regression therapist. Her aim being to help people resolve problems in their lives by understanding what the past could tell them.

"Most of my work had been helping people to remember their previous lifetimes and realise how their other lives relate to their present one," she explained. "Sometimes we recovered important memories from early childhood or even from their months in the womb."

Paulinne, was by now determined to discover the truth of that childhood summer's evening and in September 1992 underwent a regression which took her mind back 28 years to the point where she and her friend walked along a deserted country lane, chatting away.

Paulinne takes up the story: "We were caught up in an energy beam that seemed to disconnect us from the Earth's energy field and we were lifted, frozen in motion. We were literally lifted into another dimension and drawn diagonally upwards towards a craft. We passed in through a hatchway and I was aware of a constant stream of telepathic messages that kept my mind locked, that stopped me thinking. *You will go to sleep. You will remember nothing. We won't harm you, we love you, everything is fine,* the messages went on and on," remembers Paulinne.

"We were in a huge room with lots of white tables like white nylon chopping boards. There was machinery for checking and scanning. I felt paralysed and was lying on one of the tables. I was aware that this craft was beaming people in for checks.

"There were many, many people on the white tables. The beings doing all this were small and grey with spindly arms and legs and fingers like hollow straws. They had large heads and huge black eyes. They seemed to be wearing tight fitting grey suits and their eyes were covered by fine black mesh.

"I was restrained with straps and they seemed to have

taken most of my will power. I felt a lot of resistance to recalling what they did to me. They fiddled with their machines as they checked my growth and development. They recorded information.

"I learned that this was one of my regular checks and that they had a big file on me. Thought is more powerful in the dimension they work in; to think a question brings the answer immediately into mind. This is one reason they keep you in a mind lock and why you can channel information during a regression session if you are asked the right questions.

"The Grey's main interest is their breeding programme. They are seeking perfection as they create physical bodies to incarnate into. I was not regarded as a top class specimen because of my body proportions. They like a long body with plenty of room for the organs and long limbs. However, I was aware that I was on their reserve programme rather than their active breeding programme.

"A second class specimen, but I may have my uses! My eggs were regarded as too immature, they needed more hormonal exposure as I had not had enough menstrual cycles, but they did take cells for cloning from my right calf. Human cells have a lot of life force and etheric energy which the Greys are sadly lacking. They are fascinated by the life force in a body and almost hope that by seeing it they will absorb it.

"I realised that their bodies are like machines that don't function well. They are hanging onto this level of existence, trying to get energies from other beings to perpetuate their own existence. They are fighting the galactic tide of evolution and facing annihilation as a species. The Greys around my examination table made a neat surgical incision, with no bleeding as everything was frozen, and they took my cells for cloning.

"Those working with me were only learning their job. Inept, they had ruptured something deep within my leg. The cut was bleeding too fast for their usual almost instantaneous wound closure techniques. I sensed their panic and felt terrible. I thought I would die. Finally, they decided to make it look like an accident, to taper it off down to my ankle and to give the top of the cut a little twist.

"It was time to be returned. I was told: *You will remember nothing, you tripped and fell into barbed wire, you will not go to the doctor.* They knew there would be no infection and that a doctor would be suspicious of the incision.

We were beamed down and it felt like descending on ropes. I heard a sound in my head and as it stopped I found myself on my hands and knees in a field by the hedge. I lay on the ground as if I had fallen feeling shocked and numb and with no conscious memory of the events.

"They had disconnected me from the planet's energies and the shock of reconnection must have wiped out any conscious memory. I could only think of going home. But had I fallen into the field over brambles and barbed wire, as they would have me believe, I would have cut the front of my leg, not the back of my calf. I now had my answers and knew exactly why I couldn't remember going into the field or falling over. The mystery of the scar had been solved."

The end of a mystery marked the beginning of a new quest for Paulinne and Ye. Many years on, their research . . and their experiences continue.

And the Greys are not always the ones responsible.

Back in August 1996, Paulinne, Ye and their two youngest children Rose, aged seven and five year old Clio were travelling through the Grampian Region of Scotland heading for Forres on the Moray Firth where they planned a short holiday.

They had been on the road for some hours and the children were sleeping on the back seats. Ye, at the wheel of their red Vauxhall Astra was glad to be on the final leg of their journey.

"We had not long passed Granton-on-Spey when I remember we entered an area of woodland," recalls Paulinne.

"It was a bright but cloudy day and I remember our surroundings becoming darker. We suddenly became aware of a car behind us, a big dark car which had something menacing about it. Ye wanted to pull away but there was a car in front of us that was being driven by an older man, one of those careful drivers. I was very uneasy, as if I was subconsciously registering something, I don't know what.

"Then the next minute Ye was overtaking the car in front and we were heading for our destination along a clear road. The car behind us had disappeared. I felt terribly shaken and didn't feel any better until we reached Forres and I had a chance to walk around and calm down."

The family got on with their holiday, but Paulinne and Ye had already decided to delve into the events of that journey through regression at a later stage.

Back in the familiar surroundings of their consulting rooms, Paulinne quickly entered a different level of consciousness to recount the hidden details of the drive.

"We are driving along the road and we enter a beam. It is a beam of light that slants diagonally from behind us and as we drive into its path we are drawn, slowly and gently up into it," said Paulinne, describing the events as if they were happening now.

"It is like a *tractare beam* and when we enter it, we change. We are frozen and time for us has stopped. Now the car is above the trees and we are being drawn towards a spherical craft that is extremely reflective. A rotating beam, like in a lighthouse, pulses from the top.

"The car passes through a rectangular entrance, the doors are left open but the car is deposited to one side. We are taken out of the car by four or five beings. They are big, bigger than me, catlike bipeds with curly tails, upright cat ears and covered in a beige fur. I am in a trance, like a Zombie, but I see the children wake-up. They are not frightened at all. They seem to recognise these beings and the beings give out a very loving feeling.

"We are taken into a large room where the children are led off to a play area by a being they refer to as *Aunty Cat*, a female being. They are playing, scampering around. We, on the other hand, are directed to two transparent examination tables onto which we are placed.

"Telepathic messages flash into our minds saying *Don't worry, we are your friends.* We are still in a Zombie-like trance. We could not stop them from doing whatever they wanted. We are laid out on the tables and a white light comes through the bottom. The light is all around our bodies, like being encased in a coffin of light, like a bath of light.

"It is a bath of light but not solar light. There is no sensation. Now it is over and we are being taken back to the car. The children are already in the car, asleep, and as the vehicle travels back down the beam of light to the road we notice symbols on the doors of the craft. A triangle containing three circles with another triangle below it. The car continues to move down the beam then stops and we find ourselves taken out of the vehicle so we can be bathed in solar light as if to settle our energies. The first light treatment was a method of healing and it also programmed us with information, the second was to prepare us for our return."

Seconds later, they are all back in the car, Ye has overtaken the slow moving vehicle ahead, Paulinne is silent, her unease obvious, the children asleep. Ye recalled: "We almost instinctively knew something had happened but had no conscious memory of events." Paulinne and Ye believe they have been the subjects of numerous alien abductions. They have used their regression therapy skills to delve into some, but there have been so many they have not attempted to investigate every suspected missing time incident.

In fact, most of their time in the consulting room is spent investigating abductions experienced by a growing number of clients who find their way to AsSERT. According to Paulinne and Ye, there is nothing abnormal about alien abduction phenomena. It is simply a part of the rich tapestry of life in the universe.

"I suspect that most people, if not all, have had an ET encounter," said Ye. "First encounters often start in the womb and are followed up through life. We are getting more and more people coming to us for help in investigating their own experiences. Today, people are more open minded than ever before and they want to know about what is going on out there in the universe."

Paulinne agrees and adds: "I wouldn't want people to think that our only interaction is with the Greys who visit Earth for their breeding programme. They are just one type of visitor to our planet. Past life regression has revealed that I have experienced incarnations in at least five different alien forms. But the ET experience is just a part of a greater Cosmological Framework in which everything is consciousness and energy. Discovering that framework has shown me that the laws of physics are different in different dimensions."

Paulinne and Ye believe that Harvard Professor of Psychiatry John Mack summed up their joint view in his 1994 book *Abduction* in which he said: "Past life experiences provide abductees (and the investigator) with a different perspective about time and the nature of human identity. Cycles of birth and death over long stretches of time can thus be relived, providing a different, less ego derived sense of the continuity of life and the smallness of an individual lifetime from a cosmic perspective."

So what is your verdict? You have read a couple of dozen British abduction mysteries that have been deemed worthy of investigation by one or other of the UFO research organisations, so now you can decide whether it is fact or fantasy.

Are we being visited by advanced technologies from beyond the stars? Are they keeping a fatherly eye on we fledgelings in an immense and immensely dangerous universe? Or are these alien visitors playing *Big Brother,* using our population like laboratory rats in a bizarre genetic experiment which condemns some human women to a lifetime of exploitation as breeding machines for a selfish race of aliens?

Maybe that is all just so much claptrap. Perhaps Albert Budden is right. Hallucinations caused by an allergic reaction to electro magnetic fields and many other things could be at the root of the many new abduction cases that flood in every year.

EPILOGUE

Perhaps all those abductees are a significant minority of the population who are sensitive to changes in the environment. Then again, isn't it more likely that the whole phenomena has its cause hidden away inside the complex structures of the human mind?

A psychological explanation for Abduction Phenomenon has become very unfashionable in view of the big bucks being made out of Ufology in the United States. Free enterprise and super hype has virtually made alien abduction a fact of life in the USA.

As one renowned British investigator told us recently:

"It has got to the stage that if you go to any big US UFO convention these days and come up with a theory that actually questions the existence of UFOs and aliens then you're likely to get branded a heretic."

The truth about UFOs, Flying Saucers and Alien Abduction is anybody's guess. We are no further along the road to truth in this field than we were back in 1947 when the term *Flying Saucer* was born. Maybe you will become the abductee who will be in a position to offer the world incontrovertible evidence of the existence of UFOs, aliens and alien abuctions.

On the other hand maybe you won't. For those of you who may now have developed a taste for investigating the Abduction Phenomenon, there is a mass of literature available to allow you to delve even deeper.

And if you fancy trying your hand as a real investigator why not contact one of the organisations mentioned in this book.

Without Consent was intended to address the phenomenon as far as British abductees and interested parties were concerned. We wanted to set the scene for the uninitiated, for those who have never felt UFOs and Ufology as subjects worthy of serious consideration. There is an even greater mass of information from different parts of the world.

The cases we have looked at are just the tip of an enormous iceberg. And the theories we have mentioned represent a fraction, albeit a representative sample, of the innumerable explanations for Abduction Phenomenon.

At the beginning of this book we described most abductees as ordinary, sensible, rational people who had experienced a most extraordinary event in their lives. We decided to invite each and every one of them to offer an explanation of their individual experiences. Strikingly few of our witnesses have felt qualified to say what they think was responsible for their encounters.

Elsie Oakensen has an idea it could have been a spiritual event, Ted Johnson is convinced he has met beings from outer space. But the vast majority prefer to keep open minds. Their search for an explanation for the inexplicable continues. If those victims of abduction, the people at the receiving end of all the fear and trauma are capable of keeping an open mind on the subject, why aren't the rest of us?

ACKNOWLEDGEMENTS

In writing a book such as this, it is inevitable that the authors will make use of research material conducted by individual UFO investigators and various UFO research groups throughout the United Kingdom and overseas.

With this in mind we would sincerely like to give credit to the following individuals and UFO research groups.

First and foremost our long suffering partners Helen Keymer and Susan Mantle. Without their patience and tolerance, this book would not have been possible.

UFO investigators and researchers: Ken Phillips, Albert Budden, Andy Roberts, Jenny Randles, Peter Hough, Malcolm Robinson, Steven Gamble, Michael Soper, Dr John Shaw, John Spencer, Clive Potter, David Atkins, David Kelly, Margaret Fry, Geoffrey Ambler, Andy Collins, Barry King, Tony Dodd, Graham Birdsall, Nick Pope, Georgina Bruni, Budd Hopkins, Harry Harris, David Taylor, Janet Bord, Kevin Flannery, Margaret Westwood, Gloria Dixon, Paul Allison, David Haisell and any others we have forgotton to mention. UFO research groups: British UFO Research Association (BUFORA), Independant UFO Network (IUN), Contact UK, UFO Investigators Network (UFOIN), UFO Studies Information Service(UFOIS), Midlands UFO Network, Mutual UFO Network (MUFON), J.Allen Hynek Center for UFO Studies (CUFOS), Manchester UFO Research Association (MUFORA), Strange Phenomena Investigations (SPI), Project Hassdalen-UFO Norway/UFO Sweden.

Last but not least, the authors wish to express their gratitude to all of the individual witnesses who have been interviewed for inclusion in this book. Without their willingness to come forward this book simply would not have been possible. At times they have shown great strength and courage, and, despite the mountain of scorn and ridicule that has been heaped upon them, they have remained steadfast in their convictions. It is hoped that they will be an example to all of those other witnesses out there who have yet to find the courage to come forward and help us find an answer to this most enigmatic of puzzles; the Abduction Phenomenon.

CONTACT INFORMATION

The authors would like to hear from anyone who has had similar experiences to those featured in this book. They would also like to hear from anyone who has had a UFO sighting Complete confidentiality is guaranteed where requested.

**The authors Philip Mantle and Carl Nagaitis
can be contacted via the publishers:**
c/o Beyond Publications/Fortune Books Ltd,
PO Box 168, Leeds LS15 9TJ.
Tel: (0)113 260 1133,
Fax: (0)113 232 6536,
email: Philip@beyondpublications.com
Website: www.beyondpublications.com

AWAKENING

How Extraterrestrial Contact Can Transform Your Life
By Mary Rodwell

It may surprise you to know that many people around the world, from all walks of life, believe themselves to be in regular contact with beings from 'outer-space'.

Seven years ago, Mary Rodwell, trained midwife and therapist, would have considered these stories the stuff of science fiction, but through a series of events, she began to counsel individuals who claimed to be having these remarkable experiences. Mary grew to understand that these claims were not the product of an over-active imagination. They were real, happening to normal, healthy people, and what's more, it was all going on in her neighbourhood!

Through word of mouth Mary became know as a confidant and 'trustee', validating, honouring and helping people work through these bizarre and unusal experiences.

As the number of people that came to see Mary escalated into the hundreds, she realised that some people were aware of their Contact experiences, some had felt a lifelong inkling, but others were completely in the dark, being driven to find a therapist to help calm their unexpalined and 'irrational' fears.

Mary says: "The process of 'waking up' to this is not always an easy ride, but in every case, the outcome is transformational, it can be positively life-changing if the person has the right help and support."

Are you ready to ask yourself: *"Am I experiencing Alien Contact?"*
Let this book help you take the first step - why not find out for yourself?

ISBN: 1-903782-03-1
Paperback: 280 pages   Size: 216 x 138 mm
Price: RRP UK £9.99
Prices Exclude postage and packing.

Order direct from the publishers, by telephone, fax, email or online.
See page 263 for contact details

A BEGINNER'S GUIDE
TO LIFE AFTER DEATH
The Teachings of Wilhelm and John,
an experience in automatic writing

By Peter Shires

If you can open your mind, this book will open your heart.

For over thirty years Peter Shires, if he believed in anything, believed that life commenced with birth and ended with death. Then he discovered, almost by accident, that under certain circumstances, he could act as a channel, through which the wisdom of the 'other world' could be passed into the earthly realm in which we live our conscious lives.

The ability which Peter discovered he possessed, and which he has refined over many years, is that of 'automatic writing', where a loosely held pen will produce writings, which delve deeply into the nature of mankind, in this life and beyond.

**For those with an interest in understanding their own nature
and that of the world beyond, this book cannot be
other than essential reading.**

'An easy to read and entertaining insightful look at life after death. I found this book to be first rate.' **John G. Sutton, Psychicworld**

ISBN: 1-903782-00-7
Price: RRP UK £8.99
Prices Exclude postage and packing.

Order direct from the publishers, by telephone, fax, email or online.
See page 263 for contact details

263